The Effective
Incident Response
Team

The Effective Incident Response Team

Julie Lucas
Brian Moeller

✦ Addison-Wesley

Boston • San Francisco • New York • Toronto • Montreal
London • Munich • Paris • Madrid
Capetown • Sydney • Tokyo • Singapore • Mexico City

The publisher offers discounts on this book when ordered in quantity for bulk purchases and special sales. For more information, please contact:

    U.S. Corporate and Government Sales
    (800) 382-3419
    corpsales@pearsontechgroup.com

For sales outside of the United States, please contact:

    International Sales
    (317) 581-3793
    international@pearsontechgroup.com

Visit Addison-Wesley on the Web: www.awprofessional.com

Library of Congress Cataloging-in-Publication Data

Lucas, Julie, 1964–
    The effective incident response team / Julie Lucas and Brian Moeller.
        p. cm.
    Includes bibliographical references and index.
    ISBN 0-201-76175-0 (alk. paper)
    1. Computer security. I. Moeller, Brian. II. Title.

    QA76 9.A25L84 2003
    005.8—dc22   2003057743

ISBN 0-201-76175-0
Text printed on recycled paper
1 2 3 4 5 6 7 8 9 10—CRS—0706050403
First printing, September 2003

From Julie:

In loving memory of
Dale & Elaine
Wonderful parents who gave me the foundation to achieve
whatever I set my mind to attempt.

And
Dedicated to
Jason, Christie, Katie, and my family
Thanks for your help, support, and encouragement!

From Brian:

Dedicated to
Adeline
A wonderful grandmother who encouraged me to continue,
no matter how difficult I thought it was.

And
Sherry, along with the rest of my family
Thank you for your love and support.

Contents

Foreword

Computer security incidents and incident response are like fires and fire fighting.

Fires and computer security incidents can both be destructive and costly.

Small fires that are not effectively contained can turn into large fires that are more destructive and harder to control. Small computer security incidents that are not contained quickly or effectively can turn into large incidents that are more damaging and harder to contain.

Because fires and computer security incidents can be destructive and costly, we put effort into finding ways to prevent them in the first place. Think of the fire safety instruction that you probably received when you were in elementary school or when you read product usage warnings—don't play with matches, don't use candles near curtains, be careful with space heaters. Products such as children's sleepwear, consumer electronics, and construction materials are tested for fire safety. We develop (and enforce) building codes and other standards to help ensure that fires don't break out often. We do similar things to prevent computer security incidents. We create policies, develop procedures, conduct computer security awareness training, create checklists for locking down various sorts of computers and the services that run on them, install firewalls, use virtual private networks, and conduct audits.

Despite our best efforts at prevention, however, fires sometimes still break out. We have fire alarm systems to detect and warn us about these events so that we can respond to them quickly. Similarly, we design and deploy host- and network-based intrusion detection systems to detect attacks against our own computers and successful intrusions on the same.

Because fires are dangerous and we cannot completely prevent them, we devote significant resources to establishing community fire departments that respond to the fires that do occur. These groups develop procedures for effectively containing fires of various types and train people to implement those procedures in a variety of circumstances so that they can effectively handle the fires that crop up, which are unpredictable in time, type, and severity. Likewise, in the computer security world, we establish groups to handle the computer security incidents that slip past our defenses. These teams create procedures and undergo training so that they can effectively contain the incidents that crop up, which are unpredictable in the same ways that fires are.

It would be foolish to invest all of our resources in fire prevention to the exclusion of effective fire fighting or to invest in fire fighting without paying due attention to fire prevention. It is good to prevent fires, but we probably can't afford to do what would be needed to absolutely prevent them, so they will sometimes occur and we will need to respond. It would also be foolish to invest all of our "computer security" resources in incident prevention to the exclusion of effective incident response, or in incident response without attempting to prevent incidents in the first place.

These days, computer security incident response teams are involved in more than "traditional" computer intrusions. Because computers are ubiquitous in the business world, digital evidence is likely to come into play in many situations that are not directly related to computer security, such as investigations of employee misconduct, criminal activity, and research fraud. Incident response team members often become involved in computer-related investigations because they have a pool of expertise in discovering, preserving, and interpreting digital evidence. This possibility provides another good reason for forming (or improving) your incident response team.

This book focuses on forming teams to provide effective incident response. Julie and Brian approach the task as if it were a puzzle. They introduce and describe the pieces and then discuss how you put them together. Both authors have considerable experience in the computer security incident response field, and they know the questions that you will need to ask and answer as you design your own team and procedures.

Some groups may choose not to create a "formal" incident response team or may choose to outsource their incident response procedures. Although the thrust of this book is on forming your own team, it nevertheless provides a helpful framework within which to evaluate and explore these alternatives.

Have fun assembling the puzzle!

—Steve Romig

Preface

This book is about computer security incident response teams. Sometimes when we mention this phrase, people picture war-painted commandoes, late on a rainy night, in a black helicopter at treetop level, chasing the author of a computer virus through rugged mountainous terrain.

That couldn't be further from the truth. In reality, these teams consist of people who are armed with a plan and a desire to secure and investigate inconsistent, odd, anomalous events, or merely violations of policy on their network and computer systems.

This book is the first to cover the incident response team in depth—from the history and justification for forming one, to the determination of what the team will provide to the organization, to the organization of the team, to the process of attracting, hiring, and retaining the proper team members, to legal issues, to methods of dealing with incidents. It includes many examples, some taken directly from the field, and some encountered as a result of lessons learned in the field. The book takes as its perspective a normal organization—one where resources are not unlimited and where keeping the organization working smoothly, efficiently, and profitably is paramount.

We've written this book for the mid-level manager and other personnel who are responsible for the creation and day-to-day operation of an incident response team. The book also keeps the people who handle the incidents in mind. Because many other books discuss intrusion detection methodology, details about file systems, and forensics, we merely touch on those subjects and do not dive into the technical issues surrounding those items.

In building this book, we discovered a lot about how different opinions can affect the formation of a team. Both authors have been involved with incident response teams for quite a while. It's interesting to see how different dynamics and focuses can affect a team. Some teams are more technical in nature and may be branches of a company's computer security or system administration group. Others are more policy-oriented and take an "auditing" or "leading practices" approach, learning from each incident. One common thread is that each team has a strong focus, enjoys excellent leadership, and therefore garners the support of its organization to continue its mission successfully.

Another similarity shared by nearly every team we've talked with is that the team members never feel that they're doing as much as they could do. Their incident response operations aren't perfect, and they all wish they could offer more services, investigate and research more incidents, and provide the best prevention of any organization in their industry sector. Most will admit that they are doing quite a good job with the resources that they have. This attitude is a healthy one. Although the pursuit of perfection is something wonderful, it's something that will never be efficiently achieved. There's always something that will be an exception to what you've planned for. Some folks have suggested that a certain automobile is the perfect automobile. If you've ever encountered a used-car salesman, he will have several available that are the perfect automobile. There are certainly some fine automobiles on the market today, but none of them is perfect. Similarly, there are no perfect incident response teams. There will always be something new for the teams to accomplish. We mention goals several times along the way in the book—they're very important to have. They measure how well your team is doing for what's important to the organization.

In the process of writing this book, we learned that there are many different ways to do the job of incident response. Inevitably, we were asked, "Which is best?" Answering that question is one of the reasons that we wrote this book. In several places, we discuss the risks, benefits, and costs of engaging in certain activity. This factor must be considered carefully for just about any organization's product or service, but sometimes it isn't given enough consideration when dealing with computer or IT-based issues. After you've read this book, we certainly encourage you to look at your organization and do a bit of cost, risk, and benefit analysis. Are the risks of running a certain product worth the extra benefits that it provides? Are the costs of a particular architecture or computer system making the users that much more productive? Sadly, we've seen cases where organizations with wonderful business prowess seem to become giggling school kids when it comes to making decisions regarding the risks or benefits that technology can bring to them.

Management reporting is often an elusive quantity for incident response teams. Teams sometimes struggle with what to report, how much detail to include, and when to report it. It's an interesting company dynamic. We've encountered very senior-level managers in an elevator and been asked for an informal briefing regarding a recent virus infestation. Efforts spent on reporting are never wasted time. If you can quickly report trends for this month, this quarter, and this year to date, and compare them to last year's data, you will be in very good shape. Senior managers sometimes need to be reminded that their investment in a team is a good one, that the team is being productive, and that they're taking care of the important behind-the-scenes business that keeps the organization's information flowing securely. Some of the most uncomfortable meetings that we've attended were ones where we were asked about something that we didn't track. This sort of reporting and the briefings that go along with them are a very valuable tool for the incident response team manager. You'll see this material again later in the book.

The final point that we'll include here is the fact that time spent on preventing an incident is always well worth the effort. Merely investigating an incident, then closing the case without analyzing what happened and figuring out how to prevent a similar thing from occurring in other places on your network, is truly negligent. We mention this point because it is often missed. Prevention of a brand-new type of incident is something that is very difficult to plan for, and it takes skill. Preventing a recurrence of something that your team has already encountered is much easier to do. The old saying "Fool me once, shame on you; fool me twice, shame on me" certainly applies in this case.

Preventing the spread of computer crime also entails helping your neighbors do the same thing. Computer security professionals are just that—professionals. They know the value of your organization's information. They also know the value of sharing information related to computer crime so that in the future, your organization may benefit from shared information. Computer crime information and generalized information on incidents, viruses, and vulnerabilities are all very important sources that will provide your organization with the opportunity to prevent an incident without having to do the initial investigative work. By using this information and sharing your own computer crime experience (but not your organization's valuable data!), you contribute to reducing the total numbers of systems that can be considered potential victims.

Use this book as an information tool when forming your team. Organizational suggestions and examples of work flow are intended to allow your organization to maximize its technical resources. The book includes many examples of day-to-day team operations, communications, forms, and legal references. As a result, it will continue to be a valuable resource after your team becomes operational.

We've used the analogy of identifying the pieces of a puzzle and putting that puzzle together throughout the book. The "pieces of the puzzle" refer to the many considerations that should be taken into account when forming a team. Once these decisions are made, they work together to form the "picture of incident response." Some may consider certain pieces identified as merely common sense. It's been our experience, however, that even the most obvious considerations may be missed when you're challenged with the overwhelming task of forming a team. Take advantage of the experiences we've gained from having "been there and done that" and let this book guide you through the process. Good luck and enjoy the puzzle!

Some Notes of Thanks

Brian's Acknowledgments

Many people have had direct and indirect influence on the subject matter in this book. I would certainly like to list all of the names here, but that would be impossible. Even if I don't mention everyone, all of your work, encouragement, and influence certainly is appreciated. Some of the people who I'd like to acknowledge by name are Steve Romig, Adeline Moeller, Doris Moeller, Sherry Engle, Mary Kay

Jacobs, Natalie Kupferberg, Clifford Collins, Dr. Philip B. Hollander, Mowgli Assor, Frances Christman, William FitzSimmons, and Pascal Meunier.

I'd especially like to thank Julie. She's been incredibly patient, and a good sport during the writing of this book. Even during those times when we didn't think it could ever turn out as well as it did, she was always dedicated to the project, and her commitment became contagious.

Julie's Acknowledgments

In July 1991, I attended a computer security seminar in Hawaii. The keynote speaker was one of a handful of lawyers at the time prosecuting computer "hackers." I listened to him for more than two hours, but felt like it had only been 10 minutes. Following the seminar, I bought the book *The Cuckoo's Egg* and was hooked on incident response and computer security from there on. It's been a fascinating career to date, and one that I've enjoyed immensely. Much thanks to Bill Cook for his wonderful words that day and continued support of computer security professionals!

I have had the wonderful opportunity to meet and work with numerous people over the years. Their guidance and encouragement along the way has given me a world of experiences to draw upon and hopefully made me a better manager and person. Many of these people I met during my 12 years of service in the United States Navy. From the earlier days of my Navy career, VADM Richard Mayo, Capt. Barry Ketterer, Alan Saka, CDR Rich Simpson, CDR Brenda Boorda, and CDR Lynn Johnston all stand out as friends and role models for me as a young officer.

In postgraduate school, I had some wonderful teachers and guides to increase my security knowledge while I worked on my master's degree. Dr. Cynthia Irvine, CDR Gus Lott, Rex Buddenberg, and Roger Stemp—thank you for your wisdom and guidance along the way. (Dr. Irvine—*Sneakers* is still one of my favorite movies! Professor Stemp—*User* is still a four-letter word.)

I was very fortunate to finish my Navy career at the Fleet Information Warfare Center, where I had a wonderful chance to work with numerous technical experts from all ranks. Of special mention are my friends from NCIS—Tom Gillikin, Pete Mercier, Ken Knudsen, and Will Dennis. I greatly appreciate the insight you shared with me regarding computer crime and cherished our partnership. Raul Zevallos, Shawn Lenhardt, Mike Mosher, Jim Granger (aka Skippy), and all of our contractors and civilians—thanks for the continued support and laughs. To my fellow "shipmates," thank you for your wisdom, dedication, and devotion to duty. To my friends from Dahlgren and SANS Institute, thanks for your feedback and continued desire to work together toward the end goal! To those from the other service incident response teams, thanks for sharing ideas and working with us to respond to the incidents and mission. Finally, a special thanks is extended to Chuck Kasinger, one of the best officers I ever had the pleasure of working for in the Navy. You taught me so much in our two-plus years of working together. Your continued guidance, humor, and technical knowledge had a major impact on the success of our team. Thanks for being you!

Many other individuals from my Navy days contributed to my career and knowledge along the way. I could not begin to list them all here, but would still like to say thanks. You each had an impact on my life and I shall always cherish our days together! Continued wishes for "fair winds and following seas."

I have also been very fortunate to work with many people from other incident response and security teams over the years. To the members of FIRST, a special thanks for your guidance and friendship over the years. To those who stuck by me through a period of constant change during my first two jobs after the Navy, thanks! Kym Lee, Adrian Benson, Chris Rogers, Jim Lugabihl, Shawn Lenhardt, Curtis Bryson, and Jasper van der Horst—you were truly part of a wonderful team and I'm glad to have worked with you. Best wishes for continued success in your future! To those whom I currently work with and for, thanks for your encouragement along the way regarding this book. Your support has been greatly appreciated!

Finally, to my family—Connie, Jeff, Harry, Dale, Eileen, and all of my nieces and nephews: thanks for all of your help on a daily basis. Your support, encouragement, understanding, and love have made me a very lucky person. To Gene: thanks for your support and encouraging me to go into the Navy. Finally, to Jason and Christie: I'm a very lucky person to have such wonderful children. Always stay true to yourself and rely on the foundation we've built together.

Special Thanks from Both of Us

The reviewers and publishers of this book were especially helpful and always willing to lend a hand when we needed it. Our friends at Addison-Wesley had a part in this book that couldn't have been done by anyone else. Emily Frey, Jessica Goldstein, and Karen Gettman— thank you for your patience and guidance.

To all those who gave of their time to review and provide feedback, even that which was a little hard to read, a special "thank you." To our early reviewers, Wietse Venema and Steven Romig, and your comments and guidance helped tremendously to set the tone for the book and added greatly to the construction of our "puzzle." To the later reviewers, your suggestions helped us achieve the finished product and gave us additional perspective on the tone and guidance offered. Many thanks to all!

—Julie & Brian

Welcome to the Information Age

When it comes to controlling our information, too many systems have been implemented but given little or no regard to security until a compromise has occurred. Any computer system can be compromised, given enough time and resources. The key to preventing such a security breach is to ensure that enough safeguards are present to persuade a would-be intruder to move on to another target. However, when an intruder, worm, virus, or automated attack persists in targeting a computer system, having specific controls in place and a plan of action for responding to the attack or computer incident can greatly reduce the resultant costs to an organization. The implementation of a computer incident response team (CIRT), whether it is formed with internal or external resources, is one safeguard that can produce a large return on investment during a crisis situation.

This book is meant to serve as a guide to anyone contemplating or charged with forming a CIRT. The creation of such a team is not a trivial matter, and many issues must be addressed up front to ensure a smooth implementation. This book identifies most of these issues so as to help with the creation process. Once the team is formed and operational, this guide should continue to serve as a valuable resource while the team evolves to meet the demands of the constituency it serves and to respond to the ever-changing types of vulnerabilities.

With the evolution of computer systems into both local and wide area networks, the scope of computer security has increased dramatically over the past two decades. The ability to adequately safeguard information while ensuring resource availability has increasingly become a challenging task for management, system administrators, and information security personnel alike. Today, more than ever, people are discovering their vulnerability to the perils of the Information Age. As such, the topic of computer security is becoming more of a priority in many organizations. Computer security isn't a new field— it has existed since the development of the first computer. What is new is the broader view that must be taken to ensure the security of a system and the information it contains. Personnel addressing areas such as incident response must be prepared for attacks targeting any platform, exploiting any vulnerability, at any time. This uncertainty makes the world of incident response very challenging and often exciting.

This book addresses several topics that should be considered when forming an incident response team. It was written for the executive contemplating the formation of a team and for the manager charged with carrying out the directive to provide an incident response capability. Those hired to detect and respond to the incidents as they occur should find many of the topics presented equally useful, as well as those considering the world of incident response for a career. Although many technical factors are touched upon in various sections, this book was not intended to be an in-depth technical guide. Several resources are already available for that purpose. Instead, this book focuses on the decision-making aspects of creating the team, from the initial tasking through achieving an operational state.

A Brief History

Before we explore the issues surrounding computer incident response and the many considerations that apply when forming a response team, let's look at how the need for computer incident response teams first emerged. Computer systems have experienced a variety of attacks from both internal and external resources since shortly after the computer was first invented. It was not until the late 1980s, however, that some of these attacks started gaining attention in the media. One of the first widely publicized attacks was attributed to the West German Computer Club (better known as the Chaos Club). In 1987, Chaos announced that it had successfully penetrated NASA's computer systems. NASA was unaware of this intrusion until messages began appearing on its system.[1] Also in 1987, a 75-cent accounting error alerted Cliff Stoll, an astronomer turned systems manager at Lawrence Berkeley Laboratories, to another intrusion. For two years, Dr. Stoll followed the intruder as he tried to break into more than 450 computer systems (many of which were government-owned).[2] Eventually, the chase led to a small group of West German hackers with ties to the Soviet KGB. This incident was documented in the book *The Cuckoo's Egg,* which provides a very interesting account of how Dr. Stoll investigated and tracked the intruders from start to finish. (This book is highly recommended for anyone interested in computer incident response.)

One of the largest attacks to gain attention in the late 1980s centered on the computer worm released on the Internet by Robert T. Morris, Jr., a Cornell University graduate student, on November 2, 1988. In less than 48 hours, the worm spread throughout the network, infecting more than 2100 computers. Although no data were actually destroyed, the cost to fix the systems and the lost work hours were estimated to exceed $1 million.[3]

CERT

As a result of these and other early incidents, it became clear that communications and cooperation among the Internet community was not prepared to adequately and quickly respond to computer-based incidents. Consequently, after the Morris worm incident, the Defense

---

1. Stoll, Clifford. *The Cuckoo's Egg.* New York: Pocket Books Publishing, 1990.

2. Shaffer, Steven L., and Alan R. Simon. *Network Security.* Cambridge, MA: Academic Press, 1994.

3. Stallings, William. *Network and Internetwork Security: Principles and Practice.* Englewood Cliffs, NJ: Prentice Hall, 1995.

Advanced Research Projects Agency (DARPA) decided to form a response team that would provide an immediate, rapid response to major attacks on computer resources. The result was the formation of the Computer Emergency Response Team (CERT).

The CERT was funded by DARPA and co-located at Carnegie Mellon University in Pittsburgh, Pennsylvania. Soon after its creation, other incident and emergency response teams began to be formed. The CERT eventually changed its name to CERT Coordination Center (CERT CC). The CERT CC serves as an incident response team for other teams requiring assistance and for organizations worldwide that do not have teams of their own to rely upon. It should also be noted that the term *CERT* was trademarked by Carnegie Mellon University in 1998. Therefore, teams wishing to use CERT as their name or part of their name should coordinate the use of the term with the CERT CC first.

Today, CERT CC's charter is to "work with the Internet community to facilitate its response to computer security events involving Internet hosts" while taking proactive steps to increase the overall awareness of computer security issues.[4] CERT CC also conducts research geared toward improving the computer security of existing systems. Its "products and services include 24-hour technical assistance for responding to computer security incidents, product vulnerability assistance, technical documents, and seminars. In addition, the team maintains a mailing list for CERT advisories, and provides Web site http://www.cert.org, where security-related documents, CERT advisories, and information regarding security and hacking tools are available."[5] Although the CERT CC was initially funded by DARPA, it is available to perform research, conduct training, and do similar work for other government agencies and the civilian sector. Personnel working in this organization are actually employed by the Software Engineering Institute (SEI). The http://www.cert.org Web page may be referenced for more information on the services offered and for up-to-date contact information.

---

4. http://www.cert.org. CERT Coordination Center FAQ, section A1, "What Is the CERT Coordination Center?"

5. http://www.cert.org. CERT Coordination Center FAQ, section A1, "What Is the CERT Coordination Center?"

More Teams

Soon after the initial formation of the CERT, the U.S. Department of Energy formed the Computer Incident Advisory Capability (CIAC) in 1989. The CIAC was created to respond to computer security events affecting the organizations within the Department of Energy.

In the years that followed, this trend continued, with myriad organizations such as universities, private companies, and government groups forming teams to address incidents within their own organizations. The creation of teams was not restricted to the United States alone, but spread to many countries around the world. Some of the earlier international teams included the AUSCERT (the team serving organizations within Australia and New Zealand) and DFN-CERT (Germany). Some vendors actually created two separate teams: one focusing on vulnerabilities identified in their products and another addressing incidents within their company. Eventually, teams providing incident response in exchange for a fee began to appear on the scene, with companies such as IBM and Internet Security Systems (ISS) offering incident response services. Like the CERT CC, many of these teams have become well known for their security expertise and provide numerous security services such as vulnerability alerts and trend analysis.

With the large number of incident response teams emerging over the past two decades, the attention given to combating attacks on computer networks has greatly increased. Discussions of incident response can now be found in many trade journals, books, and other publications. Conferences have been organized to address the topic of incident response, training and certifications are now being offered on various aspects of the discipline, and various organizations targeting the need for computer security and incident response have begun to emerge. One of the earliest joint organizations focusing on incident response that emerged was FIRST.

FIRST

As the number of incident response teams increased, many of them tried to interact. Difficulties due to different time zones, languages, standards, and conventions soon presented many challenges. All of the teams had one central purpose: to respond to computer security-related incidents. As the source of an attack could quite easily be in any part of the world, the need for coordination and interaction between teams was readily apparent. Another major incident that involved numerous nodes on the SPAN 5 network reemphasized the need to establish an improved level of communications between teams, so a small group of the teams decided to form the organization that became known as FIRST.

FIRST stands for the Forum of Incident Response and Security Teams. The group was initially formed in 1990 with a total of 11 member teams. Since that time, its membership has grown to more than 100 teams. FIRST is an international organization which draws its members from many divisions of government and the private sector. The group's mission is to

- Provide members with technical information, tools, methods, assistance, and guidance;
- Coordinate proactive liaison activities and analytical support;
- Encourage the development of quality products and services;
- Improve national and international information security for government, private industry, academia, and the individual; and
- Enhance the image and status of the incident response and security teams (IRST) community in the outside world.[6]

FIRST is an excellent avenue for resource sharing. The organization communicates via electronic mail and holds various meetings throughout the year. Technical colloquia are limited in attendance to member teams only, but the annual meeting is open to all. The location of the annual meeting rotates from year to year, but the event typically takes place during the third week of June. Attending the annual meeting is an excellent way to meet and network with others in the field of incident response and security teams from around the world. If an organization is considering the development of an internal incident response capability, the annual conference is a great starting point for establishing contacts and conducting further research.

---

6. http://www.first.org.

What Does This Mean to My Organization?

CERT, FIRST, and several other organizations are wonderful resources for incident response teams (IRTs) to use. It is common practice for an IRT to work with such organizations to share information, share learning experiences, compare notes on incident handling, and share the burden of incident analysis.

In the authors' experience, these organizations have been very helpful to our teams in assisting us to make contact with the proper organizations, figuring out exactly what was happening with certain incidents, and providing information on patches, vulnerabilities, and workarounds to help recover from our incidents.

Examples of Incident Response Teams

There are many types of computer incident response teams in existence today. Not only do they vary in the names used to describe the teams, but they also differ in terms of their constituencies, funding, size, scope, and reporting requirements. Specific purposes and goals will also vary, but all teams share the underlying function of safeguarding the security of the information systems they are chartered to protect.

Some teams are very small, with their entire constituency being located in one building. Others have a global responsibility and may encompass multiple teams working together to cover various regions. Most of the larger computer hardware and software vendors maintain response teams of some sort for their internal systems. Some of these vendors have additional teams addressing specific vulnerabilities on their products, which in turn are responsible for writing the "vendor alerts" or advisories about vulnerabilities discovered in their hardware or software products. Some vendors, particularly consulting organizations, maintain incident response teams for hire, which will be deployed to a client's site to either assist internal personnel with responding to the incident or solely handle the incident response. For organizations with constrained resources, this avenue may prove to be a valuable alternative to funding an internal response team.

Most of the larger universities, both within the United States and abroad, have incident response teams established to address attacks on their systems. These teams have the toughest jobs, due to the open nature of most university settings and the overwhelming challenge of change control. Several big-name universities with very proactive teams are involved in FIRST. In fact, some of the founding members of FIRST were university-based teams.

Many governments and organizations around the world have also sponsored various types of IRTs. CIAC is an example of a government-sponsored team in the United States serving the Department of Energy. Other agencies and departments in the U.S. government have also formed incident response teams, such as the military teams and the U.S. Postal Service team. AUSCERT, CERTCC-KR, CERT-IT, and EWA-Canada/CanCERT are all examples of teams that handle incidents throughout their countries. Specifically, these teams respond to incidents occurring in Australia, Korea, Italy, and Canada, respectively. Examples of other international teams with a specific focus in their countries are BTCERTCC (British Telecommunications CERT Coordination Center), CARNet CERT (Croatian Academic and Research Network CERT), CERT-NASK (CERT—Research and Academic Network in Poland), and ILAN-CERT (Israeli Academic CERT).

There really is neither a rigid definition for a CIRT or information security response team (ISRT) nor a standardized set of metrics for a team to meet. Although many are referred to as incident response teams, the level of services they offer can vary greatly. Therefore, the functionality offered by the team cannot be assumed based on the team's name alone, as most teams are customized to best suit their organizations.

Some Statistics

With the implementation of several teams around the world, is there a need for additional teams? Yes! Since 1999, the Computer Security Institute (CSI), in conjunction with the Federal Bureau of Investigation, has conducted a Computer Crime and Security Survey as a public service to increase computer security awareness and to assist in determining the extent of computer crime in the United States. These surveys have identified the following trends:

- Organizations come under cyber attack from both inside and outside of their electronic perimeters.
- A wide range of cyber attacks have been detected.
- Cyber attacks can result in serious financial losses.
- Defending successfully against such attacks requires more than just the use of information security technologies.

A total of 503 organizations responded to the 2002 survey. Of that total, 80 percent acknowledged financial losses due to the attacks, yet only 223 respondents could estimate the value of that loss. The resulting costs to these organizations totaled $455,848,000! The following highlights were taken from the 2002 survey results and are quoted here to provide a sense of the need for incident response teams:

- Ninety percent of the respondents detected computer security breaches within the last 12 months.
- Eighty percent acknowledged financial losses due to computer breaches.
- Forty-four percent of those acknowledging financial losses were willing and/or able to quantify their financial losses.
- As in previous years, the most serious financial losses occurred through the theft of proprietary information (26 respondents reported losses of $170,827,000) and financial fraud (25 respondents reported losses of $115,753,000).
- Seventy-four percent cited their Internet connection as a frequent point of attack; thirty-three percent cited their internal systems as a frequent point of attack.
- Thirty-four percent reported their intrusions to law enforcement.
- Forty percent of respondents detected system penetration from the outside.
- Forty percent of respondents detected denial-of-service attacks.

- Seventy-eight percent detected employee abuse of Internet access privileges.
- Eighty-five percent detected computer viruses.[7]

The estimated losses per category of attack reported in 2002 were as follows:

- Theft of proprietary information: $170,827,000
- Financial fraud: $115,753,000
- Insider abuse of Internet access: $50,099,000
- Virus: $49,979,000
- Denial of service: $18,370,500
- Sabotage of data networks: $15,134,000
- System penetration by outsider: $13,055,000
- Laptop theft: $11,766,500
- Telecommunications eavesdropping: $6,015,000
- Unauthorized insider access: $4,503,000
- Telecommunications fraud: $346,000[8]

The most recent CSI/FBI Computer Crime and Security Survey may be obtained through the CSI Web site at http://www.gocsi.com.

The CSI/FBI survey is just one example of recent efforts to identify trends in computer crimes and incidents. Some security experts may disagree about which survey results provide the clearest and most accurate picture. Regardless of the survey selected to review for statistics and trends, the fact remains that security must be addressed as our dependence on information systems strengthens. The ability to respond to attacks on our information is a requirement that is here to stay.

---

7. Power, Richard, ed. "2002 CSI/FBI Computer Crime and Security Survey." *Computer Security Institute,* vol. VIII, no. 1, spring 2002.

8. Power, Richard, ed. "2002 CSI/FBI Computer Crime and Security Survey." *Computer Security Institute,* vol. VIII, no. 1, spring 2002.

Summary

Enormous amounts of money and labor can be spent securing a company's information infrastructure from a multitude of risks. To be completely effective, the steps taken for security must address all phases of the life cycle of a system. Today, more than ever, as connectivity and technological progress occurs, organizations are finding themselves vulnerable in the Information Age. For this reason, each organization must be prepared for an attack to its information systems. The formation of an incident response team may be the avenue selected for addressing this concern.

The rest of this book discusses many considerations that apply during the formation of such a team. In many respects, the creation of this team may be viewed as solving a jigsaw puzzle. Many pieces all work together to form one functional picture. The remaining chapters will identify the pieces of the puzzle and offer recommendations for linking them together to provide a complete picture of an incident response team. Although the primary focus of this book is to help management with the many decisions that must be made in putting that puzzle together, the book serves equally well as a resource for anyone participating on the team or for anyone concerned about ensuring the security of information systems.

CHAPTER 2

What's Your Mission?

Many people who enjoy putting jigsaw puzzles together take the same approach. That is, they find the pieces that outline the picture and put the frame together first, then proceed to identify and place the inner pieces. By having the border in place, it often becomes easier to get a sense of the overall picture, with the border serving as the foundation for completing the task at hand.

This chapter focuses on identifying those border pieces of the CIRT puzzle by providing numerous considerations that should be addressed during the formation of a team. By addressing these items first, a solid foundation can be laid for the other decisions that must be made toward the completion of the CIRT. The chapter first defines the focus and mission of the team, then moves into various operational aspects that may be considered.

Focus and Scope

Management courses frequently highlight the importance of mission statements. It is often emphasized that all members of a team or organization should understand the group's mission so they can take

---

1. Who is included in the team's constituency? In other words, who owns the computers the team will be responsible for monitoring and responding to incidents on if they are attacked?
2. How dispersed is the constituency? If it is spread out, are there regional information technology resources that may be called upon during a crisis?
3. What is the ideal manner for the team to respond to an incident: on-site, remotely, or through some combination of these methods?
4. Will the team work with law enforcement either directly or indirectly?
5. Will the team's strategy be strictly reactive, or both proactive and reactive?
6. What services or functions will the team provide?
7. What type of activity is considered to be an incident (i.e., to what sort of activity will the team respond)?
8. How will incident reports be stored and tracked?
9. How will the incidents be counted?
10. What statistics need to be provided to reflect the team's activities? Who will need these statistics and how often? How granular should the statistics be?

Figure 2-1   Questions to Help Identify the Team's Mission

ownership of the tasks at hand. The formation of a CIRT team is no different with respect to having a clearly identified mission. Establishing a mission up front by identifying the scope and focus of the team will ease the decision-making process for many later issues. The mission will also have a direct impact on the number and types of resources that need to be allocated to the team. To aid with this task, start by answering a few basic questions. (These questions are listed in Figure 2–1.)

Know Who You're Protecting: Defining Your Constituency

First, who is included in the team's constituency? In other words, who are the people who own, use, operate, and are responsible for maintaining the computers that the team will be monitoring and responding to incidents on if they are attacked? In some cases, this question is very easy to answer. For example, a university team would usually consider the students, staff, and any other authorized users to be its constituency. In other cases, the answer may not be so clear. For example, a hardware or software vendor may have a team established to address internal issues only, to address issues pertaining to its products only for its customers, or possibly to address incidents on its products and other vendors' products through a consulting arrangement. If the vendor has a partnership with another company, will the team have any responsibilities for addressing incidents as part of the partnership? Deciding who the team will support up front helps set the stage for the next set of questions that need to be addressed.

The distribution of the team's constituency or customer base will also have a major effect on many issues that must be addressed when forming a team. Will all of the team's clients be located in one building, one city, one state, one geographic region, one country, or worldwide? A large distribution will provide several obstacles or challenges when on-site support is needed and when support must be provided 24 hours per day.

Defining Response

Once the constituency is identified, the manner in which the team will respond to incidents should be addressed. If the constituency is located in one central location, this issue should not be a problem. If the computers are dispersed over a wide geographic area or worldwide, however, on-site response can be a challenge. Depending on the technical expertise of the organization's system administrators, a team may be able to remotely provide assistance by walking a local system administrator through response procedures over the phone, rather than having someone from the team fly to the location and provide on-site support. This approach should be taken whenever possible, as the reaction time will generally be quicker (thus limiting potential damage) and the cost of responding to the incident will be lower.

If on-site support is required, then a minimum of two people should be sent to the location with specific checklists and tools at their disposal. A two-person team is recommended for the following reasons:

- If problems arise during the response process, the second person can provide backup support to the primary person in completing a division of the tasks to be performed.
- If personnel are to be interviewed, having a second person can expedite the overall process: One person can conduct the interviews while the other performs the technical response.
- If the level of expertise varies between the individuals, the knowledge and experience of one may be supplemented by the knowledge and experience of the other. This is especially true for personnel who are relatively new to the incident response role.
- A two-person team can provide verification that procedures were correctly followed in case any questions arise about the tasks completed.
- One person can help with documenting the steps taken, while the other is performing the tasks at hand.

Keep in mind that the above checklist should be considered a guide to help with the incident response, but cannot cover every possible scenario that the incident handlers may encounter.

For teams that cover a large geographic region (including those with worldwide responsibility), the decision may be made to create several teams and have them geographically dispersed. This approach can help with covering various time zones and limit the potential response time for on-site support. On the downside, the possibility of detecting a wide-scale attack may be inhibited because varying resources analyze the incident data. If multiple teams are used, it is a good idea to have one central headquarters receive and evaluate the incident data from the subteams to provide wide-scale correlation. (As our tools progress in this realm, this correlation should become easier.)

Working with Law Enforcement

Another issue that should be addressed up front is how the team will interact with the law enforcement community. Will the team work with law enforcement either directly or indirectly? In addressing this question, consider the following: The computer is like any other invention that has had a major impact on our daily lives in that it has both benefits and negative consequences. A good analogy is the automobile. When the car first came along, it enabled people to do things more quickly and effectively than they could prior to its invention. People were able to travel farther, travel together more efficiently, and travel in much more comfort, thereby doing more things in a day by covering more places. Cars also had negative effects—namely, automobile accidents and automobile theft. It took people some time to learn how to deal with these negative effects, design and implement safety and security features, and establish laws to address the problems and challenges of the new invention.

Similarly, the computer is an invention that has enabled people to do many more tasks in an increasingly efficient manner and has literally changed the way we live. In fact, even an auto mechanic cannot work on a car now without a computer to run diagnostic tests. Although the positive results have rapidly expanded the use of computers, some negative uses still need to be addressed—namely, computer crime. It will take us some time to catch up to the invention by developing and widely implementing security safeguards to help protect systems better and to establish case law. With this fact in mind, enabling an incident response team to work with law enforcement can have a very positive effect on the overall safeguards that are ultimately established. In fact, the best approach when investigating any incident that potentially involves a crime uses three experts: an attorney who is familiar with high-tech crime laws, the law enforcement agent, and the technical expert. Each has valuable knowledge and insight that can be vital when taking a case to trial.

One major advantage to working with a law enforcement agency is the benefit of extended networking. Specifically, many larger law enforcement agencies have developed relationships with other law enforcement groups that may provide an added advantage in tracking an external perpetrator who has broken into a system or successfully launched a denial-of-service attack. A team trying to track an attacker on its own without any law enforcement involvement will typically find this task much more difficult, especially when the incident crosses international boundaries. It is far better (and many times easier) to provide the information to law enforcement officials and let them work with their contacts and resources to help track an intruder.

Working with law enforcement may also have some disadvantages. Often, when an organization is asked why it did not bring in law enforcement, the organization states that it didn't want the company name in the newspaper. It didn't want the publicity of a "hacking case." Although in most cases the media isn't interested in such things, this bad publicity is a real concern. There are ways to keep the company out of the news, such as using an attorney to keep the case as private as the laws will allow. Also, the organization may want to turn the case over to a prosecutor to pursue in conjunction with local, state, or federal law enforcement agents to pursue as a crime against the state or federal government, instead of naming the company in the proceedings.

An additional disadvantage of working with law enforcement may be the threat of losing control of the case. Inviting law enforcement to investigate a case may require that the case be fully investigated, even if your organization decides to stop its pursuit of the attacker. Although situations where a case cannot be stopped are very rare (all of the authors' dealings with law enforcement have been very cooperative), this outcome may be a possibility.

Even if your organization chooses to not include law enforcement as a regular part of its investigative team, it is a good idea to contact city, county, state, and federal (FBI especially) law enforcement agencies to introduce yourself and to get an idea of their services, contact information, capabilities, evidence requirements, and reporting procedures. It's always good to be prepared, even if you don't plan on using them.

Of course, legal considerations must also be addressed as they relate to privacy laws, company policies, and other issues that determine what information is shared with law enforcement. If the organization is considering the inclusion of law enforcement officials directly on the team, the first step would be to discuss the possibilities, concerns, and limitations with the appropriate legal organization as well as the management team.

If computer crime laws are to evolve so that they will better protect our information, they must be tried and tested in the criminal justice system. Organizations reporting to and working with law enforcement will facilitate this evolution. Even if an organization decides not to work directly with law enforcement, inevitably the team will encounter an incident where a law has been broken. Having contacts established up front with local, regional, state, and federal law enforcement agencies will help expedite the reporting process when this need arises. Groups such as InfraGard can help to establish these contacts.

InfraGard

Several groups have been formed in recent years to provide an avenue for networking and resource sharing between law enforcement officials and the technical community. One of these groups is InfraGard. "The National InfraGard Program began as a pilot project in 1996, when the Cleveland FBI Field Office asked local computer professionals to assist the FBI in determining how to better protect critical information systems in the public and private sectors. From this new partnership, the first InfraGard Chapter was formed to address both cyber and physical threats."[1] InfraGard's government component is staffed by the FBI and the Department of Homeland Security's National Information Protection Center (NIPC) and includes numerous chapters throughout the United States. In fact, all 56 FBI field offices have now opened local chapters with hundreds of members across the nation. InfraGard is seen as a cooperative effort between law enforcement and the private sector, with the participants being dedicated to increasing the security of critical infrastructures within the United States. From the beginning, the FBI has stated that it is not an FBI-run program, but rather a community program in which

---

1. http://www.infragard.net/history_main_pg.html.

the FBI and many other government agencies participate. The Infra-Gard program is often likened to a "neighborhood watch" program, in which businesses and agencies with similar interests share information and experiences to help reduce the risks of a networked community.

InfraGard was formed as a national organization, with individually governed and managed chapters. Working together within and between chapters, the group members strive to better protect critical information assets by enabling the flow of information between the technical community, corporate policy makers, the owners of the critical infrastructure, law enforcement, and lawmakers. Becoming involved with a local chapter provides an excellent avenue for meeting law enforcement officials, legal experts, and other technical resources in the area that may be contacted when the need arises. More information may be obtained by contacting the closest FBI office or from the national InfraGard Web page (http://www.infragard.net).

Operational Strategy

At this point, we have addressed some basic factors in identifying the focus and scope of the team. The next major section of the puzzle to consider is the team's operational strategy. Specifically, will the team be strictly reactive or both proactive and reactive in nature? If it is reactive only, the team would strictly respond to computer incidents as they are detected or reported from the constituency. Tools such as intrusion detection systems (IDSs) may be used to monitor for and detect unauthorized activity as it happens. (Some IDSs can also be configured to help stop an attack in progress.)

It is very difficult, and sometimes ineffective, for a team to remain completely reactive. For example, if an incident affects a number of systems, it may be a prudent measure to proactively examine other systems that do not appear to have been affected. This activity ensures that no damage was inflicted and confirms that proper safeguards are in place to prevent the systems from being affected in the future. Although prevention programs are difficult to justify because it is nearly impossible to quantify the number of incidents prevented, it stands to reason that an incident that is prevented consumes fewer resources than one that must be investigated.[2]

If the team is to be both proactive and reactive in nature, then services such as risk assessments, vulnerability analysis, and training may be included in the capabilities offered by the team. The number of tasks assigned to the team will have a direct impact on the number of personnel and tools required for the team to be completely operational. Keep in mind that some of these services may be outsourced or scaled appropriately for the organization, depending on the projected return on the investment for the services that are offered. More detail on the types of services that the team may consider offering is provided later in this chapter.

Defining an Incident

Regardless of the strategy taken, the type of activity that is considered to be an incident should be clearly decided up front. It is strongly recommended that a clear, concise definition be developed for the "incidents" a team will address. Generic or vague definitions such as "unauthorized activity" leave too much room for interpretation and may negatively affect operations. For example, the number of personnel assigned to the team may prove insufficient for the volume of "unauthorized activity" reported and problems may be encountered in trying to enter and track the incident data in a database or trouble ticket system.

This question leads into a discussion on the very important topic of terminology. As this topic can be quite expansive, a separate chapter has been dedicated to this one piece of the puzzle. Refer to Chapter 3 for this discussion.

Tracking an Incident

Although this is still very early in the book, you should consider your incident tracking strategy to be a part of the foundation of the

---

2. Committee on Institutional Cooperation. *Final Report: Incident Cost Analysis and Modeling Project,* University of Michigan, 1998.

incident response team. The ability to track incidents is important for several reasons:

- *Management Reporting.* The incident tracking system may be used as a tool to justify and report on the performance of the investment that has been made in the team and security tools. Reporting the type and severity of incidents encountered also helps upper management to gain a clear picture of the threats being realized in their environment. This information can then be used to focus efforts on specific areas, such as user awareness, antivirus software, and increased levels of defense, so as to improve the overall security posture of the organization.
- *Incident Triage.* A mechanism for grouping incidents can lead to streamlining incident investigation activities, setting priorities for incidents, and correlating incident data.
- *Customer Service.* The incident response team's reputation among its constituency is critical to its success. A team that permits incidents to "fall through the cracks" will lose favor with its constituency, and eventually management support. Management will naturally expect the team to handle incident information and evidence in a responsible, prudent manner. In addition to incident accountability, a team must have a well-planned method of keeping the affected constituency abreast of the status of the incident.

A dedicated database for tracking incidents, correlating activity data, and reporting statistics to upper management can be the most valuable tool that an incident response organization has at its disposal. Tracking processes and mechanisms must be established to follow the incident from the time it is reported to the time it is considered closed. Otherwise, if the team is very busy (as most are in today's environment), the chance for an incident to "fall through the cracks" is too great. Two or more tools may actually be required for this function, such as a triage tool that feeds data into a central database. The triage tool may be used for tracking open tickets, while the database is used for reviewing specific details about the activity.

Once the team is operational, the sources for reporting a computer incident to the team will typically have multiple origins. A team may accept incident reports via the telephone, e-mail, IDS, paging systems, law enforcement, or other sources. Not all information that is reported to a team as an "incident" will, in fact, turn out to be a real incident, just as a call to the emergency 911 telephone system may not be an emergency. (*Note:* 911 is the code used within the United States for emergency calls to police, fire, and medical officials. Other codes are used in different countries, such as 0, 411, and 119.)

As activity is reported from various sites or systems, mechanisms for correlating various aspects of it need to be available. For example, how often does a specific IP address show up? Have any other attacks on a specific target been reported? How many scans of a particular port number have been detected?

Finally, statistics can be a wonderful tool for any team. A database can help to quickly identify useful data, such as the number of reports received, number of open incidents, number of false reports processed, number of times that a particular Internet service provider's (ISP) addresses have attacked systems in the team's constituency, and much more. These statistics can, in turn, help to identify specific threats to the systems that the team is trying to protect as well as justify the need for the team or additional resources moving forward. (Granted, statistics can be manipulated in many ways, but it is very difficult to dispute facts that are very well defined with a good deal of granularity.)

Counting Incidents

A similar issue that must be addressed is how incidents will be counted. It is not uncommon for an attacker to gain unauthorized access to multiple sites within the same time frame or deny services to more than one system at once. A good example was the distributed denial-of-service attacks launched in February 2000. Over the course of three days, computer systems at Yahoo!, buy.com, eBay, CNN.com, amazon.com, ZDNet.com, E*Trade, Datek online, and Excite were all affected by the attack.[3] Depending on the accounting procedures implemented by an incident response team, these attacks could have

---

3. Levy, Steven, and Brad Stone. "Hunting the Hackers." *Newsweek,* February 21, 2000, pp. 39–44.

been combined into one incident or tracked separately as nine incidents with similar patterns.

Combining the activity that appears to be attributable to the same person or group of persons can help with the correlation of the activity. Conversely, by grouping the activity together, important statistics may be lost. Most teams will combine the activity that appears to come from the same source. In that case, it is recommended that the database or means of tracking statistics have enough granularity built in to depict the number of targets affected by the attack.

Services Offered

Earlier in the chapter, we touched on the decision of whether the team should be proactive or reactive. If the team will have a proactive component, a new challenge arises: What additional services will the team provide? Some of the services that teams may choose to offer are user enrollment, vulnerability assessment, penetration testing, risk assessment, and architectural review. This list certainly isn't exhaustive and will need to be adjusted to best fit the organization's requirements. The following services are presented for consideration:

User Enrollment

The process of creating, modifying, and removing user accounts and privileges on the computer systems. It also includes the definition of the authorizations, group memberships, and access profiles for users.

Vulnerability Assessment

The process of searching for possible susceptibility for a system to be accessed in an unauthorized way or to have authorized access denied. Many commercial and free vulnerability assessment tools can help streamline this process, although these tools do require a certain amount of experience to use them effectively. There are many opinions regarding the frequency with which these assessments should be conducted, but nearly all security professionals agree that they're not done often enough.

Penetration Testing

The process of attempting to gain unauthorized access to a computer system or facility. This focused attempt to break into a system or facility is usually conducted from the perspective of a "hostile" entity and attempts to measure how much effort must be expended to gain access. The network operations group or other entity that monitors the computer resources will typically not know ahead of time that the testing will be conducted. Therefore, the capability to detect and respond to an attack can be measured while searching for potential vulnerabilities.

Risk Assessment

The process of rating and evaluating vulnerabilities, threats, value, and safeguards. It takes the results of a vulnerability assessment and adds in an analysis of threats, the value of the information, and the safeguards used to protect the information. Its purpose is to help make informed decisions based on the best balance between the risk that is posed to the organization's information and the benefit of protecting it. Although several different methodologies are used for this process, it can be a very valuable tool in making decisions about how much effort to protect a system is enough.

Architectural Review

The process of evaluating the hardware, software, network, policy, and management of a system or group of systems to ensure they do what is intended, and do not do what is not intended. This service mirrors the thought that security should be part of everyone's effort—throughout the complete life cycle of information, from concept to disposal.

User Awareness Training

The process of teaching and reinforcing knowledge of policies, procedures, and strategies while maintaining a computing environment. In terms of effectiveness, user awareness training can be one of the most valuable services that a team offers. Conversely, a lack of user awareness can represent a significant threat to any network. In this forum, users can learn effective password management, the organization's information-handling policies, procedures for sharing information, virus risks, tactics to defeat social engineering, and more. As Richard Baker noted in his book *Network Security: How to Plan for It and Achieve It:*

> One of the biggest obstacles to effective computer security today is an epidemic of misplaced emphasis. Corporations spend a lot of time and money buying and installing elaborate computer security systems to protect themselves from well-publicized outsiders like youthful invaders and virus carriers. They do next to nothing to train employees to make regular backups or to avoid that stereotype of computer insecurity: the password on a sticky note attached to the monitor.[4]

Advisory Notification

The process where security notifications are distributed to the constituency. Many teams keep an inventory of the computing platforms, software, network infrastructure, and services that their organization employs. As a manufacturer, software vendor, or other source of information publishes a notification that there may be a vulnerability in the product, a virus, or a security-related upgrade, the team would verify that the advisory is authentic and then forward it to the affected members of the constituency. Other teams (such as CERT CC and vendor teams) will be responsible for writing the advisory that is initially distributed.

Research and Development

The process of creating, evaluating, testing, and integrating new products, policies, procedures, and strategies. A lab environment in which to test and discover methods of breaking into systems, techniques for securing systems, and ways to improve and implement the enforce-

---

4. Baker, Richard H. *Network Security: How to Plan for It and Achieve It.* New York: McGraw-Hill, 1995, p. 9.

ment of company policies—and as a proving ground that enforcement can be done—can be a very valuable service to the organization.

We'll go into much more detail and share some ideas on how to implement these services later in the book.

The Importance of Credibility

The importance of the team's credibility cannot be emphasized strongly enough. One bad report, advisory, or action can be detrimental to the entire team's credibility and the damage can take years to repair. Team credibility is a result of a combination of effectiveness, integrity, professionalism, timeliness, ethics, consistency, and the ability to deal with incidents discreetly, among several other factors. If the team's credibility is damaged, members of the team's constituency will lose faith in the team and stop relying on those personnel for support in responding to incidents. For this reason, advice should not be provided unless vulnerabilities and patches have been fully tested and verified. It can almost go without saying—the incident response team must practice what it preaches. In other words, the incident response team's own tools must be patched, maintained, and well managed so as to prevent incidents.

The CERT Coordination Center provides an excellent example of protecting team credibility. The center will not issue an advisory without fully testing the vulnerabilities and patches first in its lab to verify the steps that are recommended. Given the number of computer vulnerabilities that continue to appear, a team might potentially do no other activity than issue vulnerability alerts or advisories on a daily basis. In an effort to underscore the seriousness of a vulnerability discussed in a CERT CC advisory, the coordination center will issue alerts only on vulnerabilities that are considered very serious and may potentially affect multiple computer systems. When CERT CC does issue an advisory, it will include an MD5 checksum for patches that are recommended for downloading. This step is also part of integrity protection, providing an added check for administrators who are downloading a patch to ensure that it is the same patch that is intended to be downloaded.

Summary

At this point, we have identified several key pieces that should provide a border to our incident response puzzle. Although these pieces may not be clearly defined as yet, the intent was to begin the consideration process that should be given to each issue. Every question listed in Figure 2–1 and discussed in this chapter will directly affect the type and number of resources needed for the team to succeed. Many of the following chapters will return to this basic set of questions as well. It is strongly recommended that the entire book be read before attempting to answer these questions. Numerous points yet to be made will influence each of these considerations.

The chapter concluded by touching on the importance of the team's credibility. If the issues described in this chapter form the border to the puzzle, the team's credibility could be thought of as the foundation on which the puzzle is built. After all, if the integrity of the team suffers in some way, the continuity of the picture we are trying to build will suffer as well. One large corner piece of this puzzle remains to be considered—terminology. Keep reading to complete the border.

3

The Terminology Piece

This chapter focuses on terminology. Although the topic of terminology may not seem like an important piece to the incident response puzzle, it can have a direct impact on specific resources if terms are too vaguely defined and not fully thought out. A vague definition can also lead to inefficiencies in data tracking and incident-handling procedures. To explore this issue further, let's first review the definition of a computer incident and the types of activities that may be considered to be an incident.

What Is a Computer Incident?

Although the term "computer incident" is frequently used in many forums, it does not have a universally accepted definition. The following are some examples of how the term is defined in just a few publications:

- Incidents are events that interrupt normal operating procedures and precipitate some level of crisis. Specifically, incidents are computer intrusions, denial-of-service attacks, insiders' theft of information, and any unauthorized or unlawful network-based activity that require computer security personnel, system administrators, or computer crime investigators to respond.[1]

- An incident is a situation in which an entity's information is at risk, whether the situation is real or simply perceived.[2]
- A computer security incident is an adverse event in a computer system or network caused by a failure of a security mechanism or an attempted or threatened breach of these mechanisms.[3]

Publications are not alone in failing to settle on a single definition for the term "computer incident." Many definitions default to simply listing the types of activities considered to be computer incidents. If a survey were to be taken of multiple incident response teams, it would most likely find that the type of activity considered an "incident" varies greatly.

An incident doesn't necessarily need to be an international spy case, or a highly publicized case like the ones outlined in Chapter 1, for it to be important to your organization. Consider the following true example of an incident: A person has a stressful morning dealing with difficult customers, telephone problems, and a crisis that leads to broken lunch plans. In addition, this person's computer system gets infected with a fairly harmless virus that displays "You Are a Big, Stupid Jerk" on the screen. The individual decides that all of the office equipment is out to get the person, states that the computer has been broken into and now "hates" the worker, becomes very upset, and takes the remainder of the day as a "sick" day. This is the first time in our knowledge that a computer virus caused a "sick" day, and the story reveals how a very simple incident can cause a loss in productivity for an organization.

Some examples of types of activity considered to be incidents that may be addressed are described next.

---

1. Mandia, Kevin, and Chris Prosise. *Incident Response Investigating Computer Crime.* Berkeley, CA: Osborne/McGraw-Hill Publishing, 2001, p. 16.

2. Van Wyk, Kenneth R., and Richard Forno. *Incident Response.* Sebastopol, CA: O'Reilly & Associates, 2001, p. 7.

3. Chirillo, John. *Hack Attacks Denied.* New York: John Wiley & Sons, 2001, p. 358.

Successful Intrusion or Unauthorized Access.   Overall, computer intrusion is the category of activity that has the greatest potential for inflicting damage on a system, business, or organization. This category should be addressed by all entities responsible for incident response. The source of an intrusion or unauthorized access is not restricted to external entities. Internal sources can and do abuse their access privileges and gain access to systems for which they are not authorized. One recent trend in unauthorized access is the use of a victim's computer system to anonymously store files that an attacker doesn't want associated with his or her activity. Although this activity sometimes doesn't interfere with normal business, it is certainly a risk to an organization.

Examples of incidents that could be categorized under the heading of successful intrusion or unauthorized access include the following:

- An authorized user of a computer system shares an office with one of the system administrators for that system. One day the system administrator leaves his desk to go down the hall to check on something. On the way out, the system administrator does not lock his screen. The office partner is working on a college degree in computer science with a focus on computer security, and he likes to "play" with new tools as they emerge. Seeing that the system administrator has left his screen unlocked, the "insider" seizes the opportunity to give himself administrator rights on the system. He then returns to his desk and proceeds to install some unauthorized tools on his system. The unauthorized increase in his privilege settings should be considered an unauthorized access.
- An external source scans a network to identify the operating system and version installed. The source notices that the particular version of the operating system is vulnerable to a buffer overflow, which will allow the intruder to execute remote commands and gain access to the system. The intruder initiates a buffer overflow and gains access to the system.
- An individual alters a Web page after guessing that the password to the system is "password."
- A nosy employee is interested in looking at other coworkers' personnel records to see what salaries they are paid. The employee has a friend in human resources who has access to the system on

which employee records are stored. The employee begins visiting the friend frequently and watches as the coworker types in her password. Once the password is obtained, the nosy insider accesses the system and uses the coworker's ID and password to access the personnel records.

Attempted Intrusion or Unauthorized Access (Not Successful).   Depending on the granularity considered to be an attempted intrusion, this category should also be considered by most teams. After all, if someone is determined and trying to gain access to a system, that person will be back at some point. Be careful to not make the definition for this activity too granular, however. For example, the number of attempted intrusions will skyrocket if the definition includes mistyped passwords.

Examples of incidents that could be categorized under the heading of unsuccessful attempted intrusion or unauthorized access include the following:

- Audit logs reveal that someone attempted to log into an account 10 times within a 30-minute window. Upon investigation, this event may turn out to be an end user forgetting the password. However, if the end user is asked about this event and has not experienced any problems during that time frame related to logging into his or her account, it would indicate that someone else has tried to gain access. Even worse, if the end user was out sick or on vacation during that time, it would signal an attempted access.
- Firewall logs reveal several attempts to establish a Trivial File Transfer Protocol (TFTP) connection to a system within the network. TFTP was not enabled on the network, so the attempt was blocked.

Denial-of-Service Attack (Attempted and Successful).   A denial-of-service attack occurs whenever authorized users are denied the use of system resources and the denial is not attributable to normal operational problems or outages. The same reasoning used for tracking attempted intrusions also applies to attempted denial-of-service attacks. If someone is determined, the chances are good that the person will try again to create a denial of service. Because this type of attack also has a high potential for damage (e.g., financial, integrity), the attempted attacks should be included in the types of incidents that the team addresses.

Examples of incidents that could be categorized under the heading of denial-of-service attack include the following:

- An organization's network is open to broadcast e-mail and is used to send a large quantity of spam (i.e., junk e-mail). The high volume consumes a large amount of bandwidth and slows the system performance. Depending on the performance impact, this problem may be considered a successful or attempted denial of service.
- An organization's network starts receiving a large quantity of Internet Control Message Protocol (ICMP) packets. The quantity causes network resources to become "tied up," thus denying the use of the organization's computer resources to its end users.
- A facsimile machine starts receiving advertisements that are not addressed to anyone in the organization and were not requested. The machine continues to receive separate transmissions of "junk faxes" nonstop for an hour. The denied use of the facsimile machine could be considered a denial of service.
- If a category for malicious logic infections is not included separately, any worm or virus having a major effect on system operations would fall under this heading.

Virus Infection, Worms, and Trojan Horses.   Given the effectiveness of antivirus software, some organizations may decide to not consider malicious logic infections as a category for the CIRT. In this case, a central information technology department or other entity should be charged with responding to and tracking the infections as they occur and are (ideally) cleaned by the antivirus software.

Procedures for handling major outbreaks of malicious logic programs should also be documented and implemented for those cases where the antivirus software is not effective at containing and cleaning the malicious code. This lack of effectiveness may result from several problems:

- The antivirus software has not installed properly on the computer system or systems.

- The signature files have not been kept current.
- A new variant of the virus or worm is spreading and is not included in the latest signature file or the latest signature is not properly cleaning the virus. This problem does not happen very often, but it may occur when several variants of the code are rapidly emerging and spreading.
- The virus requires manual changes to be made to clean the system, which are not covered by the antivirus program.

Although many virus infections may not require much assistance to clean or eradicate, be careful not to dismiss this type of activity completely. Viruses, worms, and other such programs can have a direct impact on operations. "A survey by ICSA Labs of firms with more than 500 PCs found they took an average of 23 person-days to recover from each virus disaster in 2002. . . . ICSA Labs defined a disaster as a simultaneous attack on 25 or more PCs or an attack causing major damage."[4]

One of the best methods for gaining approval for additional security tools is to keep statistics on the activity that occurs within the organization. Tracking the number of virus infections, for example, can be an excellent way to validate the need for antivirus software. Relying on a major outbreak, such as the Slammer or LoveLetter worms or the Melissa virus, may allow some infection to catch the organization off guard in the long run. Additionally, the potential effects on a business from a major malicious logic infection should not be ignored. The I Love You virus, for example, rang "up a toll as high as $10 billion in lost work hours!"[5]

Theft of Resources.   Laptop theft, in particular, is on the rise. Valuable information may be stored on the computer system that is stolen, which can lead to the theft of proprietary or company-confidential information. Whether through the CIRT or the physical security division, organizations need to have a tracking system in place to evaluate what information is lost when a resource is stolen. The process

---

4. Bennett, Madeline. "Virus Costs Keep Rising." *IT Week,* March 31, 2003.

5. Grossman, Lee. "Attack of the Love Bug." *Time,* May 15, 2000, pp. 49–56.

should begin as soon as the resource is unaccounted for, and end users need to be aware of the requirement to report this information. Typically, theft of resources will be tracked by a corporate security group and involve a CIRT only if the system is recovered. At that point, the CIRT would try to determine what information was accessed, and when.

WARNING   Because many organizations depreciate their computer resources over time, the manner in which the equipment is handled when amortized may permit related problems to occur. First, if the equipment is to be sold through a surplus initiative, care must be taken to ensure that the disks on the system are properly cleaned prior to sale. If the disks are not cleaned, then problems related to the disclosure of privacy or proprietary information can occur. Second, if the equipment is not sent to a surplus process, it may be reused within the organization or employees may take the extra equipment home. If the equipment is still in use within the infrastructure, then it must be tracked from a change management perspective so that when operational considerations such as patch management are reviewed, the equipment is addressed. If employees are able to keep extra equipment and the equipment is no longer in the control of the organization, the same care given to a system that is sent to a surplus process should be taken. Otherwise, the control over any residual memory on the system will be lost. If an incident occurs as the result of one of these issues, it would typically involve unauthorized access or unauthorized use, rather than theft of resources. After all, the access or use would not have occurred as a result of a theft.

Pornographic Material.   Whether we agree with it or not, pornographic material is widely available on the Internet, and employees have been known to intentionally or unintentionally visit these sites while at work. The best place to address this problem is through the human resources department and in written security or human resources policies. Some groups may nevertheless decide to have their

CIRTs track or respond to violations to corporate policies such as the visiting of pornographic sites. Several tools and "naughty word" lists are available that can assist with this requirement. If the pornographic material is believed to involve pictures of a minor, then the activity may be considered a criminal offense and should be reported to law enforcement. (This determination will depend on the country in which the system is located or the suspect resides.) Chapter 10 covers the legal aspects of computer crime in more detail, but you should always consult your own legal counsel and the laws in your area before making decisions regarding legality.

The type of activity normally tracked under this heading would include the access, transmission, or storage of pornographic material. Note that this form of activity may be covered under the incident category of unauthorized use, if the organization does not wish to separate this kind of activity from other abuses. Like theft of resources, this category may be handled directly by the human resources department if the activity is not to be tracked by the CIRT.

Unauthorized Scanning or Probes.   Not all teams will consider port scanning or probes to be incidents. Unfortunately, this sort of activity will often turn out to be a precursor for other incidents, such as intrusions and denial-of-service attacks. If possible, this activity should be addressed in some way and may be viewed as reconnaissance or intelligence gathering. Do not take this activity for granted as being benign. If the external scans detected against a network appear to be "targeted" in nature, rather than part of a broad, random sweep, the activity warrants greater concern.

Scans or probes detected as originating within the perimeter of a computer environment or network will normally be addressed in a different manner than the everyday external scans and probes that are so prevalent on the Internet. An insider scanning the network would generally be considered as conducting unauthorized use.

WARNING   Internal hosts scanning external hosts should be treated with great concern! This type of activity can expose your company or organization to problems ranging from negative publicity to possible liability.

Sabotage.   This activity may be a difficult charge to prove or even identify. The result of sabotage will normally be either unauthorized access to information resources, unauthorized use of those resources, or denial of service. Unless there is specific concern for this sort of activity, it is best to include it in the category that describes the outcome of the sabotage (i.e., denial of service, unauthorized use, or unauthorized access).

Examples of incidents that could be categorized under the heading of sabotage if it is separated out include the following:

- A disgruntled employee installs a logic bomb program that will activate if his or her name is removed from the payroll system. The employee is released from the employment obligation. When the person's name is removed from the payroll, the remaining records are deleted.
- An employee with access to financial records and transactions decides to divert the partial cents (e.g., 0.9 cent) of all sales to a specific account. This event is referred to as a "salami slice attack," because the partial cents are shaved off like a piece of salami.
- An employee has a grudge against a coworker. In an attempt at revenge against the coworker, the employee gains access to the other person's performance record and lowers the ratings given by the individual's manager.
- An employee needs additional vacation days to take advantage of a wonderful trip that has been offered. The employee cannot afford to take the time off without pay and decides to pay a coworker who has access to the vacation system to increase the number of days authorized.

Some of these examples may be covered equally well under a different heading—specifically, unauthorized access and unauthorized use. The category selected to address or describe the activity reported will depend on the granularity of the definition.

Unauthorized Use (Chain Mail, Advertising Non-Business-Related Activities).
Unauthorized use covers a wide range of activities, which are normally performed by the authorized users of an organization's computer systems. How well security policies are enforced within the

organization may dictate whether this category is needed. Some of the activities, such as chain mail, can actually lead to a denial of service if e-mail servers become overloaded with unwanted, nonofficial electronic mail in a short period of time. Therefore, the categories of unauthorized access and denial of service may cover the activity to the extent that upper management would like it tracked. For organizations that wish to accurately track the amount of time wasted on activities of this nature that do not result in a denial of service or unauthorized access, this may be a good category to include as part of the group's incident definition. It is also an excellent category to place policy abuses in.

Examples of incidents that could be categorized under the heading of unauthorized use include the following:

- An employee is interested in testing the latest security scanning tool she has read about on the Internet. The employee already has administrative rights on the local system and downloads the scanning tool to her corporate computer. The user then proceeds to scan the network from inside.
- An employee wishes to establish a connection from work to another computer system via a modem. He attaches a modem to his corporate computer (most likely behind the organization's firewalls) and leaves the system attached to the phone line.
- An individual is "bored" at work and chooses to visit some unauthorized Web sites during normal working hours. The Web activity may include surfing pornography sites (if not covered under a separate category), downloading music files, or visiting other sites not authorized by the organization's security or human resources policies.
- A laptop is provided to employees for business purposes. Employees are authorized to take the laptops home for work after hours. An employee permits his teenager to use the company laptop to "surf the Web."
- An employee forwards a chain letter e-mail to friends both internal and external to the company.

Operational Versus Security Incidents

The incidents described in the preceding section focused on security issues and violations of policies. Some incident response teams, however, may have more of an operational focus than a security violation focus. Depending on the team's focus, the following additional categories may be used by a CIRT. These categories are not used to describe computer security breaches, but rather are used for tracking problems associated with vulnerability management or change management. For this reason, they are considered to be operational incidents.

Software Vulnerabilities.   Software vulnerabilities would pertain to teams that are supporting a particular hardware or software product. This category would be used to track reported problems while they are being investigated and a fix or correction is being developed. It may also be used by organizations that proactively test their networks for problems. In this case, the incident would be "open" between the time it is discovered and the time it is patched or fixed.

Software License Violations.   Configuration control is a never-ending challenge, particularly in large organizations. This category could be used to track the discovery of illegal copies of commercial software. The statistics in the category may be useful for identifying gaps in end-user awareness training regarding software licensing, deficiencies in resource funding, or problems with change management controls.

Copyright and Intellectual Property Violations.   These violations would include issues related to rights to publications or software for which the organization may or may not be the copyright or property holder. They can include things like music, source code, documents, publications, books, journals, or other types of intellectual property.

Although these categories pertain to more of an operational picture, the outcome if such things are not addressed or tracked may be a security violation that falls into one of the previous categories. The operational incident categories are mentioned here for awareness only. The remainder of the book will focus on the security incident categories.

Determining the Categories to Be Used

The sort of activity that is included in the team's incident definition will depend on the concerns of management, the type of constituency, and the laws governing the team or organization. The two types of activities that will be addressed by most teams are successful intrusions or unauthorized access and denial-of-service attacks. In addition, many teams will combine virus infections, Trojan horses, and worms into one category labeled malicious logic infections.

Regardless of the categories used to track computer incidents, one major point must be remembered when defining the term "incident" for an organization: Potential overlap between categories should be avoided to the greatest extent possible. If activity may be categorized under more than one heading, then a decision must be made as to which heading the type of activity will be entered under or whether to remove one of the categories from the list altogether. Otherwise, the statistics that result will not accurately depict the activity to which the team responded and problems will be experienced with data integrity. Furthermore, the activity covered by each category should be clearly defined in written procedural documentation to help eliminate any possible confusion.

The outcome of the activity may be the key to assigning it to the proper category. For example, scanning activity that does not affect system performance should be categorized as unauthorized scanning or probes. In contrast, scanning activity that does affect system performance should fall under the heading of denial of service.

Table 3–1 lists the various categories that may be used to describe security incidents and identifies those that may overlap with another category.

To accurately monitor the operational requirements and successes of the team, it is helpful to distinguish between the activity that is first reported and the activity that turns out to be validated as an incident. Using separate terms to distinguish between the reports received and the actual incidents processed can help to make this distinction clearer and can prove valuable for tracking statistics on the

Table 3-1   Potential Category Overlap

Category	Potential Conflict with
Successful intrusion or unauthorized access	Unauthorized use
Attempted intrusion or unauthorized access	Unauthorized scanning or probes
Denial of service (attempted or successful)	Unauthorized scanning or probes
Virus infection, worm, or Trojan horse	Denial of service
Theft of resources	Successful intrusion or unauthorized access
Pornographic material	Unauthorized use
Unauthorized scanning or probes	
Sabotage	Unauthorized access *or* unauthorized use
Unauthorized use	Sabotage, pornographic material, theft of resources

activity levels reported to and handled by a team. For example, when a report is first received, it would be classified as an event or report. The classification would be changed to an incident only when the activity reported is validated as a form of unauthorized activity that the organization considers to be an incident.

The bottom line is that no universally accepted definition for an incident exists. Therefore, the definition, as well as categories included as types of incidents, is left to the organization to determine. Much thought should be given to the definitions selected, as the choices made can have a direct impact on the use of resources and the efficiency of the incident response team.

An Incident Taxonomy

One of the best definitions and explanations of the type of activity that should be included in an incident was written by John D. Howard and Thomas A. Longstaff of Sandia National Laboratories. Together the two investigated several incident reports and worked closely with the CERT CC to understand and define a complete incident taxonomy. Their report was released in October 1998 and can be obtained from the CERT CC Web site. The taxonomy was further expanded and published as part of the *Computer Security Handbook,* fourth edition (copyright 2002). The update, written by John Howard and Pascal Meunier, provides more information regarding the process used to develop the taxonomy, defines additional terms used to classify and track incidents, and provides pointers on how the taxonomy should be applied.

The original paper was written in response to the overall lack of a common language to discuss and refer to computer incidents. The goal was to present terms and classifications that would facilitate the gathering, exchange, and comparison of information for the incident-handling discipline. The taxonomy presented serves as one of the best sources available to date, discussing the need for common definitions and presenting well-thought-out categories to facilitate those definitions. The paper is strongly recommended for anyone who wishes to delve into the topic of incident categories or definitions further, and it provides a strong foundation for developing an organization's own incident definition and classification schemes. (The quoted sections in the following paragraphs and all definitions were taken directly from the paper, which may be downloaded from the CERT CC Web site.)

The term *taxonomy* is defined as "a classification scheme that partitions a body of knowledge and defines the relationship of the pieces." *Classification* refers to the "process of using a taxonomy for separating and ordering." The proposed taxonomy for computer incidents uses terms such as *event, attack, action, target,* and more to classify the actions that are included in an incident from start to finish. Figure 3–1 presents an overview of the incident taxonomy in its entirety.

The following definitions were taken from the paper and are presented here as an overview of the taxonomy. The reader is strongly

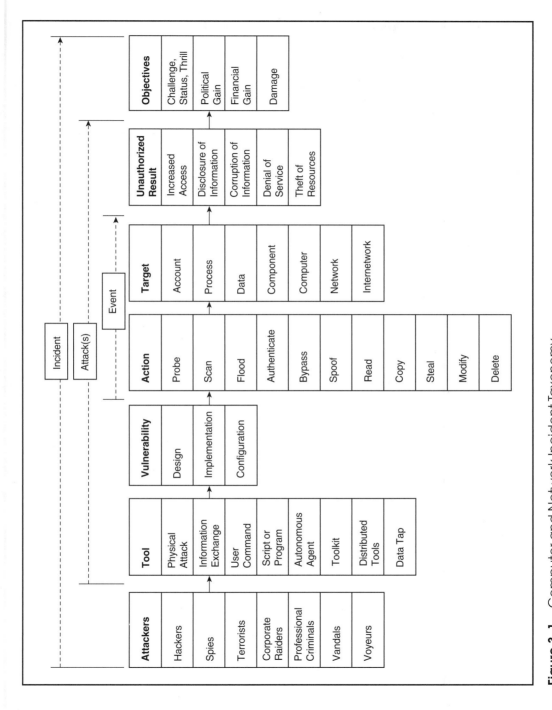

Figure 3–1 Computer and Network Incident Taxonomy

Source: John D. Howard and Thomas A. Longstaff, "A Common Language for Computer Security Incidents,"
Sandia National Laboratories, October 1998.

encouraged to download the paper from the CERT CC Web site to gain a full appreciation of the work presented.

The taxonomy begins by explaining that "the operation of computers and networks involves innumerable events," which are actually changes in the state or status of a system or device. With respect to computer incidents, these events result from actions that are directed toward or against specific targets. The paper defines these three terms—event, action, and target—as follows:

- *Event:* An action directed at a target that is intended to result in a change of state (status) of the target [IEEE 96: 373].
- *Action:* A step taken by a user or process so as to achieve a result [IEEE 96: 11], such as to probe, scan, flood, authenticate, bypass, spoof, read, copy, steal, modify, or delete.
- *Target:* A computer or network logical entity (account, process, or data) or physical entity (component, computer, network, or internetwork).

These terms serve as the building blocks for the incident taxonomy and help to provide a logical link between the action and the target. This link will not stand alone as an incident definition, however, for two reasons. First, although an action must be taken against a target for an event to have occurred, this link does not specify or indicate whether the action was successful in changing the state. Second, it does not differentiate between authorized and unauthorized activity. The taxonomy classifies the types of actions that may be taken against targets as follows:

- *Access:* Establish logical or physical communication or contact [IEEE 96: 5].
- *Probe:* Access a target so as to determine its characteristics.
- *Scan:* Access a set of targets sequentially so as to identify which targets have a specific characteristic [IEEE 96: 947, JaH 92: 916].
- *Flood:* Access a target repeatedly so as to overload the target's capacity.
- *Authenticate:* Present an identity of someone to a process and, if required, verify the identity so as to access the target [MeW 96: 77, 575, 714; IEEE 96: 57].

- *Bypass:* Avoid a process by using an alternative method to access the target [MeW 96: 157].
- *Spoof:* Masquerade by assuming the appearance of a different entity in network communications [IEEE 96: 630; ABH 96: 258].
- *Read:* Obtain the content of data in a storage device, or other data and medium [IEEE 96: 877].
- *Copy:* Reproduce a target, leaving the original target unchanged [IEEE 96: 224].
- *Steal:* Take possession of a target without leaving a copy in the original location.
- *Modify:* Change the content or characteristics of a target [IEEE 96: 661].
- *Delete:* Remove a target, or render it irretrievable [IEEE 96: 268].

The possible targets against which the action is taken so as to make an event occur fall into seven possible categories. Some of these categories are "logical" and some are "physical." *Account, process,* and *data* are the logical categories, and *component, computer, network,* and *internetwork* account for the physical entities. The targets are further defined as follows:

- *Account:* A domain of user access on a computer or network that is controlled according to a record of information that contains the user's account name, password, and use restrictions.
- *Process:* A program in execution, consisting of the executable program, the program's data and stack, its program counter, stack pointer and other registers, and all other information needed to execute the program. [Tan 92: 12; IEEE 96: 822].
- *Data:* Representations of facts, concepts, or instructions in a manner suitable for communication, interpretation, or processing by humans or by automatic means [IEEE 96: 250]. Data can be in the form of files in a computer's volatile or nonvolatile memory, or in a data storage device, or in the form of data in transit across the transmission medium.
- *Component:* One of the parts that make up a computer or network [IEEE 96: 289].
- *Computer:* A device that consists of one or more associated components, including processing units and peripheral units, that is

controlled by internally stored programs, and that can perform substantial computations, including numerous arithmetic operations, or logical operations, without human intervention during execution. A computer may be stand-alone, or it may consist of several interconnected units [IEEE 96: 683].

- *Network:* An interconnected or interrelated group of host computers, switching elements, and interconnecting branches [IEEE 96: 683].
- *Internetwork:* A network of networks.

The next building block that the taxonomy explores is the definition of an attack. It has several elements, which involve "a series of steps taken by an attacker." The attack is conducted by using some tool to exploit a vulnerability so as to cause an event to occur. If the event has an unauthorized result, then an attack has taken place. The term *attack* is fully defined as "a series of steps taken by an attacker to achieve an unauthorized result." An *unauthorized result* is any outcome that was not approved by the owner or administrator of the system.

The attack sequence always begins with a *tool,* which is simply defined as "a means of exploiting a computer or network vulnerability." The types or categories of tools used to launch an attack are defined as follows:

- *Physical attack:* A means of physically stealing or damaging a computer, a network, its components, its supporting systems (e.g., air conditioning, electric power).
- *Information exchange:* A means of obtaining information either from other attackers (e.g., through an electronic bulletin board) or from the people being attacked (commonly called social engineering).
- *User command:* A means of exploiting a vulnerability by entering commands to a process through direct user input at the process interface. An example is entering UNIX commands through a TELNET connection, or commands at an SMTP port.
- *Script* or *program:* A means of exploiting a vulnerability by entering commands to a process through the execution of a file of com-

mands (script) or a program at the process interface. Examples are a shell script that exploits a software bug, a Trojan horse login program, and a password-cracking program.

- *Autonomous agent:* A means of exploiting a vulnerability by using a program or program fragment that operates independently from the user. Examples are computer viruses and worms.
- *Toolkit:* A software package that contains scripts, programs, or autonomous agents that exploit vulnerabilities. An example is a widely available toolkit called rootkit.
- *Distributed tool:* A tool that can be distributed to multiple hosts, whose operation can then be coordinated to anonymously perform an attack on the target host simultaneously after some time delay.
- *Data tap:* A means of monitoring the electromagnetic radiation emanating from a computer or network using an external device.

The vulnerabilities that these tools are used to exploit are divided into three categories. The term *vulnerability* itself is defined as "a weakness in a system allowing unauthorized action" [NRC 91: 301; Amo 94: 2]. The three categories are broken down and defined as follows:

- *Design vulnerability:* A vulnerability inherent in the design or specification of hardware or software, whereby even a perfect implementation will result in a vulnerability.
- *Implementation vulnerability:* A vulnerability resulting from an error made in the software or hardware implementation of a satisfactory design.
- *Configuration vulnerability:* A vulnerability resulting from an error in the configuration of a system, such as having system accounts with default passwords, having "world write" permission for new files, or having tolerable services enabled [ABH 96: 196].

For an attack to have occurred, the event or change of state that occurs after the tool exploits the vulnerability must be an unauthorized result. An *unauthorized result* is defined as "an unauthorized consequence of an event." Five categories are used to describe and define these results:

- *Increased access:* An unauthorized increase in the domain of access on a computer or network.
- *Disclosure of information:* Dissemination of information to anyone who is not authorized to access that information.
- *Corruption of information:* Unauthorized alteration of data on a computer or network.
- *Denial of service:* Intentional degradation or blocking of computer or network resources.
- *Theft of resources:* Unauthorized use of computer or network resources.

At this point, the taxonomy has established two main building blocks to identify the activity that occurs within the context of a computer incident. First, for an event to have occurred, some action must have been taken on a target resulting in a change of state. Second, if this event has an unauthorized result and is caused by a tool being used to exploit a vulnerability, then an attack has taken place. With this foundation, the term *incident* can then be described. The taxonomy defines an incident as "a group of attacks that can be distinguished from other attacks because of the distinctiveness of the attackers, attacks, objectives, sites, and timing." *Attacker* and *objective* make up the last two elements of the incident definition:

- *Attacker:* An individual who attempts one or more attacks in an effort to achieve an objective.
- *Objective:* The purpose or end goal of an incident.

Seven categories were used to identify the types of attackers who might seek to initiate computer incident:

- *Hackers:* Attackers who attack computers for the challenge, status, or thrill of obtaining access.
- *Spies:* Attackers who attack computers for information to be used for political gain.

- *Terrorists:* Attackers who attack computers to cause fear or achieve political gain.
- *Corporate raiders:* Employees (attackers) who attack competitors' computers for financial gain.
- *Professional criminals:* Attackers who attack computers for personal financial gain.
- *Vandals:* Attackers who attack computers to cause damage.
- *Voyeurs:* Attackers who attack computers for the thrill of obtaining sensitive information.

"The concept of success or failure is embedded in the overall incident taxonomy, as well as within the seven individual blocks. Overall success is achieved by an attacker only when the objective is achieved." These objectives that motivate the attack are as follows:

- Challenge, status, thrill
- Political gain
- Financial gain
- Damage

If an unauthorized result is achieved, then the individual attack is deemed successful.

The original paper describing this taxonomy was briefed in the fall of 1998 to a group of computer security professionals representing at least 20 incident response teams. In the discussions that followed the presentation, the group tried to find types of attacks and events that were not covered by the taxonomy. No exception was found, and the group concluded that the taxonomy was comprehensive in the classifications and definitions described. Not only does the Howard/Longstaff paper serve as a great tool for understanding and defining computer incidents, but the elements of the taxonomy could also be used to establish an incident database. The references used in the definitions provided in this section are listed in Figure 3–2 to facilitate further research.

In addition to the terms defined as part of the taxonomy itself, the updated taxonomy provided in the *Computer Security Handbook* provides other terms that may be used to define incidents. These terms

[ABH 96]	Derek Atkins, Paul Buis, Chris Hare, Robert Kelley, Carey Nachenberg, Anthony B. Nelson, Paul Phillips, Tim Ritchey, and William Steen. *Internet Security Professional Reference.* Indiana: New Riders Publishing, 1996.
[Amo 94]	Edward G. Amoroso. *Fundamentals of Computer Security Technology.* Upper Saddle River, NJ: Prentice-Hall PTR, 1994.
[IEEE 96]	John Radatz, ed. *The IEEE Standard Dictionary of Electrical and Electronics Terms,* 6th ed. New York: Institute of Electrical and Electronics Engineering, 1996.
[JaH 92]	K. M. Jackson and J. Hruska, eds. *Computer Security Reference Book.* Boca Raton, FL: CRC Press, 1992.
[MeW 96]	*Merriam-Webster's Collegiate Dictionary,* 10th ed. Springfield, MA: Merriam-Webster, 1996.
[NRC 91]	National Research Council. *Computers at Risk: Safe Computing in the Information Age.* Washington, DC: National Academy Press, 1991.
[Tan 9]	Andrew S. Tanenbaum. *Modern Operating Systems.* Englewood Cliffs, NJ: Prentice Hall, 1992.

Figure 3–2   References Used in "A Common Language for Computer Security Incidents"

Source: John D. Howard and Thomas A. Longstaff, "A Common Language for Computer Security Incidents," Albuquerque, NM, and Livermore, CA: Sandia National Laboratories, October 1998.

are not necessarily used to classify the events themselves, but represent information that is needed to respond to the incident. Most relate to identifying the dates and sites associated with events. A definition for corrective actions and an incident number are also provided.

Common Vulnerability and Exposure (CVE) Project

As stated earlier in this chapter, there is no universally accepted definition for the term *computer incident.* An action that is considered to be an incident by one organization may not be an incident to another organization. This inconsistency with respect to definitions does not end with this term, but also applies to many of the terms associated with an incident. For example, *vulnerability* is another term with several variations in its definition. The variations do not apply to the term "vulnerability" only, but also to the manner in which many well-known exploits are referred to and described. The problem with these inconsistencies is not merely one of semantics. Rather, the inconsistencies have presented many challenges with respect to the tools used to detect, combat, and track incidents.

To address this problem, a community-wide effort emerged in the late 1990s to standardize the names used to describe the publicly well-known vulnerabilities. This project resulted in the establishment of the Common Vulnerability and Exposure (CVE) dictionary. (People frequently mistake the culmination of this effort for a database, but it is actually a dictionary.) The goal of the CVE project is to standardize the names of security vulnerabilities so that users, vendors, and security professionals alike can use a common language when discussing them. This common language makes it easier to share data across various vulnerability databases and security tools.

The CVE project is a collaborative effort involving numerous security organizations. Security tool vendors, educational institutions, and government groups are all represented, along with some prominent security experts. Together, the representatives form the CVE Editorial Board, which oversees the terms entered into and defined in the dictionary. Mitre Corporation maintains the dictionary and moderates board discussions. The dictionary and more information about the CVE project may be obtained from http://cve.mitre.org.

If a security tool is advertised as being CVE compatible or compliant, then the vulnerability naming conventions and reports generated by that tool must incorporate the names provided in the CVE dictionary. An end user of the tool can be assured up front which problems are handled by the tool, as CVE compliance provides a baseline for evaluating the tool's coverage. The use of CVE-compatible tools and databases should enable better coverage with fewer interoperability issues and lead to enhanced security.

Summary

As the discipline of incident response continues to evolve, there remains a lack of consistency in defining what a computer incident is or encompasses. Defining an incident is difficult "because attacks and incidents are a series of steps that an attacker must take. In other words, attacks and incidents are not just one thing but rather a series of things."[6] An action that is considered to be an incident by one organization may not be considered an incident by another organization. In many regards, the definition of what a computer incident is remains subjective and should be outlined by the organization. When defining the term for an organization or, more importantly, considering the types of activity to be considered an incident, due consideration must be given to all implications of the chosen terminology. Definitions that are too broad or too narrow will directly affect resources and the ease with which incident data are depicted and stored.

The paper titled "A Common Language for Computer Security Incidents," written by John D. Howard and Thomas A. Longstaff, provides a strong foundation for understanding and defining computer incidents. Although this paper has not received as much attention to date as it should, it does a fantastic job of breaking computer incidents down into three basic building blocks: events, attacks, and incidents. The taxonomy (or common language) defined provides the granularity needed to track the activity identified, but also permits activity attributable to the same person or group to be correlated as one incident. The taxonomy was further expanded upon and published as part of the *Computer Security Handbook,* fourth edition. The 2002 update, written by John Howard and Pascal Meunier, provides more information regarding the process used to develop the taxonomy, defines additional terms used to classify and track incidents, and provides pointers on how the taxonomy should be used. The original taxonomy was presented in depth in this chapter. Readers who are interested in learning more are strongly encouraged to download and

---

6. Bosworth, Seymour, and M. E. Kabay. *Computer Security Handbook,* 4th ed. New York: John Wiley & Sons, 2002, p. 319.

read the paper or the chapter in the *Computer Security Handbook* in its entirety.

The lack of standardization in terminology does not simply stop at the term "computer incident." Rather, it applies to many other terms associated with computer incidents, such as "vulnerability." These inconsistencies have resulted in interoperability issues in sharing incident data between varying tools and databases. To address this problem, the Common Vulnerability and Exposures (CVE) project emerged. Through the efforts of many security professionals working together on this project, a common dictionary of vulnerability terms has been identified and defined. Although these terms and definitions are not considered absolute, the dictionary provides an excellent way to baseline the coverage that a tool (or database) provides and eliminates many of the interoperability problems previously experienced. Many security tools are now promoted as being CVE compliant, which means that the terms defined in the dictionary are used and included with the tool.

The consistency (or lack thereof) in definitions used within an organization and between organizations can have major implications for the incident response team's communication capabilities. Consistent terminology facilitates the exchange of information and allows for better tracking of incidents. The statistics that may be tracked by the team will provide a better picture of the environment if the terminology used is clearly defined. The clearer definitions may also help to identify security shortcomings within the environment and assist in identifying business needs and effects on productivity.

Although the definitions presented in this chapter have not met with universal acceptance, a tremendous amount of progress has been made in addressing the need for a common computer incident language. The bottom line for any organization forming an incident response team is to realize that there are some inconsistencies in definitions, that there is a lack of universally accepted definitions, and that the manner in which terms are defined can affect both resources and daily operations. This impact is why the terminology piece is considered to be a corner piece in the border of our overall puzzle. Chapter 4 will build on the discussion presented here by providing more details on specific types of attacks that may be considered to be computer incidents.

4

Computer Attacks

No book on computer incidents or incident response would be complete without a discussion of the various types of attacks that may be launched. This chapter provides that discussion, building on the terminology presented in Chapter 3. As this book is not intended to be an in-depth technical guide, such attacks will be described only at a high level. The chapter begins by examining some of the major consequences that can result from an attack, and then looks at some specific vectors used to launch such attacks. It ends with an in-depth discussion of malicious logic, especially the computer virus. Steps that can help organizations reduce their potential for virus infections will also be presented as part of the malicious logic discussion.

> **NOTE** A more thorough discussion of computer viruses and other such code is presented because many managers find themselves dealing with this sort of incident on a frequent basis. Adding to the interest is the level of attention given to the topic of computer viruses by the media over recent years. Viruses are not necessarily the most significant threat that a CIRT will address. In reality, they are only one of many problems that an organization might encounter and must be prepared to handle.

Computer security professionals from various organizations have worked together to establish a list of the most commonly exploited vulnerabilities. This list is maintained by the SysAdmin, Audit, Network, Security (SANS) Institute and maintained at its Web site (http://www.sans.org). The development of the list included input from the FBI, CERT CC, and many other organizations and individuals. The original list was posted in 2000 and included the top 10 most frequently exploited Internet vulnerabilities. The list expanded to the top 20 vulnerabilities in 2001. The top 20 list is actually a combination of two top 10 lists—the top 10 vulnerabilities associated with UNIX and the top 10 vulnerabilities associated with Windows operating systems. Despite the best efforts of many security professionals, this combined list still accounts for the most frequently exploited vulnerabilities.

Anyone charged with securing an information infrastructure should begin by using the SANS list as a checklist for possible vulnerabilities and proceed from there. In some cases, it may be quite difficult to totally prevent the vulnerability from being present in an infrastructure. For example, poor password choices are a vulnerability that is frequently exploited to gain unauthorized access to a system, yet passwords are needed in most cases as one level of security. Nevertheless, some specific steps may be taken to lessen the exposure of the potential vulnerability, such as conducting frequent password scans, conducting password training for end users, and invoking automated password rules. Similarly, sendmail is a mail server application used with many UNIX installations that has had numerous vulnerabilities identified over the years. Ensuring that the most recent version of sendmail is loaded and used on the system can help prevent some of the problems associated with the program. The same holds true for patching other operating systems as vulnerabilities are discovered and versions of the software are updated or patched.

Consequences of Computer Attacks

Computer Intrusion, Unauthorized Access, or Compromise

A compromise occurs when someone gains unauthorized access to a computer resource. Typically, we tend to think of people outside an organization when discussing compromises. In reality, a compromise can also be accomplished by an authorized user of a system or an internal employee. For example, if a person is authorized to use a system and has set privileges at an end-user level, bypassing security countermeasures to increase that privilege level should be considered an unauthorized access or compromise. Additionally, if an internal employee gains access to a system that he or she is not authorized to use, that breach should be considered a compromise.

System compromise can be achieved through both physical and electronic means. Access through physical means would be accomplished if an unauthorized person gained physical access to a system and was able to log on. The following scenarios provide examples of how such an event might happen:

1. Sam, an authorized user who happens to be a system administrator, is logged onto the computer system. While working on the computer, he realizes that he needs a tape that is stored down the hall and walks out of the room to get it. Unfortunately, Sam is in a hurry and forgets to lock his screen before leaving the room. Fred is a curious employee whose own office is currently being renovated so he is sharing the office space with Sam. Seeing that Sam forgot to lock his system, Fred decides to increase his user privileges to do some corporate snooping. He sits down at Sam's computer and quickly changes his privilege level to that of system administrator. He returns the computer to the screen that was up when Sam left the room and goes back to his own desk. Sam returns with the tape and continues to work, with Fred now able to perform tasks as a system administrator. This increased access will most likely allow Fred to view files that he was previously unable to see.

2. Sherry is a receptionist for Company X and is very diligent about watching who comes into the office space. In fact, no one is able to

get into the offices without first going by her. Sherry's managers like to make administrative tasks as simple as possible for their employees, so a pool of computer resources are maintained in a room behind Sherry's office. Because Sherry is so good at her job and sits close to this resource pool, Company X does not see the need to require passwords on the computer systems located in the room. After all, it's there to provide greater ease of use for the employees.

Sherry takes her annual vacation. The boss hires a temporary employee to fill in as receptionist while she is away.

Tom works for Company X's main competitor and is determined to get access to its computer system to see the firm's latest developments. He disguises himself as a copier repairman and appears at the office shortly after noon during the week that Sherry is on vacation. He gets past the temporary employee to "repair the copier," which happens to be in the same room as the pooled computer. Most of the regular employees are at lunch at this time, so Tom has ready access to the computer system for at least 30 minutes. During that period, he is able to access some files that he saves to a diskette, which he then slips into his repair bag. Tom informs the temporary employee that the copier is repaired and walks out of the office with his findings.

3. Emily has had some problems with her supervisor and is very concerned that her personnel file contains some negative remarks. One night she notices the door to the human resources department has been left open and decides to investigate her personnel file. Emily obtains a boot diskette from her desk and inserts it into the A drive before turning on the system. After the system boots, she is able to search the contents of the system's hard drive to look for personnel files and anything else she is able to access.

Requiring employees to wear identification badges and teaching them to challenge unknown personnel who are walking alone through a space will help to protect against a compromise occurring from an external resource through physical means. Ensuring that security countermeasures (e.g., passwords) are used and educating personnel on the importance of locking their screens will help to safeguard against the internal compromise threat. Additionally, systems should be programmed to lock or initiate a screen saver after a short period of being idle.

Although physical access is one avenue used to get into a computer system, many more compromises occur through electronic means. A wide variety of methods are used to gain access to a computer system, and many excellent resources outline these means. The "Attack Vectors" section later in this chapter describes some specific attacks or avenues used to gain access electronically to a system. These methods provide a small sampling of the attack avenues that may be used to gain unauthorized access to a system. Entire books have been written on such attack methods, so this chapter is not intended to provide a comprehensive examination of all avenues. Rather, the intent is to highlight some methods to demonstrate that threats may come through a multitude of means and from many directions.

Denial-of-Service Attacks

A denial-of-service attack accomplishes exactly what its name implies—it denies authorized personnel the use of a computer resource or resources. It is normally accomplished by flooding the target with signals so that its bandwidth is so consumed it cannot take further instructions. Several types of denial-of-service attacks may be used, some of which have familiar names such as LAND and smurf. (Smurf will be described in more detail later as an example of a denial-of-service attack.)

Port Scans or Probes

Some organizations do not recognize port scans or probes as incidents. However, experience working in an incident response team will reveal that many successful attacks (compromise or denial of service) are often preceded by some type of scanning activity. Rules must be set to not track too granular a level of probing, yet allow the recognition of this type of reconnaissance when it occurs.

Network scanning tools are frequently used to conduct a scan of a network. By scanning the network, the intruder is trying to glean as much information as possible that may be used to gain access. For example, determining the type and version of the operating system used on a network will give an intruder hints about the associated vulnerabilities that may be tried. Most network scans will be readily apparent, as they will come from the same or a handful of IP addresses. This information can easily be identified and even protected against with most intrusion detection systems. More skilled attackers may change the scanning parameters to lessen their chances of being detected. Similarities in the ports scanned or timing of probes can help with the detection of these tests.

Attack Vectors

The following subsections describe some specific attack avenues that may be used to gain unauthorized access to a system, deny the use of information system resources, or conduct reconnaissance on the network. As noted previously, the avenues described here represent merely a sampling of possible attack vectors. Numerous other books provide more in-depth reviews of various types of attacks, and the reader is encouraged to continue research into a larger sample of attacks.

The Human Factor

Default Accounts and Passwords

Most vendors ship hardware and software products with default accounts and passwords already set. Before computer security started gaining more attention over recent years, these default accounts and passwords were used by vendors to help troubleshoot or fix problems when they arose. However, these settings soon became known to less helpful people and provided an easy route into computer systems. Although many vendors have tried to strengthen the security in their products over recent years, many continue to ship products with such accounts and passwords enabled. Before placing any system into production, all default accounts should be disabled or have their associated passwords changed.

The passwords selected and used by authorized end users represent another major avenue for unauthorized access to systems. Numerous programs are available that may be used to crack or decrypt passwords from the password file. Typically, an intruder will obtain a copy of the password file, run one of these programs on it long enough to identify a couple of login accounts and corresponding passwords, and then use these account login IDs and passwords to further their exploration of a system.

L0phtCrack is a well-known program that is used by many security professionals during penetration tests or vulnerability assessments. If permitted to run long enough, L0phtCrack will eventually reveal all passwords in the file. It does so not through a decryption algorithm, but rather through a pattern matching scheme. LC4 is the latest version of L0phtCrack and is designed to crack passwords on Windows systems. (More information on L0phtCrack and LC4 can be obtained from http://www.atstake.com.)

Table 4–1 provides examples of other password cracking software that may be used to reveal passwords. Most of the tools listed in the table as being able to crack Windows NT passwords can be used on all versions of Windows platforms (e.g., XP, NT, 2000).

Another popular method for obtaining passwords is through a brute-force attack. This type of attack involves simply guessing the user's password. This guessing of passwords may be done either manually or by using an automated tool that attempts to guess the password by cycling through every possible combination of passwords. (This is actually how L0phtCrack identifies passwords through its pattern matching capability.) Educating end users on good password selection techniques, requiring passwords to be changed periodically, and not permitting the reuse of passwords are all measures that can reduce the likelihood of a successful brute-force attack. The stronger the password, the more likely the entity trying to guess the password will give up and move onto another target. The Tips for Selecting Good Passwords sidebar lists a few recommendations to consider in selecting good passwords and may be used as a starting point to help address this topic in training programs.

Table 4-1   Examples of Password Cracking Software

Name	Purpose
Gammaprog	Cracks passwords of Web-based e-mail (e.g., Yahoo!, Hotmail) and POP.
Hypnopaedia	Remotely connects to a POP3 mail server and attempts to guess the password of a specific account.
John the Ripper	Popular UNIX-based password cracker that can attack UNIX, Kerberos, Andrew File System (AFS), and Windows NT passwords.
Mssqlpwd	Cracks Microsoft SQL Server passwords.
PalmCrack	Runs on Palm PDA and can crack UNIX, NT, and some Cisco router passwords.
PGPPASS	Cracks PGP key rings. Note that the Caligula virus is designed to steal PGP key rings by FTPing them from the victim's PC to a server on the Internet.
Slurpie	UNIX password cracker designed to work in a distributed mode, so the cracking task can be shared by multiple machines (the same concept followed by the commercial cracking tool from AccessData).
Webcracker	Remote brute-force tool to crack password-protected Web sites.
Aimpw	AOL Instant Messenger Password Cracker.
!Bios	Decrypts the passwords used in common BIOSs, including those from IBM, American Megatrends, Award, and Phoenix.
Zipcrack & PkCrack	Cracks encrypted ZIP and PKZIP files.
Cain	Anyone with access to Windows 9x can use Cain to locate and retrieve cached passwords in the Registry or in .pwl files. It typically recovers passwords for logon, local and remote shares, screen savers, and dial-up access. An associated agent called ABLE, when placed on a victim's machine, can be remotely accessed to collect passwords.

Source: Warren G. Kruse II and Jay G. Heiser, *Computer Forensics Incident Response Essentials*. Boston: Addison-Wesley, 2002, p. 145.

Tips for Selecting Good Passwords

DO

Use a phrase to create a strong, easy-to-remember password. For example:

- Create a phonetic sentence using the pronounced sounds of letters, numbers, and special characters.

I10D24GET	"I tend to forget"
RULOSTIM	"Are you lost? I am!"

- Use short, unrelated words with numbers and special characters.

    GO2SEPT   ROSE49SPORT

- Use the first letter from each word in a phrase.

4s&7yaoff	"Four score and seven years ago our forefathers"

Use more than just A to Z.

Use mixed-case and embedded numbers.

Use a minimum of seven characters.

Use punctuation, spaces, and symbols where possible (not all systems support them).

DO NOT USE

- Words found in the dictionary
- Common acronyms or words associated with the work environment
- Proper names
- Foreign languages
- Consecutive keys on the keyboard

- All the same character (e.g., 1111111)
- Personal numbers (e.g., Social Security number, phone number)
- Words that are easily personally identifiable (e.g., pets' names, children's names, license plate numbers, addresses)

OTHER TIPS

- Do not write passwords down.
- Do not tell anyone your password.
- Be alert—watch for shoulder surfers.
- Change passwords often.
- Use unique passwords (do not reuse passwords).
- Do not use the same password for every system.

Social Engineering

A very popular method to bypass or exceed normal computer access is social engineering. Social engineering occurs when an intruder successfully convinces someone with authorized access to divulge information that may be used to gain access to a system. This can be accomplished without the authorized user even realizing it is being done. The intruder may lie about his or her identity, position, location, or other factors to convince an employee or authorized user that access should be granted.

A person posing as a member of the information technology department and requesting an authorized user to provide a password to conduct system checks is just one example of social engineering. Although this approach may not seem to be an avenue that is easily used, it is surprising how often it succeeds. For this reason, many Internet service providers post warnings on their Web sites to not divulge passwords when requested. Addressing the threat of social engineering and posting security alerts within an organization when such threats are being targeted toward a group are the best tactics to prevent a successful compromise via this route.

Wireless Attacks

Many organizations are now using wireless connectivity to communicate within their environment. Unfortunately, the same wireless capabilities may be used by unauthorized users to gain access to the systems if proper security is not implemented. Numerous consulting firms now conduct "war driving" exercises to check for unsecured wireless access points that may be used as points of access into a system. (*War driving* refers to scanning for wireless access points that may not be authorized, just as *war dialing* refers to the search for modems.) Numerous cases have been documented where systems were able to be accessed via the wireless access points. For example, if two companies share a building and both have wireless networks, without proper controls employees from one company may be able to access the other company's network. There have also been cases where access was obtained from the parking lot of a company with a wireless network. The best way to protect a wireless network is to include a security architect as part of the initial design of the system to address security concerns.

TCP/IP Design Limitations

SYN Flooding

A network connection is normally accomplished through a series of signals and responses. First, the client wishing to connect to the server sends a SYN message to indicate a connection is needed. Next, the server responds with a SYN-ACK signal, recognizing or acknowledging the request. Finally, the client responds back to the server with an ACK signal and the connection is opened, enabling data to flow between the two.

In a SYN flood attack, numerous SYN signals are sent to the server with addresses that are actually unavailable. The server will allocate records for these connections as if they were legitimate requests. As the number of "false" requests increases, the server becomes tied up in dealing with the "false" requests and is no longer available to accept legitimate connection requests.

Smurf

Although many readers will tend to think of a little blue cartoon guy when hearing this term, smurf is actually a type of denial-of-service attack that has been around for many years. A smurf attack relies on routers being configured to allow directed broadcasts and requires an intermediary site that may also become a victim of the attack. Basically, the attacker sends a "ping" or Internet Control Message Protocol (ICMP) echo request packet to the broadcast address of a network. The source address of the ping request is modified so that it appears to come from a specific host that is the victim of the attack. When the broadcast address receives the request, it forwards the packet to every live host on that network, which may include hundreds or even thousands of systems. Each host replies to the ping request with an ICMP echo reply. The hundreds or even thousands of replies are all sent back to the source address of the victim, potentially overwhelming it with network traffic and creating a denial of service. Note that the smurf attack is not a design limitation of the TCP/IP protocol suite, but rather an abuse of behavior that is normal and expected within the protocol.

Coding Oversight

Multiple vulnerabilities exist in various platforms due to oversight or holes in the program code that intruders can discover and use to their advantage. For example, sendmail in UNIX programs has experienced several problems over the years that have been manipulated to gain unauthorized access to systems. This is one reason that new versions of sendmail (and other programs) have been released over time.

The best safeguard to prevent coding problems from being used as an attack avenue for a system is to monitor vendor advisories and alerts for problems as they are discovered. Patches and updates should be implemented as appropriate. If the vendor provides an MD5 checksum for the patch, the patch's or program's checksum should be checked to ensure that it matches the one provided by the vendor prior to installing the program. In a few cases, patches that were made available to address a vulnerability have been compromised and altered so that personnel downloading the patch actually installed a Trojan horse version that presented new problems. Checking the MD5 checksum helps to prevent the installation of invalid patches.

Buffer Overflows

A buffer is an area of the computer's memory used to temporarily store data. Typically, a buffer of a set size is created with enough memory for the needs of the program. However, when a larger-than-normal amount of data is sent to the buffer, the data is routinely appended at the end of the buffer, possibly overwriting other instructions or memory. This may cause data to be lost or corrupted, or even cause the program to crash. The use of buffer overflows to create a denial of service has increased over the past four to five years. In some cases, malicious commands may be embedded in the overflow data, then executed on the computer when the program freezes or crashes.

Common Oversights in Web Common Gateway Interface (GCI) and Network Interfaces

Many Web applications have been written to accept unfiltered user input from any source and act on that input. As a result, the Web server can be tricked into doing something that is neither intended nor expected by the authorized users. For example, Common Gateway Interface (CGI) programs are used with Web servers to provide input from a Web page that may be beyond HTML's ability to manipulate. Some problems have arisen with some of these programs accepting input without question and passing it to a shell program for execution. As a result, intruders have been able to gain unauthorized access to systems as well as "hack" multiple Web pages.

One notable CGI program that has been used to gain access to Web servers is called phf. Multiple teams have provided advisories on the exploits associated with phf, and Web servers should be checked to ensure that proper safeguards are in place to prevent this program from being manipulated. Ways to manipulate this program have also been detailed in hacker publications and on hacker Web sites.

The vulnerabilities associated with CGI programs have been known for several years, yet some Web pages still fall prey to this sort of attack. Other, more recent tactics used to trick or manipulate Web servers, Web server applications, or the underlying operating systems include the following:

- Entering malformed URL requests and HTTP headers
- Creating a buffer overflow by exceeding the expected length of input in form fields
- Embedding metacharacters in URLs or form input data
- SQL injection, where malicious SQL commands are issued.

Malicious Logic

Malicious logic—viruses, worms, Trojan horses, and logic bombs—robs its victims of productivity and jeopardizes every organization's information security and infrastructure. These computer programs, which are written with spiteful intent, perform unauthorized routines to damage and destroy data or to degrade system performance. Although the level and type of damage varies, the impact can be enormous, with the greatest costs usually tallied in the form of person-hours expended on recovery. There is virtually no way to keep an organization completely free from malicious logic, but there are steps everyone can take to proactively address the problem. First, one must understand the types of codes and recommended courses of action.

The Computer Virus

The form of malicious logic that is familiar to most people is the computer virus. A virus is a self-replicating program whose purpose is to propagate to as many different places as possible. Viruses accomplish this goal by modifying other programs to include copies of themselves through an (unknowing) act of a user. Although viruses have received much attention from the media in recent years, they have actually been in existence since 1980. In his thesis written in 1984, Fred Cohen termed the phrase "computer virus" because of its similarity to a biologic virus, which also replicates. Table 4–2 compares computer and biologic viruses.

A virus is normally named based on some function that it performs or a name that is used in its "signature." For example, Wazzu is

Table 4-2 Comparison of Computer and Biologic Viruses

Computer Virus	Biologic Virus
Computer viruses are parasitic. They need another program in which to exist and reproduce.	Biologic viruses are parasitic. They need a cell in which to live and reproduce.
Once a program has been infected, it is forced to make new copies of the virus.	Once a cell has been infected, it is forced to make new copies of the virus.
Computer viruses are seldom used to infect the same program/disk twice.	Biologic viruses rarely, if ever, infect the same cell twice.
Specific computer viruses target specific program types (e.g., .exe, .com, .sys, boot record).	Specific biologic viruses target specific cell types.
An infected program does not always show obvious signs of infection.	An infected cell can go on living for a long time without obvious signs of infection.
After an incubating time of varied length, a computer virus often releases some kind of payload, which can prove fatal to the whole system.	After an incubating time of varied length, a biologic virus often releases some kind of payload, which can prove fatal to the whole living system in which the infected cell lives.
A typical computer virus has a size of some 1000 to 3000 bytes. If the DOS interrupt subroutine is added to that, the size can easily be multiplied by two.	The DNA of a typical small virus, such as the polio virus, contains information that if reproduced on a computer would add up to some 5000 bytes. The smallest virus discovered to date is equivalent to about only 200 bytes.

Source: Rune Skardhamar. *Virus Detection and Elimination.* Cambridge, MA: Academic Press, 1996, p. 14.

a macro virus that first appeared in the late 1990s. When the virus launched its payload, it would randomly insert the term "Wazzu" throughout the contents of an infected Microsoft Word document.

Frequently, virus writers will change an existing virus slightly and re-release the modified code to create a new strain of the virus. These new strains are usually identified with the original virus name and an alphabetic extension. For example, the Wazzu macro virus was modified several times to create new strains of the virus denoted as Wazzu.A, Wazzu.B, and so on.

New strains of existing viruses account for the population explosion among computer viruses over the years. In 1992 and 1993, the average number of new computer viruses per month ranged from 100 to 150.[1] Most of these "new" viruses were not actually brand-new viruses, but rather new strains of existing viruses. In January 1997, the average number of new discoveries was 200 per month, with a total of more than 8500 known computer viruses. The numbers have continued to rise with time. In October 1999, Symantec released an updated signature file for its Norton antivirus software that increased the number of detected viruses by 646 in just four days! As of March 2003, the Norton antivirus software included signatures to detect more than 63,000 viruses.

Virus Types

There are five main types of computer viruses: file infectors, partition-sector viruses, boot-sector viruses, companion viruses, and macro viruses. The type of virus is determined by how the code propagates.

- *File infectors* replicate by inserting themselves into executable files. Usually, the virus code is written at the beginning of a targeted file, so it is executed immediately, or appended to the end. If the code is written somewhere other than the beginning of the file, the start-up sequence of instructions in the file is normally modified to transfer program control to the malevolent code.
- *Partition-sector infectors* contaminate the partition record of a hard disk. First, the virus copies and stores the whole partition sector somewhere else on the hard disk. Then the virus copies itself to the partition sector and executes when the computer is booted from the hard drive.

---

1. Skardhamar, Rune. *Virus Detection and Elimination.* Cambridge, MA: Academic Press, 1996, p. 12.

- *Boot-sector viruses* infect both floppy diskettes and hard disks by changing or replacing the boot-sector program with a copy of itself. This type of virus is most frequently spread by forgotten floppy diskettes left in disk drives. It can be considered a special case of the file infector virus, which infects only the boot-sector program.
- A *companion virus* searches for executable programs with the .exe or .bat extension and creates a copy of itself with the same name but a .com extension. The virus is activated when a user tries to execute the legitimate file from the command line. After the virus completes its routine, control returns to the original file. Companion viruses tend to spread only within a computer system and are normally easy to spot through both manual and automatic means.
- *Macro viruses* were discovered in the summer of 1995. Instead of infecting an executable program file or disk boot sector, this type of virus infects an application's document files. The virus contains a set of application-specific macro commands that automatically execute in an unsolicited manner and then spread to the application's documents.

In addition to these types of viruses, two other terms frequently used to describe viruses are *multipartite* and *polymorphic*. A multipartite virus combines two or more different infection methods, and a polymorphic virus changes itself with each virus infection. The polymorphic virus normally includes some sort of "mutation engine" to change itself during an infection in an attempt to elude detection.

Symptoms indicating the presence of a computer virus vary. Some of the typical signs indicating a virus may be present include the following:

- Display of an unusual message
- Missing files
- Files of increased size
- A slowdown in the operation of the computer
- A sudden lack of disk space
- Inability to access the disk drive

These symptoms may be attributed to other problems as well, so one should not assume the problem is automatically a virus without undertaking further investigation.

Important Steps to Remain Virus-Free

Regardless of the type of virus, some basic steps can go a long way toward ensuring that your computer system remains virus-free:

- Document and share standard antivirus procedures.
- Train users to consistently follow standards.
- Conduct regular scans with antivirus software.
- Update antivirus software as new signature files become available from software vendors.
- Use antivirus software at various levels within the information infrastructure.
- Keep computer users informed of the latest threats.
- Remind end users not to open unknown e-mail attachments without first scanning for viral code.
- Do not leave diskettes in floppy drives when computers are turned off.
- In Microsoft Word applications, the global template, typically a file called Normal.dot, should be scanned for viruses and set to read only.
- Any auto-run and auto-open features on e-mail programs and browsers should be disabled.
- The CMOS boot sequence could be changed to start with the C drive first, then the A drive.

Ultimately, a particularly nasty virus may escape detection and cause the loss of critical data on workstations or file servers. In those situations, a conscientious file backup program is absolutely essential. Even if the virus code is backed up on tape or other media, system administrators can update virus definitions to remove it. The code will not run until the operating system is running again, so restoration of data onto a new PC updated with antivirus protection becomes possible.

Other Forms of Malicious Logic

The following descriptions provide a breakdown of the other main types of malicious logic. As the writers of these types of code build off of one another's knowledge, the programs that result from their aggregate work is beginning to cross or blur some of these definitional boundaries. In some cases, it may be very difficult to determine whether the code is a virus, a worm, or a Trojan horse. The following definitions are the commonly accepted terms as of the writing of this book:

- A *worm* is "an independent program that reproduces by copying itself from one system to another, usually over a network. Like a virus, a worm may damage data directly or it may degrade system performance by tying up resources and even shutting down a network."[2] The worm written and released by Robert Morris, Jr., in late 1988 and LoveLetter are examples.
- A *Trojan horse* is a program or routine concealed in software that appears to be harmless. Trojan horses are not viruses and do not replicate like viruses, but they may contain or include a worm or virus as part of the package. The most common way to remove a Trojan horse is to simply delete the identified Trojan application. Trojan horses are quickly becoming one of the top security threats to computer systems. Back Orifice, Back Orifice 2000 (or BO2K), and Netbus are all examples of Trojan horses.
- A *logic bomb* is a software program that is triggered by a timing device (e.g., a date or event) to launch its payload. The payload may release a virus or worm, or perform some other type of attack. This logic bomb is a popular device among disgruntled employees.

Most antivirus software vendors try to include worms and Trojan horses in their signature strings, but their success rates for detection and eradication vary greatly. System administrators cannot assume the antivirus software will detect and solve all malicious code problems.

---

2. Russell, Deborah, and G. T. Gangemi, Sr. *Computer Security Basics*. Sebastopol, CA: O'Reilly & Associates, 1991, p. 426.

Virus Hoaxes and Urban Legends

Any discussion of malicious logic should address the topic of virus hoaxes and urban legends. Although these problems do not actually involve malicious code, they are a major nuisance for system administrators and can present potential security risks. For example, the forwarding of messages to multiple recipients has been known to shut down e-mail servers. This problem should be addressed through end-user education programs.

"A virus's true prey is not the computer, but the good will and ignorance of the users."[3] Similarly, virus hoaxes and urban legends prey on users to spread fear throughout the Internet. A virus hoax is an e-mail warning of some new virus rumored to be in circulation on the Internet. Some of the warnings are very well written and convince well-intentioned users to forward them to others. Unfortunately, mass-forwarding of the false e-mail spreads panic and productivity suffers (not to mention the time wasted in debunking false allegations, reading bogus postings, and tying up resources with multiple forwards of group mail).

Urban legends are very similar to virus hoaxes, except they forward a warning about some other major event, problem, or impending catastrophe. The story that aired on *Dateline* in late 1999 about the use of suntan lotion causing blindness in children is an excellent example of an urban legend, as well as the e-mail stating that Congress is planning to pass legislation that will tax all e-mail. Several Internet resources may be used to confirm whether a story is a virus hoax or urban legend. One of the best sites is http://www.vmyths.com/. If the warning directs the recipient to "forward the e-mail to everyone you know," it's a pretty safe bet that it is a hoax.

The bottom line—do not e-mail virus hoaxes or urban legends. If in doubt, check with a reliable source regarding their validity before taking any further action. The safest action is to press the Delete key. Some organizations have experienced serious system performance degradation when well-intentioned users forwarded warnings to multiple sites. It is far better to leave the warnings to the experts than to

---

3. Skardhamar, p. 15.

try and spread the "word," which merely adds to the hype and may hurt one's reputation in the process.

In some cases, well-intentioned people have caused denial-of-service attacks by responding to hoaxes received via the Internet. In the late 1990s, a hoax circulated on the Internet concerning a young girl who was dying from cancer. Her dying wish was to raise money for cancer research. If the recipient responded by e-mailing the American Cancer Society, the sender promised to donate $0.02 toward cancer research. The response from well-intentioned recipients was so great that it overloaded the systems at the American Cancer Society, which suffered a denial-of-service attack.

Computer viruses rob workers of productivity, redirect the attention of system administrators from more severe security threats, and can jeopardize the security of the organization's information infrastructure. Yet, there is virtually no way to keep an organization completely free from the viral code. To keep the problem in perspective, an organization must take steps to proactively address the problem.

The first step is to increase the overall awareness level of all end users. Addressing topics such as the importance of the macro warning box in Microsoft Word applications and the need to scan attachments for malicious code prior to opening them can go a long way toward eliminating large-scale infections. Increased awareness will also help eliminate problems attributed to the virus hoaxes.

In conjunction with awareness education, implementing antivirus software throughout the enterprise with automatic updates of signature files remains the best course of action developed to combat viruses to date. The signature file updates may be programmed to occur during off-peak hours if desired. Whenever possible, antivirus software and signature file updates should be implemented in a way that cannot be bypassed by end users.

Finally, a check of configuration settings should be made to ensure that auto-open features are disabled and global templates are set to read-only access. These two changes alone may help reduce the penetration achieved by the next rapidly spreading virus. By implementing a proactive antivirus program, the effects of malicious code can be greatly minimized.

Summary

This chapter presented an overview of the major categories of computer attacks as well as some specific attack vectors. Although the attacks described are in no way inclusive of all the attacks known, the descriptions should provide some insight into some of the many "needles in a haystack" that the incident response team must be prepared to detect and manage. The chapter concluded with a discussion of malicious logic infections, particularly viruses. Several pointers for protecting a computer or network from a virus infection were presented.

Incident response teams must be prepared to deal with any type of attack that may be launched against the operating systems used in their infrastructure. Not every form of attack may be used on every operating system. For example, UNIX users should ensure that they are using the latest version of sendmail to prevent problems associated with that program. The best advice for any incident response team about identifying and knowing the specifics of attacks is to first take a look at the SANS top 20 list and see how it applies to your infrastructure.

One of the biggest complaints voiced by system administrators is that there are too many vulnerabilities to keep up with. Table 4–3 shows the number of vulnerabilities reported to CERT CC and the number of advisories the center issued regarding the most serious vulnerabilities. Although the problem of so many vulnerabilities cannot easily be reduced, the best way to avoid becoming overwhelmed is to always remain alert to the advisories and bulletins issued. The CERT CC advisories serve as a good starting point. Vendor Web sites and bulletins should also be monitored as applicable for the systems in one's infrastructure. Some consulting firms and managed security service providers have begun offering services in recent years that focus on vulnerability management as well. These services may provide a good avenue for keeping current with the latest announcements, but they should not stand alone in addressing the vulnerabilities in an organization's infrastructure. The warnings or advice presented must be coupled with knowledge of the internal environment to identify vulnerable platforms and decide what and when to patch. The best advice to remember about monitoring vulnerabilities

Table 4–3 Number of Vulnerabilities and Number of More Significant Problems Reported Annually to CERT CC that Resulted in Advisories

Year	Vulnerabilities Reported	Advisories Issued	Vendor Bulletins Issued
1995	171	18	10
1996	345	27	20
1997	311	28	16
1998	262	13	13
1999	417	17	
2000	1,090	22	
2001	2,437	37	
2002	4,129	37	

Source: http://www.cert.org.

is to rely on multiple sources and not keep "all of the eggs in one basket." Relying heavily on only one source will eventually catch the organization off-guard.

Chapters 3 and 4 focused on the corners of the incident response puzzle by discussing the importance of terminology and identifying numerous types of attacks. Although this book is not intended to be an in-depth technical review, the information presented in this chapter should give some idea of the threats that an incident response team must be prepared to address. We now return to putting the puzzle together, by identifying the other considerations that should be taken into account during the initial formation of a team. Let's continue by discussing operational and resource issues.

CHAPTER

5

Forming the Puzzle

At this point, we have formed the border of our incident response puzzle, laying the foundation on which the team will be built. Now it's time to start filling in the middle sections to complete the picture of the team. The first major corner section we will address is resources. Although there are many types of resources to consider, the most valuable resource for any incident response team is always the people—the incident handlers, the system administrators, and the team leaders. Without the proper mix of personnel, the team will not be effective even if it has the latest and greatest hardware and software at its disposal. Therefore, several sections will be devoted to discussing considerations that directly affect the selection of personnel.

Other pieces of the puzzle to be addressed in this chapter include the facilities to house the incident response team, training plans for enabling professional development, interaction with the media, and ideas for convincing management to fund the team. When combined together, these pieces will add another layer to the incident response puzzle.

Putting the Team Together

Coverage Options

Before selecting the members of an incident response team, several considerations must be addressed that will have a direct impact on the number of personnel needed. The first consideration is the hours of operation for the team. The underlying requirement that must be met is the provision of the proper amount of coverage. Because attacks can and do happen at all hours of the day from all points of the globe, the best coverage is to ensure around-the-clock (24×7) monitoring and response capabilities. This coverage may be provided in three ways: through direct resources available on-site around the clock, through on-site coverage during mission-critical hours with outsourced or on-call coverage after hours, or through a completely outsourced arrangement.

24×7 Staffing

The ideal coverage is provided by a dedicated staff that is on-site and directly available at all times. The number of personnel required reflects, at a minimum, the number of services provided, the size of the constituency, the number of operating systems for which expertise is needed, and safety concerns.

Number of Services Provided. As more services are offered, the number of personnel required to effectively provide that level of functionality will increase. If intrusion detection systems are to be monitored, the team personnel should be able to monitor the number of sensors deployed. In the past, the rule of thumb for monitoring many intrusion detection systems has been one person for every 10 systems. More recently, advances in security management tools and intrusion detection systems are addressing scalability issues and permitting one person to cover more systems simultaneously. As technology continues to improve and scalability becomes less of an issue, this ratio should increase even further.

Size of the Constituency. Lack of responsiveness is one of the first problems that can hurt the reputation of an incident response team.

If the number of personnel selected cannot keep up with the demands placed on them, the team will not be effective. This consideration may be a difficult factor to gauge up front. Therefore, a business case that outlines the potential for growth, if the demand exceeds the initial estimates, should be made early on in the team formation process.

Number of Operating Systems. Many organizations now use multiple operating systems within their infrastructure. An incident response team must have at least two experts for every operating system used, in addition to other types of expertise. A minimum of two experts is recommended for simultaneous attacks and for coverage during vacations or absence of one of the experts.

Safety Concerns. Safety concerns call for at least two people to work in an area at any given time. This redundancy provides support in the case of sudden illness, fire, or other unexpected event. Other regulations governing manpower requirements in the interest of safety might also need to be considered.

There are two main options for creating the dedicated, on-site staff. The first, and easiest, method is to hire people for various shifts and have them work the same shift throughout the week. The second option is to work rotating shifts similar to military watch schedules, where the personnel rotate between day, evening, and midday shifts. Multiple watch rotation schedules can be devised to ensure that personnel work 40 hours per week, with days off scheduled appropriately. Some watch rotations are built upon a 12-hour work day, while others stick to an 8-hour day. The schedule that works best will depend on the specific requirements and resource availability of the organization. If deciding between a 12- or 8-hour work day, it should be noted that personnel will typically begin to fade or lose attentiveness after the 8-hour mark. Therefore, the 8-hour work day is strongly recommended over a 12-hour day, whenever possible.

Partial On-Site Staffing

Resource constraints may prohibit constant coverage from being provided by a dedicated internal team. Because shift work generally requires shift differentials to be paid to employees and may increase other costs such as those related to utilities and physical security, it may be deemed less appropriate to staff an internal team around the clock. In this case, a beeper response or an outsourced response may be used to help ensure 24-hour coverage.

With a beeper response, personnel remain on-call via a beeper or pager. If on-site support is needed, then the person with the pager is required to provide the necessary response. This approach can work in a limited-resource situation, but it has a strong potential to overwork very qualified people. To lessen the burden placed on the team personnel, it's best to establish a "watch schedule" that rotates the on-call status between employees. The pager method also has the potential to catch an organization off-guard, as the amount of monitoring after normal business hours will be severely limited or almost nonexistent.

In this model, notification typically results through three avenues:

- An authorized user of the system notices something that is suspicious and reports it by sending a page. For example, Bob, a project manager, comes into the office over the weekend to work on an important project. When he opens the sensitive files, he notices they have been altered from their original state. Bob first contacts other members of the team who are working on the project to see whether they made the alterations. When the answer is consistently no, he escalates his concern by notifying the on-call person through a page.
- Some automated tools provide the capability to send a page when specific events occur. For example, an intrusion detection system may be programmed to send a page when someone logs into a particular account. In this case, the organization may have already been compromised and the account used by the perpetrator to gain access has been identified.
- Attackers routinely use intermediary systems to hop between IP addresses. This *IP hopping* is used to cover the intruder's tracks. If a system is compromised or used in an attack on another site, then the next victim may try to notify the organization of the attack coming from its systems via the pager, if it is advertised on a Web site or through some other means. Alternatively, the notification may come in response to an attempted denial-of-service attack in

which the organization's systems are used to broadcast the attack. In either case, notification will succeed only if the third party has access to the contact information.

Outsourcing

An outsourced response may be able to provide more thorough coverage than the pager response method can. The incident response functionality may be outsourced entirely or for after-hours coverage only. To obtain the best results, this option requires hiring a security company to monitor and manage security devices such as firewalls and intrusion detection systems. The vendors offering this type of service are referred to as managed security service providers (MSSPs). The number of MSSPs increased overall during 2001.

Just as the number of providers varies, so the level of service (i.e., coverage) offered by these vendors varies. If considering this option, pay particular attention to the services provided and the service level agreements. Some vendors will only monitor the security devices (i.e., watch for the alarms); others will both monitor and manage the devices. Some companies offer an incident response for any unauthorized activity detected; others limit the response to a phone notification of a provided point of contact within the customer's organization. Regardless of what level of service is provided, a routine report should be given to the MSSP's client, providing feedback on the services provided and the activity detected.

Split Coverage: Internal Team and MSSP

Although the monitoring of security devices may be split between an internal team and an MSSP for after-hours coverage, it is really best not to choose this dual-provider route. It results in two separate teams monitoring the devices, which may have a negative effect on the correlation of activity detected throughout the day. Unless a daily turnover takes place regarding the activity detected by each team, the best approach is either to outsource the function completely or to handle it entirely in-house. Because attacks can happen at any hour, the monitoring coverage should be provided 24 hours per day, 7 days per week. Anything less increases the chances for a successful after-hours attack and may lead to more extensive damage.

Determining the Best Coverage

To determine the best route for an organization, a business impact analysis should be undertaken. Costs such as those for personnel salaries and benefits, tools, training, and facilities should be weighed against the costs that would be incurred if the function were outsourced. Considerations such as retention of personnel, the geographic dispersal of systems, the availability of security resources at each location, and the value of the systems protected should also be discussed with respect to advantages and disadvantages of each coverage option. (Many of the issues discussed in Chapter 2 will help to provide starting points for describing the advantages and disadvantages.) Once all of these issues are addressed, management can make a sound decision about whether to provide the functionality in-house or to outsource it. Providing the capability completely in-house or completely outsourcing it are the two options recommended. A pager or on-call response method should be viewed as less viable and used only if it is the last option available, other than no monitoring.

Regardless of whether the organization decides to monitor security devices, steps to respond to a computer incident must be in place. If it is determined that the return on investment is too low given the costs that would be incurred to staff an internal team, then the organization should, at a minimum, have potential external resources identified to respond to an attack when it occurs.

Some professional services organizations offer an incident response team service that can be activated as the need arises or hired on a subscription basis. This service can be provided separately or in conjunction with a managed security offering. Generally the costs will be much higher for contracting this work in an emergency situation. The subscription service is analogous to paying an insurance fee on a monthly basis for coverage when it is needed and may be a more economical route to take. Additionally, if a subscription service is used, the preliminary processes entailed in engaging the response team will have already been completed, meaning that the required personnel can initiate the response much faster. Because the consultant provided by the outside company is not likely to have intricate knowledge of the client company and its resources, an internal resource should be provided to assist the consultant who is responding on-site to any incident.

Team Roles

If the decision is made to provide the incident response capabilities through an internal team, the next major milestone is to identify the roles to be included in the team and the skill sets required for those roles. This exercise will also help to determine the total number of personnel needed. The services to be provided by the team will have a direct impact on the roles needed. A good rule of thumb is to first identify the services to be provided, then identify specific tasks that must be completed to satisfy those requirements. The Team Roles sidebar identifies some suggested roles that should be considered for including in the team.

Team Roles

Core team members include the following personnel:

- *CIRT leader:* This manager is responsible for the day-to-day operations of the team.
- *Incident handlers:* These personnel receive the reports, review the incident data, correlate events, and provide the response required, whether on-site or remotely.
- *Database administrator:* The amount of data received by the typical incident response team will require a database for its storage and processing. A database administrator is vital to the success of this particular requirement. He or she can also help to program and maintain a trouble ticketing system that can feed reports to the database.
- *Legal counsel:* This expert is responsible for guiding the team with respect to laws and regulations governing the team's operation and providing advice on particular incidents.

Experts who will provide depth to your team include the following:

- *Malicious logic experts:* These personnel are good at detecting and responding to malicious logic infections. They also fall into the realm of incident handlers, but are mentioned separately to ensure that this area is addressed.
- *Subject matter experts:* These personnel are involved in the day-to-day operations of a particular network, system, application, or department. They are sometimes called upon by the core investigative team to help analyze data, information, or evidence collected that involves their area of expertise. Rarely are these experts deployed with the investigative team.
- *Research and development:* These positions are responsible for testing new vulnerabilities and patches to those vulnerabilities, as well as recommending new tools for the team. If the team has an advisory function, these team members may be responsible for writing and disseminating the advisories. These personnel are usually not members of the investigative team, although in some cases they may be called upon to analyze some incident data or evidence.
- *System administrators:* These personnel ensure that the security tools and information resources of the team are available and in good working order. Although not formal members of the investigative team, the system administrators keep the "back office" running for the team.
- *Communications:* A communications expert helps the team communicate regarding incidents to its constituency, the media, and regulatory or governmental entities. It's always better for people to hear news directly from the communications staff rather than on the 6 o'clock news. Also, a communications component of the team will help the organization prevent incidents from happening by keeping the team's constituency informed about techniques to avoid incidents.

- *Human resources:* The human resources (or personnel, or employee relations) department can provide the core team, along with legal counsel, advice on handling of internal incidents.

Several additional roles may enhance the team coverage or operations:

- *Security operations center (SOC) personnel:* In an organization that proactively monitors devices such as intrusion detection systems, these team members watch the security devices to detect unauthorized or suspicious activity. They may also conduct vulnerability assessments periodically on the systems they are guarding. The name used to describe the position may take other forms, but typically will involve shift work to ensure that 24 × 7 coverage is provided. These positions are responsible for providing what is normally referred to as level 1 support.
- *Shift leader:* As the team grows or if there is a need to cover 24 × 7 operations, a management position may be needed for each shift. This person is responsible for the operations during the scheduled time of work.
- *Help desk:* These personnel provide user support through e-mail and phone calls to address questions and concerns as they arise. The help desk may be a separate, designated role or it may be staffed by the SOC personnel. The roles of the help desk personnel may include resetting passwords, making the initial incident report entries into the database, and answering general security-related questions.
- *Law enforcement representative:* If the decision is made to work directly with law enforcement agencies, a law enforcement position may actually be incorporated as part of the overall team. This individual would serve as a liaison to the appropriate law enforcement group, in addition to working the computer crime cases detected and reported. In most cases, a representative from law enforcement will be provided only for teams associated with federal, state, or local governments. Other teams will need to fill this connection through a liaison role.

This list is meant to provide a guide to some positions that may not have been previously considered for inclusion within the team. The actual roles selected will vary from team to team, and not every role listed above may need to be incorporated. Some roles may actually be combined with other roles. The skills desired will also vary from position to position, and must fit the organization. Although each role has its own value and significance, those that are most vital to consider are the incident handler, database administrator, investigative team members (i.e., CIRT), shift leaders, and legal counsel. Although these roles are important to an incident response team, several of them overlap significantly with the roles on a security team. You certainly should consider using the two types of resources in conjunction with each other.

Once the desired roles are determined, a description should be written for each position. The Sample Incident Response Team Leader and Sample Incident Handler Position Description sidebars provide sample position descriptions for the team leader and an incident handler. These samples may be edited as appropriate for the organization. Additionally, the tasks needed to provide each service offering may be a good starting point for constructing other position descriptions.

Team Skills

Incident Handler

When filling the role of incident handler, ensuring that the candidate has a few basic skills can help achieve a successful fit with the team. Some of the skills are more of an inherent nature and are not unique to incident handling; others are more technical skills. The following list summarizes the basic skills needed for incident handling:

- *Patience.* One of the first skills to look for is patience. Incident handling requires a great deal of patience as the person will many times be challenged with a "needle in the haystack" situation.
- *Common sense.* Although a skill that may be difficult to measure, common sense is also critical to the position. Jumping to conclusions and overreacting to "events" without keeping things in perspective can be very damaging to the team's integrity in the long

run. An ounce of common sense and the ability to view the "big picture" can help to keep this tendency in check, providing an effective balance to the goal of incident response.

Sample Incident Response Team Leader Position Description

**Computer Incident Response Team Leader
Job Specification**

Scope
Responsible for the daily operation of the computer incident response team. Develops organizational policies related to incident response and secures authorization for their implementation. Provides general direction to and review of subordinate team leaders. Recognized as the organization's expert on computer incident response, security threats, and vulnerabilities. Liaisons with law enforcement and other incident response teams as needed.

Job Complexity
Works on computer security problems attributed to both internal and external threats. Tracks incident response trends to identify and evaluate fundamental security problems and needed improvements within the organization. Addresses managerial, financial, marketing, and security issues related to the protection of corporate information assets. Must be able to act quickly and decisively in a crisis situation.

Discretion
Can commit company resources needed in the course of incident response. Must be able to escalate concerns/issues when needed.

Interaction
Regularly interacts with end users, managers, senior managers, and executives. Interactions can involve controversial situations, resource negotiations, or situations calling for influencing and persuading other senior-level managers and executives. Actions can influence policy making, resourcing, company reputation, possible litigation, deployment of human resources, or the like.

Sample Incident Handler Position Description

Incident Handler
Position Description

An incident handler will use a wide range of technical and personal skills to detect and respond to computer incidents within the organization. This person will provide guidance to end users and system administrators alike, concerning computer security threats and vulnerabilities. This position reports to the computer incident response team leader, and works closely with help desk and security operations center (SOC) personnel.

Responsibilities

- Respond to suspicious activity reports received from end users and the IT staff
- Identify potential vulnerabilities with corporate information resources
- Enter and process trouble tickets on reported vulnerabilities and incident reports
- Provide input to the help desk regarding new security vulnerabilities and threats
- Test patches advertised to resolve pertinent vulnerabilities
- Write company security alerts, including information on recommended courses of action
- Track incident statistics and summarize weekly performance in the company trend report
- Respond on-site to computer incidents as required, preserving evidence of wrongdoing for possible prosecution
- Support law enforcement efforts on any computer crimes detected on corporate information systems
- Brief managers and end users on the company's incident trends, vulnerabilities, and other related information
- Prepare media briefs for management on specific incidents
- Provide end-user training on incident reporting and security countermeasures
- Other duties as assigned

Qualifications

- Knowledge of major protocols and operating systems used by the company
- Two to three years computer security experience
- Strong written and verbal communications skills
- Strong deductive reasoning skills
- Completion of at least two GIAC certifications

- *Deductive reasoning and problem-solving skills.* The incident handler needs to be able to quickly identify the relevance of data, any missing information, and the important information.
- *Good memory.* A good memory can be very helpful when correlating activity that may be attributable to the same source or may appear similar in nature. It is also not uncommon to be asked about incidents that may have been reported in the past, and a good memory can expedite the response if reports do not have to be recalled and reviewed to answer the questions.
- *Strong communication skills.* The ability to communicate effectively through both oral and written means is vital to making a high-quality incident response. The incident handler will need to communicate through a variety of channels, including e-mail, reports, and procedural documents. Similarly, the incident handler will need to brief individuals or groups of people, including other team members, experts, members of law enforcement, constituents, and possibly the media.
- *Diplomacy.* An incident handler must often interact with people who are excited or even angry. He or she must remain professional at all times and ensure that the necessary information is exchanged.
- *Integrity.* Incident handlers routinely deal with highly sensitive information. The integrity of not only the individual but also the team must remain a priority at all times. The incident handler must be able to handle sensitive information with confidence and according to team policies and procedures.
- *Team player.* Successful incident handling requires a great deal of teamwork. Therefore, it is imperative that the incident handler be

able to function in a team environment while being a cordial and productive team member.

In addition, the incident handler must be able to follow policies and procedures to ensure consistent, reliable methodologies are adhered to during the response process. He or she must be able to admit when help is needed. Events can occur quite rapidly during a computer incident, and incident handlers must acknowledge when they have reached the limit of their knowledge or when they find themselves out of their depth for any given situation. Finally, the incident handler must be able to cope with stressful situations, such as when the workload becomes excessive, human life may be at risk, or when an angry or excited caller demands a response.

In addition to these basic skills needed for incident handling, the following technical skills are required for an incident handler:

- *Security basics:* Incident handlers should have a good understanding of the basic security principles. Specifically, they should understand the goals of computer security, including confidentiality, integrity, availability, and nonrepudiation. Additionally, they should understand the mechanisms used to ensure authentication, access control, and privacy.
- *Security vulnerabilities and weaknesses:* Incident handlers should have a firm grasp of the many vulnerabilities and weaknesses that can affect the overall security of the network. They must recognize elements of an attack that may be attributed to physical security, protocol design flaws, implementation errors or flaws, user errors, malicious logic, and configuration problems.
- *Internet knowledge:* Incident handlers should have a good understanding of the Internet, including its structure and components. Examples of these components include the Internet Network Information Center (InterNIC), root name servers, network access points, and major archive sites.
- *Network protocols:* Because many attacks occur over networks, a good understanding of the major protocols, especially the Transmission Control Protocol (TCP) and Internet Protocol (IP), is very important. Other protocols that should be addressed and under-

stood by the team include the User Datagram Protocol (UDP), Internet Control Message Protocol (ICMP), Address Resolution Protocol (ARP), and Reverse Address Resolution Protocol (RARP). For each protocol, the incident handler should understand its purpose, basic specification, and basic method of operation.

- *Network applications and services:* Each incident handler should understand some of the common network applications and services used by the team's constituency. As with the network protocols, the incident handler should understand the purpose of the application or service, its basic method of operation, and the common uses of the application or service. Examples of Internet-based applications and services of which the incident handler should have an understanding include the Network File System (NFS), Domain Name Service (DNS), TELNET, File Transfer Protocol (FTP), HTTP, and others.

- *Malicious logic foundation:* It is quite helpful if the incident handler has a basic understanding of the various forms of malicious logic, including how to prevent, detect, eradicate, and recover from an infection.

- *Incident analysis:* Given raw data, the incident handler must be able to identify what details are missing and determine the scope of the activity reported. When clarification or more data are needed, he or she must be able to communicate what is needed. Review of the data should enable the incident handler to identify the vulnerabilities exploited and the magnitude of the incident.

- *Basic knowledge of relevant applications:* The incident handler should have a general idea of how these applications are used in the organization.

Finally, the incident handler should be well versed in the operating systems used by the constituency. He or she should know how to harden the operating system (i.e., securely configure it) and should be familiar with the security tools used to evaluate system logs, configuration settings, and security-related settings. Every incident response team should include a minimum of two experts for every operating system in use. This number is required for coverage in instances when more than one site needs a response simultaneously, as well as when the "one expert" is sick or on vacation. Depending on the size of the team's constituency, the number of required experts should increase proportionally.

Incident handlers are the core of the incident investigative team. For this reason, their backgrounds and previous experience should be scrutinized very carefully.

Database Administrator

An incident database is a vital tool for computer incident response, so the role of database administrator is also critical. The database administrator should have a good understanding of the requirements associated with incident response and, even more importantly, very strong skills in configuring, maintaining, and troubleshooting the database software used. If a trouble ticket system is used, he or she should also have a strong knowledge of that system to determine the appropriate interfaces needed. Ideally, a trouble ticket system will be used to track open incidents and provide the interface for the storage of incident data in the main database.

Typically, the database administrator does not participate in the investigative efforts. Nevertheless, he or she must be a trusted member of the team, as the database administrator will likely have access to all of the records and digital evidence that the team collects.

Response Team Leaders

The CIRT team leader is the glue that holds everything together. He or she should possess many of the skills of an incident handler while also being a proven manager and leader. Likewise, shift leaders are vital to the daily operations of the team. Good communication skills are essential for ensuring a smooth transition between shifts. The shift leader needs to make quick decisions as events occur, have a good grasp for the "big picture," and know when to escalate problems to the next level.

Response team leaders are often incident handlers who have earned a promotion. Like incident handlers, response team leaders are part of the core investigative team, and they often serve as coordinators during a team deployment.

Legal Counsel

Legal counsel experienced with high-tech crimes is an extremely valuable resource and one that is not always available to incident response teams. Having a dedicated lawyer can be extremely valuable for translating laws as they apply to the area of incident response and for addressing potentially volatile situations in a short time frame. If the organization does not have a legal counsel who can directly support the incident response team, then access to outside counsel should be considered. The attorney selected for this role must be experienced in issues such as privacy, contracts, and employee relations, and must have strong knowledge of the industry regulations, laws, policies, and practices that are unique to the organization.

Although some organizations don't include a member of the legal team as part of the core investigative team, we strongly recommend that legal counsel be involved in at least an advisory role when your team is deployed. As questions may arise later regarding the procedures that your team followed when initiating its investigation, your organization's legal team can direct the response team leaders on proper, legally sound investigative techniques. In major deployments, the authors' team meets with our organization's legal staff so that everyone knows exactly what each member is to do, and so we all know the legal ramifications of the situation under investigation.

Promotions and Growth

To provide for growth and promotions within the team, it is strongly recommended that the team roles be established in a manner that permits individuals to build upon their expertise and accept increased responsibilities. For example, it may be determined that the roles of shift leader, incident handler, intrusion detection system monitor, and help desk staff are needed for a particular team. New members of the team may be introduced in the role of help desk staff. As they master this job and gain a better understanding of the responsibilities of each team role, they may be promoted to intrusion detection system monitor. Following success at this role, a promotion to incident handler may be deemed appropriate, and then finally a promotion to shift leader for those individuals who demonstrate leadership and management abilities in addition to mastering each position held. Other promotion sequences may also be used, and it may be necessary to introduce new personnel somewhere in the middle, rather than at the beginning level, if the need arises and their experience warrants a higher starting position.

Some of the positions associated with manning a security operations center may be considered "dull" if little activity is reported, particularly for individuals working evening and midnight shifts. Therefore, allowing growth and variety in the job can be very important considerations for promoting a healthy team setting. Providing for promotions and the ability for personnel to increase the scope of their jobs is an excellent way to increase employee retention and enhance job satisfaction. Another strategy is to rotate personnel between positions over set periods of time (e.g., monthly, quarterly, biannually). For example, a rotation between monitoring stations, the help desk, and other positions may increase the overall knowledge of team members while preventing employees from becoming too stagnant in one position.

Interviewing Candidates

The discipline of incident response requires teamwork and can be very stressful at times. Interviews conducted with prospective candidates should include team exercises, if possible, and focus on both interpersonal and technical skills. One suggested test is to put the candidate on the spot by asking him or her to give an impromptu technical presentation. This exercise not only tests the candidate's communication skills, but can also provide a measure of how well he or she handles stress.

An informal interview over dinner or lunch can also be quite revealing as to how the candidate interacts with others. The meal should include other members of the team who may have already been hired or who may have been part of an existing team for some time. Feedback from these members can be a good gauge as to how readily the candidate will be accepted into the team.

Role playing can also be a revealing exercise, particularly if the candidate lists previous incident response experience on his or her résumé or application. Other members of the organization may take on the role of a victim or system administrator trying to report an incident, and the candidate should serve in the role for which he or she is being considered. The role play should "throw some curves" to the would-be incident handler to see how the candidate would respond.

Finally, the candidate should be interviewed by multiple people within the organization. It is best if these interviews are conducted one-on-one, so that the interviewers can later compare notes about their impressions of the candidate. An evaluation sheet of characteristics desired for the open position may serve as a useful tool while the interviews are taking place. Background checks, including calls to references, should be included in the overall hiring process. With the proper amount of due diligence, qualified candidates should emerge to help build a successful team.

As always, the team should adhere to all of the human resources department's policies regarding interview procedures and etiquette, and ensure that all candidates are handled consistently.

Facilities

The facilities in which a team will operate is another consideration that must be taken into account when determining the number of resources needed to staff a team. The monitoring of devices such as intrusion detection systems is normally accomplished in an area that is referred to as a security operations center (SOC). The security functions may also be incorporated into the network operations center (NOC). The main difference in these two types of operations centers is the focus of the activity. As the name implies, the focal point of operations in an SOC is computer security, featuring activities such as monitoring and managing firewalls and intrusion detection systems. The focus of the activity in an NOC is network operations—ensuring that the network is operational and taking care of requirements such as adding new users and helping users with access issues. An NOC is typically manned by the organization's system administrators and help desk personnel.

Due to resource constraints, it may be easier to add the security functionality to an existing NOC, rather than establishing a completely separate SOC. This is particularly true for smaller organizations that do not have a large constituency to monitor. If this route is chosen, however, there should be some level of physical separation between the two areas. Many aspects of computer security are based on a "need to know," and it may not be effective to have security problems identified to the NOC's full audience. Additionally, security principles require a clear separation of duties between those personnel who are maintaining the networks and those who are guarding or monitoring them. Therefore, the incident response capabilities should never be accomplished by the same people who are responsible for maintaining the systems. Many people believe that combining these two functions, or even combining their facilities, is analogous to having "a fox watching the hen house."

Regardless of the physical location of the incident response team, a clear communication channel must be established between the team and the network operations personnel. This communication will assist in differentiating between activity caused by network problems and that associated with cyber attacks. For example, backhoe operators and falling trees have been known to take down entire networks or sections of networks. If an SOC does not have an established communication channel with the corresponding NOC and begins receiving reports of access problems, the event may initially appear to be a denial-of-service attack. However, if the NOC communicates about the outage, it will help to quickly shift the attention to the actual cause of the problem and may prevent valuable hours of work from being wasted.

At this point, the hours of operation, the roles of various team members, and the facilities for housing the team have all been discussed. The answers to the various questions raised about these topics should help to identify the number of people needed to staff the incident response team. On all accounts, the size of the team should be proportional to some extent to the size of the team's constituency and their geographic coverage. We will now move on to the next major piece of the puzzle, which focuses on the tools used by the team.

Products and Tools

The type of tools needed by an incident response team will depend on the number and types of services that the team will provide. Many tools are now available, including both free and commercial off-the-shelf products, which can be very useful to a team. As a precursor to the identification and functional descriptions of these tools, this section will describe the categories of tools that may be used to perform various tasks. These categories are not fully inclusive of all tools that may be used to facilitate incident response, but they do provide a good foundation for considering the tools needed by a team. The tools described in this section overlap in some cases with a well-managed security operation, and they do not apply only to an incident response team.

Penetration Testing Tools

A variety of tools can prove very useful in conducting vulnerability assessments or penetration tests. Some focus on the overall network; others are geared more toward testing at the host or application level. Typically, a combination of tools and techniques will prove to be more effective in giving a true picture of the security of an infrastructure as opposed to the use of one single tool.

Vulnerability scanners are the category of tools typically thought of when planning penetration tests. These tools provide a quick and easy way to identify vulnerabilities on a network or specific systems. Scanning tools are available for testing systems at the network, host, and application levels. Network vulnerability scanners send packets out over a network to identify potential vulnerabilities that may be used to gain unauthorized access or cause a denial of service. The most common form of network scanning entails scanning a server or network from the Internet to check for open ports and services that can be exploited. Other scans are conducted by using network diagnostic tools such as Finger and WHOIS to obtain information that may provide an entry for attacking a system.

If a network is vulnerable to a denial-of-service attack, then the use of some vulnerability scanners can cause such an event to occur. For this reason, caution should be taken when using these tools so that the team is either able to prevent a problem from occurring or prepared to quickly restore operations. Mission-critical systems should be identified up front, so that they may be avoided during testing or recovery procedures. Also, the times of least impact should be known so that if a system is deemed mission critical at certain times, the system is not tested during those hours. For example, if weekly accounting reports are generated on Friday afternoon and they consume a large amount of CPU cycles, it may be a good idea to steer clear of testing those systems on Friday afternoon. (Of course, this tendency may also be noted as a potential vulnerability.)

Some very good network vulnerability scanners are available today that can prove quite useful in identifying potential weaknesses in a network. Unfortunately, the results these scanners generate are not always 100 percent accurate. The generation of false positives is a never-ending challenge with vulnerability scanning tools. A false positive occurs when a vulnerability is identified that does not actually exist. To eliminate the false positives, it is strongly recommended that the team use more than one tool and compare the results generated by each tool. The results should also be reviewed and investigated to eliminate any additional false data. Experience with conducting such tests will help to eliminate the number of false positives over time, as the person conducting the test can learn to quickly recognize problems associated with specific tools.

The host base vulnerability scanner is used to compare the configuration settings on a particular host to sound security practices. Discrepancies between the two should be noted and reviewed for potential threats. The host level should be included whenever possible while conducting a penetration test or vulnerability assessment. All critical systems (e.g., servers) should be tested as well as a random number of end-user workstations.

Other tools that can be quite useful when conducting penetration tests are those associated with war dialing. War dialing is the scanning of phone numbers to search for modems and facsimile machines. If a modem or fax machine is found, it should then be tested for security features. Examples of security features that may be present include the request for a password or a call-back feature. In the commercial sector, some companies opt to eliminate the war dialing feature in their test plan to cut costs when hiring an outside firm to conduct a penetration or vulnerability assessment. This step is not recommended, as modems represent a very viable threat to the security of an infrastructure. More often than not, organizations are surprised to learn that they have more modems in their infrastructure than originally thought.

The final category of tools that are frequently used in penetration testing includes password cracking tools. Weak passwords continue to represent a major vulnerability category in many organizations worldwide. The use of a password cracking program can help to identify password problems as well as individually weak passwords. Such programs do not actually decrypt the passwords in a file, but rather utilize a pattern matching scheme. Essentially, password cracking programs use known encryption algorithms to generate passwords with known key values. If the password generated with the known key (e.g., words in the dictionary) by a password cracking program matches the password in the file being "cracked," then the key used to generate the password has been identified. The key used to generate the password is actually the password itself. Most operating systems today have known password cracking tools that can be used to identify easily guessed passwords.

The information that is gathered from scanning can provide a good basis to a team to have an idea of what possible vulnerabilities were available on a system that could have been exploited to cause the incident. It is possible that an organization may deliberately not eliminate all known vulnerabilities as part of its risk/benefit analysis.

In addition to the tools listed here, many other resources may be used to conduct a penetration test, including the phone, trash dumpsters, the Internet, and the phone book. Although this book will not go into great detail on how these tests can be conducted, it is important to note that the tools or resources available to run such a test do not have to end with technology. Any penetration test should use multiple avenues to attempt to gain access to the identified target.

Intrusion Detection Systems

Various categories of intrusion detection tools exist, providing for application-, host-, and network-based monitoring, as well as integrated tools that combine two or more of these levels. As their name implies, application intrusion detection tools focus on collecting information at the application level. Audit logs generated by Web servers and firewalls are examples of application-level monitoring. Although application intrusion detection is not as widely used as network-based intrusion detection, this type of monitoring is gaining in popularity.

Host-based intrusion detection systems (HIDS) monitor the activity of a specific system. Sensors are installed on the monitored system to collect and analyze information. Most HIDS are configured to report the activity detected to a central management server for consolidation and further analysis.

Network-based intrusion detection systems are the level normally thought of when referring to the area of intrusion detection. This level is typically referred to with the acronym IDS (intrusion detection system). Sensors gather information directly from the network through packet sniffing. The IDS may analyze the traffic by comparing the traffic patterns to a known attack signature pattern, by undertaking protocol analysis, by comparing the traffic patterns to a baseline of activity, or by using a combination of these methods. When suspicious activity is detected, an alarm is normally sent to a central management console or server. The IDS can be thought of as a smoke alarm on the network's perimeter that sounds when smoke (i.e., suspicious activity) is sensed.

Intrusion detection systems can be very valuable to an incident response team. When selecting an IDS, the following specific features are recommended to enhance incident response capabilities:

- The ability to add custom signatures to the attack signature file
- The ability to alert incident response personnel through alphanumeric pagers
- Session playback support
- Alerting mechanisms that are performed externally to the system being monitored

An intrusion detection system can also be used once an incident has been discovered, as a mechanism for gaining further information or evidence. When a wiretap order (or Title III) is written for a computer system during a computer crime investigation, an IDS may be the tool of choice to actually implement the order.

In addition to the intrusion detection tools that focus on specific levels of monitoring, some products combine the functionality of two levels into an integrated intrusion detection product. For example, some products combine sensors for both the network and host levels in one product. Similarly, some firewall appliances combine network-level intrusion detection systems with their firewalls. Provided inter-operability between the products is not an issue, this approach can be a way to expand the granularity of coverage with one product.

Mandy Andress provides an in-depth look at each level of intrusion detection system tools in her book *Surviving Security: How to Integrate People, Process, and Technology*. The advantages and disadvantages of each type of tool are discussed in detail in Chapter 8 of her book and summarized in Table 5–1.

Network Monitors and Protocol Analyzers

Network monitors and protocol analyzers are diagnostic tools used by both incident response teams and system administrators alike. For incident response, they are primarily used for conducting low-level attack analysis and for storing network data to disk for further analysis. "In short, these tools are like microscopes that reveal the inner contents of the data" involved with a computer incident.[1] To be completely effective, the monitoring tool must perform its tasks silently and invisibly on the network. Otherwise, its obvious presence would defeat its purpose in the task of incident response.

Forensics Tools

A variety of hardware and software products can be extremely useful when a computer crime scene needs to be preserved. Some commercially available software programs can expedite the forensics process by helping to identify the files present on a computer system and maintaining copies of the drive being investigated. Most forensics programs will enable a bitstream image to be made of the drive and can document the system date and time. Additionally, such programs

---

1. Van Wyke, Kenneth, and Richard Forno. *Incident Response.* Sebastopol, CA: O'Reilly & Associates, 2001, p. 113.

Table 5-1 Advantages and Disadvantages of the Various Levels of Intrusion Detection Systems

Level of Intrusion Detection	Advantages	Disadvantages
Application intrusion detection	• Provides a high level of granularity	• Too many applications to support • Covers only one component
Host intrusion detection	• Verifies success or failure of an attack • Monitors specific system activities • Detects attacks that network-based systems miss • Well suited for encrypted and switched environments • Requires no additional hardware • Lower cost of entry	• Network activity is not visible to host-based sensors • Running audit mechanisms can use additional resources • When audit trails are used as data sources, they can take up significant storage • Host-based sensors must be platform-specific • Management and deployment
Network intrusion detection	• Lowers cost of ownership • Detects attacks that host-based systems miss • More difficult for an attacker to remove evidence • Fast detection and response • Detects unsuccessful attacks and malicious intent • Operating system independence	• Unable to determine outcome • Unable to read encrypted traffic • Unable to save all packets on a switched network • Unable to handle high-speed networks
Integrated intrusion detection	• Trend analysis • Stability • Cost savings	• Interoperability issues • Feeling too secure

Source: Mandy Andress. *Surviving Security: How to Integrate People, Process, and Technology.* Indianapolis: SAMS Publishing, 2002, pp. 171–177.

automate keyword searches for specific types of information that may be stored, and they provide a mechanism for authenticating the data stored on the device. Overall, forensics software programs can expedite the analysis process, while providing an avenue to help prepare for prosecution in a court of law.

In addition to software, several other tools can be quite useful for computer forensics purposes. A forensics computer that has an extra bay and hard drive will prove quite helpful in forensic investigations. In addition, system components for backing up or preserving data will be needed, such as tape drives, Zip and Jaz drives, a CD-ROM burner, and various cards, cables, and converters. Given the scope of the investigation, video, still, and digital cameras also normally prove useful for obtaining and preserving evidence.

Because computer forensics is a developing discipline and can be vital to a successful incident response, an entire chapter has been devoted to this topic later in the book (see Chapter 11). The processes to be followed in a forensics investigation and some of these components will be discussed further at that time.

Other Tools

Numerous other tools may prove very helpful to an incident response team in the course of operations. Again, the value of many of these tools depends on the services selected for the team to perform. Two of the most vital tools for any response team are a database and a trouble ticketing system.

The database should have enough room to store all of the fields of information to be tracked for every event and incident over an extended period of time, as well as room for growth. It is not uncommon for an incident to span an extended period of time—lasting weeks, months, or even years. To correlate activity that appears to originate from the same source, the information from each event needs to be readily available in the database. Having to search through archives of data may hamper the correlation efforts. Therefore, the database needs to have a significant amount of memory so as to store large amounts of data.

A trouble ticket system will prove extremely valuable, particularly if the incident response team becomes very busy. (Regardless of the size of the team's constituency, this overwork is guaranteed to happen. Like a computer compromise, it's just a matter of time.) Entering new reports, updates to existing reports, requests for information, and other types of reports or inquiries into the system can help to ensure efficiency in responding to the information, as well as help to track statistics regarding the types of reports or inquiries received. Additionally, the trouble ticket system can serve as the front end to a database by being the tool that feeds the appropriate data directly to the master incident database. This system should assign a unique tracking number to each report and inquiry for easier tracking when an update is received or when a customer calls with an inquiry.

Encryption tools are valuable in helping to ensure confidentiality of sensitive incident data. Encryption should be used for communicating any remotely sensitive information over unclear channels, such as the Internet. In addition, if incident data are to be transmitted between subteams (for large-scale operations), encryption through a virtual private network (VPN) can ensure the confidentiality of the reports.

Finally, networking components such as modems, CD-ROM burners, external hard drives, and other various forms of removable media can meet specific needs of the team as operations progress. Each planned service should be analyzed to determine the specific functional requirements that must be met by the team's computer infrastructure. As the network components are identified, they should also be examined to ensure that room for growth is available. Although this section has identified numerous components that a team may choose to include in its infrastructure, the list is not fully inclusive and other tools may be needed prior to operations commencing.

Funding the Team

Every organization needs to have a computer incident response capability, whether that capability is provided through internal or external means. The real challenge in many cases is gaining management's approval to fund the requirements to establish a team, acquire specific resources, or even outsource the requirement. All too often, organizations wait until they become the victim of an incident to provide the funding necessary to respond quickly. This section outlines a few methods commonly used for convincing management to fund the internal response team up front, *before* a major incident occurs. Although this book focuses on computer incident response, these techniques may be applied equally well to any expenditure associated with computer security.

Marketing Campaign

Gaining the support of management is essential for the successful implementation of the team. Convincing management to spend precious dollars on computer security or an incident response team is not always an easy task, however. The best approach to take is to ensure that management fully understands the threats to the computer systems and the proposed safeguards that an incident response team can provide to help protect against those threats. It may be necessary to undertake a marketing campaign to gain the support needed from management. Personal interviews may be conducted with key decision makers to gain insight into the business requirements, identify existing concerns related to the establishment of a team, identify any other projects that may be competing for the same funding, and evaluate the perceived effectiveness of such a program.

Presentations or papers may be provided to management to help clarify and describe the requirements for the team moving forward. These requirements should be stated clearly and accurately, so that management fully understands the problem. Acronyms and technical terms should be avoided unless the presenter is absolutely sure that the targeted audience understands the language. Finally, the presentation or paper should be kept as simple as possible, include possible alternatives, and focus on the business issues.

Once approval is gained either in full or in part, the marketing campaign should continue by keeping management apprised of progress made to date and any additional issues that may arise. Marketing is an area that is just starting to emerge within the security space and will be an important aspect of successful projects in years to come.

Risk Assessment

One of the most common methods used to justify costs associated with computer security in the recent past is the conduct of a risk assessment. A risk assessment evaluates the overall infrastructure to identify the organization's information risk. By assigning numeric values to each element, the following equation can be used to quantify the organization's risk:

$$\text{Information risk} = [(\text{vulnerability} * \text{threat}) / \text{safeguard}] * \text{value}$$

where

- *Vulnerability* is a point in a system that, if acted upon, may cause the system to produce unpredicted results, increased privileges, or unnecessary access. An example of a vulnerability is an account that does not have a secure password.
- *Threat* is a factor that may act on a vulnerability. It may arise from many different sources. Sometimes a simple mistake can be a threat—for example, a person accidentally deleting all of the files on a shared directory.
- *Safeguard* includes those techniques employed to protect an information system against threats and vulnerabilities. Safeguards can be very simple or very complex. It's important to tailor the safeguards to be in a balance with your threat and vulnerability level. No one installs a vault door on a grass hut.
- *Value* is the information's worth to the operation of a business.

Calculating the value used for each component of the equation and thus the information risk itself is dependent upon the goals and objectives of the organization. Numeric values are normally assigned to the vulnerability, threat, and safeguard fields, and the value and information risk fields are represented in dollar amounts. These values will not be the same across the board for all organizations. Nevertheless, the results of the calculation can offer an indication of the level of risk that the organization is willing to assume and the additional dollars that are needed to reduce the risk.

The existence of an incident response team should be noted as a safeguard. The availability of internal resources to quickly respond to an incident will normally reduce the potential damage that can (and typically does) result from many types of incidents.

The outcome of a risk assessment may be done in conjunction with the marketing campaign previously described. Other methods may also be used to quantify risk, as this model has several drawbacks. Quantifying risk is certainly no simple task. Any model that you choose needs to be consistent, repeatable, and understandable.

Business Case

Another way to approach the funding issue is through the establishment of a business case that identifies the projected return on investment. As the dollar amount of the benefit associated with an incident response team may not be readily quantified, the return presented may be based more on cost avoidance. In other words, how much money can the organization save by having the incident response team in place to quickly respond and limit the potential damage? Because many executives do not fully understand the costs that can be incurred following a security breach, the business case should begin by offering statistics on computer crimes and the costs associated with them. Both tangible (e.g., lost sales, effects on shareholder value) and intangible costs (e.g., effects on goodwill and reputation) should be identified. The incident response team can be promoted as an insurance measure to help avoid or limit potential risks. Identifying the team as an enabler for the business can also provide a convincing argument in favor of funding.

Placement of the Team

In some cases, the placement of the team within the organization will provide a method for recouping some of the expenses. For example, an organization may establish the team as a corporate entity, with the bulk of the funding provided as overhead. When an incident occurs, the team will respond to the needs of specific business units within the corporation and the corresponding business unit will be charged for the team's time and materials. Under this setup, each business unit can have the response functionality readily available without having to separately fund the requirement, yet the team can recapture some of its expenses. It is necessary to be very careful about this model, however. A "chargeback" model may encourage business units to cover up incidents, thereby making the organization as a whole less secure.

Although the corporate placement of the team can be political at times, it can also provide an advantage to the organization by allowing the "full picture" to be tracked and monitored by one central entity.

Worst-Case Scenarios

An approach that may be taken either separately or in conjunction with other methods is to have management personnel state how much down time they are comfortable accepting and use that as the selling point to acquire additional resources. When all else fails, a reality check using worst-case scenarios for "what if" situations may be used to convince management to expend additional funds. For example, what if an intruder gained access to the company's computer system? The worst-case result may be the company's competitor stealing plans for a new product under development.

Management's support of computer security is vital to the protection of the company's information assets, so the importance of gaining these executives' support cannot be emphasized strongly enough. In some cases, it may be necessary to use more than one method to obtain the funding required to support the establishment of the team and the purchase of needed resources. Different methods may be used over time as the need for funding of resources is renewed. Maintaining accurate statistics reflecting the level of support provided by the team can prove extremely valuable when revisiting the funding requirements after the team has been established and operational for some time.

Training

Training requirements for the incident response team should be considered up front when the team is being formed. As the discipline of incident response is continually evolving, ongoing training should be planned for all members of the team. Various types of training are available, and a mixture of all forms should be included in the team's training plans. Training subjects can include incident response procedures, vulnerability awareness, specific tool operation, legal concerns, and much more.

In-house training should be offered periodically and can be used to provide an overview of processes and procedures specific to the organization and the team. Topics may include a wide variety of technical subjects as well, and can be either obtained from external sources or developed internally. Whenever possible, actual hands-on training is strongly encouraged on new techniques and products. For larger, more dispersed teams, it may be necessary to develop a "train the trainer" program where specific resources are identified for administering training requirements on a larger scale.

The establishment of a lab that is separate from any operational systems can be an extremely useful tool for in-house training and should be included in funding considerations. In addition to training, the lab can help with incident response by providing an avenue for testing new vulnerabilities, verifying patches, investigating code that allegedly contains a virus, and much more. The lab does not have to be huge and located in a separate room to itself. Rather, it can be small and fit in the corner of the facility. The main concern is to have computer systems available that can be used to train and learn on that will not affect overall operations should a problem be encountered. Additionally, the operating systems selected for the lab should mirror those used by the team's constituency.

The number of external resources providing training specific to incident response is beginning to grow. In some cases, the training is offered through a conference setting, such as the System Administration Networking and Security (SANS) Institute conferences; other sources provide training in a classroom setting. Many vendors now offer training that can be conducted on-site for multiple attendees at once, allowing a team to train several members while reducing the costs associated with travel and registration.

In addition to education specific to incident response, training plans should include courses on specific hardware and software to be used by the incident response team. Many vendors offer training on their products either directly or through qualified partners. In some cases, the training can also be used as an avenue to gain certifications on specific products. Some vendors will include a set number of seats for free training when a purchase is made or offer a discount for groups.

Certifications

Finally, the topic of certifications should be addressed for team members. The number of computer security certifications has increased in recent years, and the certifications vary in the complexity and testing requirements used to complete the process. The following is a summary of the best-known security certifications available as of the writing of this book.

Certified Information Systems Security Professional (CISSP).   The "CISSP certification was designed to recognize mastery of an international standard for information security and understanding of a Common Body of Knowledge (CBK)."[2] It is administered by the International Information Systems Security Certification Consortium [also known as (ISC)²] and is generally considered one of the two more prestigious and valuable certifications. The examination given to prospective certification candidates takes up to six hours to complete and consists of 250 multiple-choice questions focusing on 10 distinct security domains:

- Access control systems and methodology
- Applications and systems development
- Business continuity and disaster recovery planning
- Cryptography
- Law, investigation, and ethics
- Operations security (computer)
- Physical security
- Security architecture and models
- Security management practices
- Telecommunications, network, and Internet security

---

2. http://www.isc2.org, CISSP Description.

To be considered for the CISSP certification, a candidate must meet the following requirements prior to taking the examination:

- Subscribe to the (ISC)² Code of Ethics.
- Have a minimum of four years of direct, full-time security professional work experience in one or more of the 10 test domains of the information systems security Common Body of Knowledge (CBK) or three years of direct, full-time security professional work experience in one or more of the 10 test domains of the information systems security CBK with a college degree or equivalent life experience. Valid experience includes information systems security-related work performed as a practitioner, auditor, consultant, vendor, investigator, or instructor, or that which requires IS security knowledge and involves direct application of that knowledge.

More information regarding the certification and examination schedules may be obtained from the (ISC)² Web site at http://www.isc2.org.

System Security Certified Practitioner (SSCP). The SSCP certification is also administered by (ISC)². This examination takes up to three hours to complete and includes 125 multiple-choice questions covering seven domains:

- Access controls
- Administration
- Audit and monitoring
- Risk, response, and recovery
- Cryptography
- Data communications
- Malicious code/malware

Candidates wishing to achieve the SSCP certification must meet the following requirements prior to taking the examination:

- Subscribe to the (ISC)² Code of Ethics.
- Have at least one year of cumulative work experience in one or more of the seven test domains in information systems security.

Valid experience includes information systems security–related work performed as a practitioner or that which requires IS security knowledge and involves direct application of that knowledge.
- No affiliation with any organization is required.

As with the CISSP certification, further information and testing schedules may be obtained from the (ISC)² Web site.

Certified Information Systems Auditor (CISA).   The CISA certification program is administered by the Information Systems Audit and Control Association and Foundation (ISACA). Established in 1978, the program is the other high-end security certification generally recognized by the information security industry. "The program has been the globally accepted standard of achievement among IS audit, control and security professionals."[3] Unlike the CISSP program, which offers tests several times during the year, the CISA examination is given only once per year and covers the following domains:

- IS audit process
- Management, planning, and organization of IS
- Technical infrastructure and operational practices
- Protection of information assets
- Disaster recovery and business continuity
- Business application system development, acquisition, implementation, and maintenance
- Business process evaluation and risk management

To qualify for the certification, candidates must meet the following requirements:

- Successfully complete the CISA examination
- Have a minimum of five years experience in information systems auditing, control, and/or security work
- Agree to subscribe to the Code of Professional Ethics
- Agree to adhere to ISACA's Information Systems Auditing Standards

---

3. http://www.isaca.org, CISA Description.

More information on the CISA certification and the examination schedule can be obtained from the ISACA Web site at http://www.isaca.org.

Global Information Assurance Certification (GIAC).   The GIAC certification program was started in February 2000 and is administered by the SysAdmin, Audit, Network, Security Institute, better known as SANS. An evolving program that includes in-depth technical training, it is gaining tremendous momentum in the security space. Through the certification process, a candidate can demonstrate the depth of his or her knowledge and abilities. This certification program is one of the best available as of the writing of this book and is strongly recommended for security practitioners or managers who are seeking significant value from their training dollars.

"For each GIAC certification, the candidate must complete a written 'practical assignment' that demonstrates their ability to put their skills into practice. GIAC is the only security certification that requires candidates to submit a practical assignment in order to demonstrate this real-world, hands-on mastery of security skills."[4] Following the practical portion of the certification process, the candidate must also take and pass one or more technical examinations.

The following GIAC certifications were available as of March 2003:

- GIAC Security Essentials Certification (GSEC)
- GIAC Certified Firewall Analyst (GCFW)
- GIAC Certified Intrusion Analyst (GCIA)
- GIAC Certified Incident Handler (GCIH)
- GIAC Certified Windows Security Administrator (GCWN)
- GIAC Certified UNIX Security Administrator (GCUX)
- GIAC Information Security Officer (GISO)
- GIAC Systems and Network Auditor (GSNA)
- GIAC Certified Forensic Analyst (GCFA)
- GIAC IT Security Audit Essentials (GSAE)

The GIAC Security Engineer (GSE) is a certification that combines a track of study, resulting in this higher-level certification.

---

4. http://www.sans.org.

Each certification can be obtained either independently or in conjunction with the other certifications. Also, to ensure that the certified security practitioner is staying current with the latest threats and security concerns, GIAC requires the certification to be renewed annually. More information on the GIAC program and conference schedules can be obtained from the SANS Institute Web site at http://www.sans.org.

NOTE   All of the security certifications discussed here have varying requirements to keep the holder of the certification current. The specific requirements and time frames vary with the particular certification program. The Web sites of the certification bodies give specifics on these requirements.

Constituency Training

The subject of training should not end with the requirements of the team members, but should also address the general training of the constituency. If the end customers are educated on topics such as the process for reporting an incident, the information to be provided in an incident report, and the importance of preserving the computer crime scene, it can smooth the way for a successful incident response. This training can be provided through a variety of means—a topic that leads into the next section, marketing the services of the team.

Marketing the Team

One of the biggest mistakes an incident response team can make is assuming that people will know it exists and will use it as intended. In other words, incident response is not "the field of dreams" in which you can "build it and they will come." The degree to which managers and end users understand, adopt, and invest in the incident response program will be proportional to the marketing efforts made to promote the program and its effectiveness. Therefore, a marketing campaign to advertise the team's establishment and guidelines for working with the team must be included in all planning efforts. The training and marketing should not end with the team's initial announcement, but should incorporate continual marketing endeavors to keep the constituency apprised of the team's successes and encourage continued reporting and use. Marketing can also be used to offset negative publicity or rumors if those emerge as well. In some cases, reporting suspicious activity to an incident response team may be deemed mandatory by end users (e.g., government teams). Despite the mandate to report, do not be fooled into thinking that the team does not require a marketing campaign. Every team requires marketing!

Marketing of security programs and services is an endeavor that is expected to increase significantly in organizations over the coming years. The Meta Group produced a white paper titled "Global Networking Strategies" in October 2001 that described the importance of marketing in conjunction with computer security programs. The paper's authors estimate that only 10 percent of all organizations will actually formalize their marketing efforts over the next two years, while others will "elect to ride the wave of 'interest' generated by high-profile security events (e.g., CodeRed, Nimda)."[5] As security programs mature, the Meta Group expects this percentage to increase to 30 percent and 60 percent of all organizations having security marketing programs established as a well-defined discipline by 2003 and 2005, respectively.

A marketing program should identify the audiences to which the program is to be advertised, with a communication plan being developed for each group. The communication plan should identify the method of advertising to be used, including media and style formats, and the schedule of events to be followed. A SWOT analysis can be very useful for addressing specific requirements for each target audience. SWOT stands for Strengths, Weaknesses, Opportunities, and Threats, with each letter in the acronym identifying an area to be considered when analyzing the target audience. When marketing a computer incident response program by using this analysis, the perceived strengths and weaknesses of the target audience with respect to the program should be identified. The best opportunities the program can

---

5. Bouchard, Mark. *Global Networking Strategies.* Meta Group, October 31, 2001.

provide should also be identified, as well as any perceived threats to it. Once these four key areas are fully identified, the message for the target audience can be crafted.

Several methods may be used to advertise the existence of the program and the services it provides. The following are just a few examples of potential marketing avenues:

- Conferences
- Training seminars
- Poster campaign
- Memoranda and e-mail
- Webcasts
- Flyers
- The organization's intranet or Internet Web page
- Company policies

Typically, a combination of methods works best to spread the word to the greatest number of constituents. The costs associated with completing each type of advertisement should be incorporated into the team's budget as appropriate.

Dealing with the Media

Just as it's not a matter of if, but when, an attack will occur against an organization's information resources, so it's a question of when the media will inquire about the activities of the incident response team or a specific incident. Therefore, plans must be made up front regarding how to deal with media inquiries and who should serve as the spokesperson for the organization.

Existing public affairs policies and procedures governing the disclosure of information regarding an attack, disaster, or emergency are valid guidelines for deciding whether and how to release information regarding attacks on information assets. Sometimes significant benefits can be realized by establishing a specific public affairs strategy, associated with handling a particular incident. Withholding or releasing information about an incident and how it is handled can be a powerful defensive tactic.

Intruders often seek ways to evaluate the success or results of their attack. Incident-handling methodologies can reveal useful information to an adversary who is conducting an attack, or to one who might target the organization at some future time. There are potential advantages to gain from denying attackers the satisfaction of knowing what they achieved or damaged. It is highly valuable to deny potential attackers the information they desire. For example, knowledge about incident-handling methodologies and successes could lead to more sophisticated or targeted attacks by an adversary. Likewise, incident-handling information could be used to identify or exploit weaknesses and vulnerabilities of the information infrastructure and the community that protects it.

Policies and procedures that document team requirements should address dealing with the media in detail. Under no circumstances should any member of the response team provide information about an incident over the phone or directly to a member of the media without the authority to discuss such activity. Team members should be cautious when responding to phone calls inquiring about specific incidents, as they may actually be social engineering attempts to gain details for a story. Information should be provided only to individuals having a "need to know" for that information, and all efforts to accurately identify callers must be made. The safety and security of the constituency and its information resources must remain paramount at all times. The best rule of thumb for members of a team receiving an inquiry from the press (or an individual) is to ask for the caller's name and phone number, and then have the appropriate resource follow up.

Typically, a leak to the press regarding a computer incident is viewed as a negative event. In reality, organizations that choose to control the spin provided in the news regarding a compromise (for example) can actually receive positive publicity from the attention. An organization with a sharp security staff that quickly identifies and contains an intruder can be viewed positively by shareholders and customers alike, rather than becoming the target of the negative publicity after trying to cover up an incident once a leak to the press has been made. However, when such an event occurs, any statements made should not allow it to appear as if the organization has experienced more than one incident.

Summary

This chapter focused on some key issues regarding the formation of a computer incident response team. Decisions such as the number and type of services to be offered, the roles and responsibilities of team members, required skills for team members, and interviewing prospective candidates were discussed in detail. These issues are vital to determining not only the right number of personnel to include in the team, but also the right mix of resources. The facilities to house the incident response team, training plans for enabling professional development, ideas for convincing management to fund the team, and strategies for dealing with the media were also presented. All of these pieces add another layer to the puzzle, helping to achieve the total picture of a cohesive incident response team.

Our picture of incident response is almost complete, with only the center sections remaining. This chapter included a description of the categories of tools that may be used by an incident response team. A brief recess will be taken from forming the puzzle to highlight the importance of teamwork in incident response in Chapter 6, and to explore some of these tools in greater detail in Chapter 7. Chapter 8 will then proceed with completing the incident response team puzzle by discussing operational issues and focusing on the processes and procedures that should be incorporated by a team. The remaining chapters of the book will then expand upon various important topics.

CHAPTER

6

Teamwork

All too often in the world of incident response, those responsible for responding to an attack are looking for a very specific, discrete occurrence of an event that occurred on a computer. With so many vulnerabilities prevalent today and so many points of access to computer systems, it would be impossible for one person to identify, respond to, and recover from an attack all alone. Similarly, it is nearly impossible for an incident response team to succeed if the team members try to cover all bases alone. Teamwork, both within the team and in relation to resources external to the team, is vital to successful incident response.

This chapter is devoted to teamwork to reemphasize its importance to successful incident response. It starts by briefly looking at other areas within a company or organization with which teamwork should be considered, and then touches on the importance of teamwork within the team.

External Team Members

Suggestions about forming a team have appeared throughout the book. Some of the components of your team are already in place, even if you haven't officially started forming a team. Once the existing components are identified, relationships with resources outside of the team need to be established. The reason for considering these relationships is to establish lines of communication and have knowledge of each partner's areas of responsibility and capability. Having these relationships built beforehand will allow for very efficient operations when an incident occurs.

One way to establish relationships between organizational components and your incident response team is simply by letting these entities know about your team. A brochure explaining your team's responsibilities, capabilities, constituency, and contact information is certainly a step in the right direction toward establishing these relationships. Meetings and briefings with members of other departments or business units can also prove valuable to establishing these contacts.

Some of the partners with which your team should consider establishing a relationship include the following:

- *Legal department.* The legal department should be very interested in the incident response team, and a strong relationship should be formed with it. In some cases, a legal department will assign an attorney liaison to maintain ongoing contact and participation with your incident response team. This relationship is formed with the benefit of both the incident response team and the legal department in mind. The incident response team can assist the legal department with investigations, and the legal department can be very involved in protecting the organization from liability. The legal department can also provide expert opinions on enforcement and the limits of policies and laws. In addition, it (or, in some cases, the human resources department) can help defend the investigative team if questions arise regarding the procedures or the legality of the investigation.
- *Vendors.* The importance of establishing a relationship between your incident response team and the people who supply computer

and network equipment is sometimes overlooked. This relationship can benefit the incident response team if the need arises to explain the unique performance or behavior of a particular piece of equipment. Most vendors have means to distribute notifications regarding upgrades, patches, and security notices for their equipment and software. This relationship goes beyond the vendor's sales executives, to involve with the vendor's security or incident response team.

- *Business units.* Sometimes, it's helpful to compare an incident response team to a fire department. The fire department has the experts on staff to deal with certain incidents—namely, fires. In most offices, one or several liaisons are familiar with fire department procedures for evacuating an office area. These office marshals are trained as first-responders and reporters of an incident. Although they're not necessarily formal members of the incident response team, they are specially trained in how to communicate with the incident response team, what to do (and not do) when they encounter an incident, and how to locate resources. In one example involving the authors, the site contact was able to arrange for special parking privileges and have the proper keys to the areas of the building where the investigation was to take place. Such personnel are highly familiar with the details of the layout of a building or area, and they can be absolutely instrumental in making sure the incident response team knows where critical resources (such as a good place for take-out Asian food for that very long investigation) are located.

- *Law enforcement.* Most larger law enforcement agencies have capabilities to respond to computer-based crimes. For example, locally the authors know that two federal agencies (the FBI and the Secret Service) have agents assigned to computer crime. The state has various capabilities (the State Patrol has computer crime agents, and the attorney general's office has a computer crime lab); the city police have several officers to investigate computer crime; and the county sheriff's department has computer crime investigation capabilities. In addition, the federal Department of Homeland Security is developing a "cyber-terrorism" group. Although these capabilities will vary depending on the area in which you live, it is important that you are aware of the capabilities of law enforcement, and that you utilize these agencies' services to the best benefit of your incident response team.

- *Business partners.* Contact between your incident response team and business partners can be a place where incident response team managers may begin to have concerns about confidentiality and conflicts of interest. This contact should be created and maintained to ensure that your business partners know that you have an incident response capability, and are aware of the responsibilities of your team. Remember, the primary goal of your incident response team is to protect your constituency.

- *Marketing department.* The marketing department contact can be a wonderful tool in two ways: to assist in "selling" your department to the constituency, and to promote your department (if appropriate) to your company's clientele. Members of this group will most likely be able to help with the production of promotional and educational materials as well.

- *Communications department.* As mentioned elsewhere in the book, there may be a need to issue a press release or have someone be interviewed by the media. The communications department is usually the source of people who are trained in these skills. It is the place where all communications outside the team (especially to the public) should originate. (Depending on the structure of the company or organization, this function may actually reside in the marketing department.)

- *Physical security.* The physical security group can be a great asset to the incident response team. In many cases, these personnel have alarms, cameras, building maps, wiring diagrams, locks, keys, safety and hazard information, access logs, building rosters, and other equipment that may be of use during an incident response team deployment. It's also likely that the physical security group members have contacts with local police, fire, and disaster teams that can prove very beneficial in the response process.

There are other resources external to the team and the organization with which the incident response team should also establish contacts. As many of these relationships were described earlier in the book, we will not reiterate them here. The main point to remember is that teamwork does not end with the incident response team itself, but should branch off in many different directions.

Internal Teamwork

Teamwork within the group is paramount to the success of an incident response team. A team that doesn't work well together will create dire and sometimes insurmountable challenges that threaten your incident response capabilities. Therefore, the ability to operate successfully in a team environment should be considered when a member is selected to join the team, and should continue to be assessed through daily operations. This section touches on some considerations that should be given to selecting and retaining good team members.

Selecting Team Members

When selecting the members of your team, you should look for more than just technical skills. Team members should be able to communicate well and have an understanding of the importance of their job. Although some "loners" may have superior technical skills, they're not usually compatible with a team environment. Technical skills are very important, but you should select personnel who are resourceful, adaptable, and able to ask questions. One of the best team members with whom the authors worked had very few technical skills, but was always asking questions, cross-checking facts, and taking wonderful notes. Although this person didn't understand all of the technology involved, he asked all of the right questions, making sure that he (and other members of the team) had a complete understanding of the incident. His background was not technical, but he was very dedicated and loyal to learning everything possible about the incident, even going so far as to read the documentation on every tool, technique, and computer command that was used in the incident.

The ability to work well within a team environment is a very difficult criterion to gauge in an interview. One tactic that may be used to gauge this ability is to ask a candidate to teach you how to do a simple task, and then measure how much the candidate ensures that you understand. Another tactic is to take the candidate to lunch with other members of the team and watch how they interact. Speaking with references who are former or current coworkers is also a very good way to gauge a candidate's ability to work well with a team.

Retention and Cohesiveness

Once you have selected and built your team, you should celebrate this accomplishment. You've brought together a team of experts whose skills and capabilities are unique and in high demand. Your next challenge is to keep the team together and productive.

As with nearly any other field, a team member needs to have a career path. A sample career path may look something like this:

Entry-level incident analyst →

Incident specialist →

Senior incident analyst →

Response coordinator →

Incident briefing specialist →

Incident coordinator

The existence of such a career path will encourage members of the team to continue growing by working toward the next level.

Incident response has been known to become very tedious and tiring work. To counter this problem, an incident response team manager may choose to have members rotate through the services that the response team offers to the constituency. For example, a member may spend a few months on the incident analysis team, then a few months on the forensics team, then time with the vulnerability assessment team. This rotation will keep the job exciting for the member, give him or her the chance to work with other members of the team, and build the individual's knowledge and capabilities within the team.

Team-building exercises may also be used to enhance teamwork within a group. Some activities, such as incident "dry runs" or simulations, can be very productive team-building experiences. Several organizations offer leadership and team-building exercises that vary from working retreats to obstacle courses and paintball excursions. Some may be accomplished within the work site; others, such as rope climbing courses, will require the members of the team to go off-site. The off-site events can be particularly effective, as many people will tend to relax more away from the office. If such events cannot be undertaken, then simple activities such as office potlucks, rewriting a poem or story such as "How the Grinch Stole Christmas" with a "hacker theme," or having a cake on team members' birthdays can go a long way toward promoting retention and the sense of a team.

As many management books will reflect, rewards are a very valuable tool in retaining employees. Many of these books recommend keeping rewards simple and frequent. An opportunity to celebrate a team member's accomplishment should not go unnoticed. In the past, the authors have been involved in some very unique reward programs, and some of the most impressive ones were also some of the most unorthodox. For example:

- A staff meeting held at a baseball game
- An afternoon at an amusement park
- A picnic at the boss's house
- A family event at the zoo or museum
- Leadership/teamwork lunches to review a book such as *The Seven Habits of Highly Effective People*

All of these examples involved simple rewards that made a lasting impression. Not only do such efforts reward the individuals for hard work or specific accomplishments, but they also tend to promote teamwork when the entire team is included.

Recognition of an accomplishment by a team member or a significant event should be celebrated as a team. A team member who achieves a certification or one who puts in the extra time to make a difference should be recognized, noted, and rewarded. By including the entire team, the importance of the recognition is strengthened. Your constituency and management structure should also be aware that you've formed a very effective and cohesive team. Word of both individual and team successes should be shared as appropriate.

Of course, as nearly every leadership book points out, one of the most effective ways to keep a team together is to do things as a team with strong leadership. A leader who leads by example is a respected leader, and that leads to loyalty.

Another way to help promote teamwork within the group is to manage incidents as a team. Assign an entry-level analyst to shadow your more experienced incident handlers. Occasionally, you may assign an experienced incident handler to prepare and give a briefing to senior management. Perhaps you could have a member of the team (or the whole team) prepare a presentation for a conference. These activities can be used to stave off employee burnout and to raise the combined skills of your team.

Managing an incident response team is not all that different than managing any team of professionals who must work well together. Numerous management and leadership books on the market offer fantastic pointers on building and retaining a successful team. We merely point out a few methods or tools that may be considered for your incident response team.

Summary

A wise man once said that if you put your ego aside, and ask questions to learn about how things work, it will lead to a much deeper understanding. A team whose members can put their egos aside, at least while working together, will be a very successful team. The importance of teamwork, both internally and externally, cannot be underestimated. This chapter reemphasized the importance of teamwork to the world of computer incident response. As we look at the picture of incident response that we have formed throughout this book, we note that the picture will quickly become cluttered if the teamwork that glues the pieces together is missing. There is a very good reason that most organizations with incident response capabilities use the word "team" in the name given to that group.

Selecting the Products and Tools

A threat is an avenue through which a person or event may exploit a vulnerability to adversely affect the system. Examples of threats include a person who steals organization resources, viruses, disgruntled employees, accidents, uninformed end users, and natural disasters that cause your accounting systems to crash, just to name a few. This chapter will explore some of the products and tools that may be used by security professionals, including computer incident response teams, to prevent threats from being realized. Although this list is nowhere near inclusive of all tools and products currently available, it does present a good overview of areas to consider.

Training as a Tool

An effective user awareness training program is an excellent tool that may be used by an incident response team to proactively protect computer systems. Defining terms that end users may have heard in media reports, but may not totally understand, can provide a high return on the investment in time required to create such a program for any organization. For example, "social engineering" is a term that some end users may have heard, but may not understand completely. By defining social engineering, identifying the potential effects it can have on an organization, and describing methods end users can take to prevent falling prey to social engineering techniques, an organization can make tremendous strides in limiting the potential impact of an attack that uses social engineering to gain information on the systems.

Another topic that should be addressed in any computer security awareness program is password selection. Passwords remain a major avenue used by attackers to gain unauthorized access to computer systems. By educating end users on good password selection techniques, an organization can greatly increase the security of its systems. (Figure 4–1 listed a few recommendations to consider in selecting good passwords that may be used as a starting point to help address this topic in training programs.)

These are just a few examples of topics that may be covered in a user awareness training program. Two additional points should be addressed concerning this function. First, it is not enough to simply put a training session together, present it to all end users, and expect the awareness level to increase and stay at a sufficient level. To be effective, computer security awareness needs to be addressed up front and continually revisited. Second, the training can be given in multiple ways and reinforced through creative measures. For example, training sessions can be provided in an auditorium setting or through a Web broadcast, computer-based training (CBT), an intranet link, or written documentation. This training can then be reinforced through follow-on training, tests, organization-wide e-mail that highlights specific tips, or even games.

An example of a game reinforcement would be having the end users compete against one another in solving a crossword puzzle. The puzzle answers would correspond to the training given. The puzzle should be given out after the training session is completed so end users have to pay attention during the training session. Completing the puzzle must be worthwhile to the end users, so an award should be decided upon and advertised up front. For example, the first division to have all members complete the puzzle correctly and turn it in could receive an extra 30 minutes for lunch one day. Granted, this approach may be a stretch for some organizations, but the point is to make the training and reinforcement of good security practices fun. Computer security does not have to be dry!

Sound Security Practices

Lack of training is not the only source of threats emanating from the users of a system. The estimated share of system penetrations stemming from fully authorized users who abuse their access privileges to perform unauthorized functions has varied over the past decade from 50 percent to 80 percent. Although these estimates fall within a considerably wide range, the bottom line is that the "insider threat" should not be ignored.

The following areas are points where systems may be vulnerable to attacks and should receive extra attention:

- *Controls over data handling.* Controls need to be implemented for every form of data, not just the data that reside on the computer systems. These controls need to be documented and enforced, and must apply to every phase of information flow (creation, storage, processing, distribution, and destruction). The following are examples of questions that may indicate a need for data-handling controls: Are inventories kept up-to-date? Is there an inventory for physical media, especially those that may contain sensitive corporate data? Can an authorized user simply put a diskette in his or her pocket and walk out of the building? How is paper eliminated from the office space? Are shredders used to make removal of sensitive documents from trash cans more difficult?
- *Weak or missing physical controls.* Physical security measures that limit the access to computer systems can be just as important as the hardware and software features added to some systems to protect the information they contain. Are key elements of a network located in a shared location? In many cases, the security of a system may be bypassed by simply booting the system from a floppy diskette. Does the organization require employee identification badges to be worn? More importantly, if employees notice someone walking around the building without a badge, are they trained to question the person or bring his or her presence to

someone's attention? These are just a few questions that address physical security concerns that can affect the security of a computer system if left unchecked.

- *Inadequate procedural controls.* Clear, concise, written procedures can help to eliminate confusion over specific processes and to ensure that management security objectives are implemented. They can also help to fill voids when trained personnel leave the company or move to other positions. The problem is that many people do not like to write down procedures, and many descriptions are written without the procedures being fully implemented.

- *Poor programming practices.* For years the practice of writing backdoors into software programs to enable programmers to enter and fix problems later has been followed. This practice creates two major problems. First, programmers sometimes forget to remove these backdoors prior to code being shipped. Second, backdoors are an avenue that many would-be attackers search for and like to use to gain unauthorized access to systems. Software programs need to be written with security as part of the foundation, which includes the use of sound programming practices.

- *Operating system weaknesses.* The biggest security challenge for most system administrators is keeping up with the latest patches for operating systems. This is a real challenge for software vendors as well, because resource-sharing functions typically contradict the security requirements. Therefore, a tradeoff is typically made to try and balance the two. Operating systems need to be hardened before being placed on production systems. Once they become operational, system administrators need to remain vigilant, watching for new vulnerabilities and patches as they may be discovered. Teamwork between system administrators, the security community, and vendors is the best way to guard against operating system weaknesses.

A "newspaper effect" within some organizations may cause some system administrators to focus on highly publicized external threats such as hackers and viruses. As a result, too little attention may be given to basic countermeasures such as backups and passwords, which can prevent more serious problems from within the organization. Networks, in particular, suffer from an additional weakness caused by system administrators who focus on the end system and not the network as a whole. For example, many network administrators expend much effort and resources to protect the hosts on the network, yet pay little or no attention to the overall network. This trend reflects the fact that it is generally easier to protect the hosts than the entire network, and intruders are more likely to go after the data on the host. Nevertheless, there are sound reasons for protecting the overall network. Focusing on the host alone may leave the entire network open to overlooked vulnerabilities. For example, an intruder may be able to divert transmitted data to an off-site host for examination or to search for passwords. Human error, in the form of a misconfigured host, could lead to a degradation in service for network users. Or, a denial-of-service attack may be generated without the attacker ever penetrating the system. By focusing on the entire network, company personnel should be able to identify vulnerabilities such as these.

To avoid such problems, a computer incident response team (or another part of the organization) may wish to conduct periodic vulnerability assessments. Most companies offering security services today provide one form or another of a security assessment, so outsourcing this function is also a possibility. Branding or marketing spins used by different vendors may lead to confusion over the actual type of assessment needed (or outsourced). *Information Security Magazine* presented an excellent four-part series of articles beginning in July 2000 that examined the many types of assessments that may be performed. The following points were taken from the first article of the series and are summarized here to differentiate between the types of testing:[1]

- *Penetration test.* A correctly performed penetration test is a covert test in which a consultant or trained insider plays the role of the hostile attacker who tries to compromise system security. Because the ultimate goal is penetration, the test is carried out without warning, in something close to complete secrecy. Ideally, there should be no support from the organization being tested (or attacked); at most, guidance should be restricted to what the penetration team should avoid. If the organization is outsourcing the

---

1. Winkler, Ira. "Part I: Audits, Assessments & Tests (Oh, My)." *Information Security,* July 2000, pp. 80–85.

tests, the client should let the consultant know what the specific goals are for the test. Penetration testing is also used to improve executive management's security awareness and convince them of the need to financially support security related programs. The Penetration Testing: Myth versus Reality sidebar, which was taken from Part 3 of the assessment series ("Penetration Testing Exposed"), provides some interesting insights into some myths regarding penetration testing.

- *Audit.* An audit is used to determine how an organization measures up to specific standards. Its goal is to provide guidance on improving the organization's adherence to the standards. An audit is probably the most straightforward security test, but it has specific purposes and limitations, which must be clearly perceived. With a security audit, you have a set of security guidelines, standards, or policies against which systems should be compared for compliance. A good standard should address both physical and technical security.

- *Assessment.* An assessment involves going beyond an audit by looking past a checklist. While an audit addresses specific issues, an assessment typically involves the use of scanning tools to identify and examine the extent of the system's vulnerabilities. Detailed recommendations for improving the overall security of the system by limiting potential threats should result from the assessment. An assessment is usually the most valuable form of security tests that can be performed. Assessments can vary in scope, and can be approached in several different ways. The scope of a vulnerability assessment focuses on developing an inventory of possible vulnerabilities. A risk assessment includes the components of the vulnerability assessment, but also includes a methodology to attempt to estimate the threats, costs, and likelihood of the vulnerability being exploited.

If a penetration test is conducted with the attackers having no real information about the system up front, then it may be referred to as a "zero-knowledge attack." This sort of attack or test is designed to mimic an outsider who tries to penetrate the system's defenses. If the attacking person or team has as much information about the target environment as possible, then the test may be referred to as a "full-knowledge attack." This type of test simulates an attacker who has intimate knowledge of the target systems, such as an employee or other insider. Regardless of the amount of information provided up front, the test should include information gathering to determine how much intelligence can be collected on a system from available resources.

Penetration Testing: Myth versus Reality

Myth: Penetration testing is black magic and voodoo that only self-appointed gurus can perform successfully.

Reality: Penetration testing is a process with objectives, techniques, and best practices. Successful penetration testing begins with a rank assessment of goals. The test should mimic a real-world attack and the tester should have clearly defined objectives.

Penetration testing requires quantifiable security and network knowledge. The tester need not have links to shadowy underground figures or a mysterious government background, but should be aware of published exploits and techniques—anything that was ever published in PHRACK or Bugtraq, for example, should be in the tester's toolkit. A fundamental understanding of TCP/IP is required.

One note about great penetration testers—their minds work a bit differently than most folks. They are extremely inquisitive individuals with a thirst for knowing in great detail how everything works. This allows them to answer the endless "what ifs?" running through their heads: "What if I send the first packet with a SYN-ACK rather than a SYN?" "What if machine A trusts machine B implicitly?" So, to the extent that some individuals have an innate ability to solve problems in a creative manner, penetration testing depends on the personnel involved.

Myth: Running a commercial vulnerability scanner is penetration testing.

Reality: Penetration testing is designed to simulate a real-world attack, and few attackers use the latest commercial scanners to try to penetrate systems. Most commercial scanners are like Swiss army knives—they perform many functions, but don't do any one function particularly well. Commercial scanners can be great tools and serve a valuable security role, but their usefulness in a penetration test is limited. Given that a common goal of a penetration test is to gain access to sensitive information without getting caught, it should be obvious that commercial scanners are inappropriate—they light up intrusion detection systems like a Christmas tree!

A more realistic approach is to pick the most appropriate tool for each phase of the penetration test. This could mean starting a test with only slow scanning for a limited number of commonly vulnerable services using SYN half-scans; alternatively, it could mean simply grabbing application version information from known Web servers. The specific techniques necessary for this approach are not available in commercial scanners. Note that comprehensive freeware scanners, such as NESSUS and SAINT, are also great programs for identifying vulnerabilities, but not necessarily great for penetration testing.

Myth: Popular freeware and shareware tools are the cat's meow.

Reality: Individual shareware tools provide great capabilities, but also have "issues." Basically, you get what you pay for. While free tools often provide innovative capabilities, they can have unexpected results or prove difficult to use. Nmap is a personal favorite and is an example of the best in freeware tools. However, while attempting to circumvent some router access control lists, we used nmap with the option to bind to a source port of 20. While reviewing network traffic logs, we noticed that nmap used a source port of 20 only for the first packet—if we had trusted the tool to act as advertised, our test would have given us a false sense of security. (*Note:* This bug is now listed as a limitation on the nmap Web page.)

We tend to cobble together multiple freeware tools using scripting languages to achieve optimal results. Based on an understanding of the capabilities of each tool, and on the state of IDS and other security technology, we'll put together scripts like the ones at www.hackingexposed.com/scripts/scripts.html.

The difficulty is not in finding good tools, but in using them appropriately. Tools such as nmap, netcat, hping, firewalk, and icmpquery are indispensable components of our toolkit, but require extensive testing for optimal use.

Myth: Exposing potential vulnerabilities is good enough; there's no need to actually break in.

Reality: One of the primary goals of penetration testing is to demonstrate the consequences of exploited vulnerabilities. Has anyone tried to explain to a CEO why TCP 139 shouldn't be accessible from the Internet? He'll be turned off faster than a light bulb. But show him a printout of this quarter's earnings projections, and you'll be surprised how effective your message is.

For diagnostic host reviews or audits, consider skipping the exploitation. But for the penetration review, exploitation is a critical phase.

Myth: The penetration team didn't break in. That means I'm secure.

Reality: Penetration testing is not the best way to find all vulnerabilities. Network assessments that include careful diagnostic reviews of servers and network devices will identify more issues faster than a "black box" penetration test. Penetration tests are a "snapshot in time" of a system or network's security exposure. As such, testing is limited to known vulnerabilities and the current configuration of the network. Just because the penetration test was unsuccessful today doesn't mean a new weakness won't be posted on Bugtraq tonight—and exploited tomorrow. And just because a testing team didn't discover the vulnerable points of your system doesn't mean others haven't— or won't.

Myth: I just finished a penetration test. There is no need for a security audit or diagnostic review.

Reality: Penetration testing is often done for two reasons: to increase upper-management awareness of security issues or to test intrusion detection and response capabilities. If the goal is to comprehensively determine all vulnerabilities, then a diagnostic host review performed with full knowledge of network topology is preferred. The penetration test is often (and rightfully)

> used to gain the budget necessary to correct security deficien-
> cies, which are addressed through audits and host reviews.
>
> Source: George Kurtz and Chris Prosise. "Part 3: Penetration Testing Exposed." *Informa-
> tion Security,* September 2000, pp. 92–93.

Most incident response teams performing assessments on networks will actually conduct penetration tests. Penetration testing has
two benefits for an organization's incident response capability. First,
it can be used to simulate attacks to the organization. If this type of
testing is conducted, at least one key member of the response group
should be aware of the testing to help mitigate situations that can
arise as a result of the test. For example, if the testing is conducted
strictly internal to the organization and incident response procedures
require law enforcement to be notified, the key member should be able
to stop the response prior to law enforcement being contacted.

Finally, another type of proactive service that an incident response
team may consider offering is an advisory capability. Typically, an
advisory is generated in response to a specific type of threat or vulnerability that has been discovered. However, advisories can also be
proactive in nature by helping to increase awareness levels for potential problems or providing an accurate picture of the types of attacks
being detected. Advisories are an important element for many teams
and will be discussed in greater detail later.

The Tools of the Trade

The classic methods of attempting to find vulnerabilities, assess them,
and create reports based on them are just as effective today as they
ever were. An experienced staff member might take inventory of the
system, attempt to attack it, and manually create reports of the findings. Unfortunately, this methodology is not effective in doing a comprehensive and repeatable assessment due to the human factors
involved (i.e., variations).

The tools used for this work are generally targeted at different
areas. We'll attempt to sort them out here and identify their most
effective uses. After all, you can use a screwdriver as a chisel in some
cases, but it's not always the best way to get the job done.

Network-perspective scanning tools are loaded on a network-connected system and attempt to use network connectivity to search for vulnerabilities on the targeted systems. The results from using these tools can vary based on their placement on the network between the scanning system and the target systems. For example, you should hope that different results are noticed when the scanning system and the target systems have a firewall between them. The following are examples of network-perspective scanning tools:

- Internet Security Systems ISS Internet Scanner, http://www.iss.net
- NMAP "Network MAPper," http://www.insecure.org
- eEye Digital Security Retna, http://www.eeye.com
- Nessus Security Scanner, http://www.nessus.org
- SARA (Security Auditor's Research Assistant), http://www-arc.com/sara
- SAINT (Security Administrator's Integrated Network Tool), http://www.saintcorporation.com

Host-perspective scanning tools are generally loaded onto the target systems and then executed. This setup gives the software access to configuration files, network services, software lists, software version information, registry entries, users, and hardware information. As a consequence, the host-perspective tools have much more information to work with than the network-perspective tools do. The following are examples of host-perspective scanning tools:

- Internet Security Systems ISS System Scanner
- Bindview, http://www.bindview.com
- RSA/Security Dynamics Kane Security Analyst, http://www.rsa.com
- Symantec Enterprise Security Manager, http://www.symantec.com
- Microsoft Configuration and Analysis Snap-In, http://www.microsoft.com

Intrusion detection is a capability that you may choose to add to your incident response team toolbox. It can provide a means to report incidents to the team, monitor network traffic, and gather important information about the running state of your network. Several books have been published about the benefits, challenges, and strategies of intrusion detection. The following are examples of intrusion detection products:

- Internet Security Systems RealSecure
- Cisco Intrusion Detection, http://www.cisco.com
- Enterasys Dragon, http://www.enterasys.com
- NFR Intrusion Management System, http://www.nfr.com
- SNORT, http://www.snort.org
- DOE-CIAC NIDS (Department of Energy Computer Incident Advisory Capability Network Intrusion Detector), http://ciac.llnl.gov[2]

Forensics tools are used to investigate the information stored on computer disks. These tools can assist in recovering "deleted" data, and some have specialized tools to assist in gathering evidence from computer systems. The following are examples of forensics tools:

- Guidance Software's Encase, http://www.guidance software.com
- TCT (The Coroner's Toolkit), http://www.porcupine.org/forensics/tct.html
- NTI Computer Incident Response Suite, http://www.forensics-intl.com

Application-perspective scanning tools are specifically focused on a certain application. They are usually similar to host-perspective scanning tools, where access to configuration information is most easily accessed.

Although *checklists* may not be automated tools similar to the scanning tools, they are valuable in assessing systems. They have a more general perspective than the scanning tools, and they often cover some of the infrastructure-related issues that affect vulnerabil-

---

2. The DOE-CIAC Network Intrusion Detector is available to only authorized agencies.

ity, threat, and risks to information by surveying things such as facilities, physical controls, and policy issues. Some examples of checklists are found at the following organizations' Web sites:

- SANS Institute (SysAdmin Audit and Network Security Institute), http://www.sans.org
- National Institute of Standards and Technology (NIST), http://www.nist.gov
- CERT/CC (Computer Emergency Response Team Coordination Center), http://www.cert.org
- Microsoft
- AusCERT (Australian Computer Emergency Response Team), http://www.auscert.org
- NSA (U.S. National Security Agency), http://www.nsa.gov/snac/index.html

Risk methodology tools are used to not only assess vulnerabilities, but also take into account the value of the information or service, the cost of the equipment and support, the threats to the information or service, the likelihood that a threat may be able to exploit a vulnerability, and all of the safeguards that have been implemented. These tools are very valuable in helping make risk-, benefit-, and cost-based decisions about where to concentrate on security. Sadly, risk methodology tools for information security are difficult to find, and are mostly home-grown, specialized tools that aren't available for sale to the general commercial world.

Using the Tools

If you're reading this chapter and think that it's covered a lot of intricate puzzle pieces, you're right. You don't have to use all of the pieces to create a good incident response team.

If you're only concerned with vulnerabilities from the network perspective (i.e., you have only trusted people with physical access to the systems themselves), you may decide that a simple vulnerability scanner is enough for your team.

If you're making decisions based on risks (i.e., attempting to balance the right level of security with the right level of ease of use for your e-commerce business), you may want to invest in tools and practices that will help you gather the best available information for making these decisions.

In all of these cases, a human factor is still involved in evaluating the information gathered with these tools. In some cases, the tools may not take all of these factors into consideration. A low-value system with no information on it that isn't connected to a network, but has a vulnerability, is almost certainly a much lower priority than one of your legal staff's laptops. Someone must still make a decision regarding which vulnerabilities and threats get addressed, in what order, and in what time frame, and how much effort will be spent to address them. There are many, many ways to solve a problem, and human thought is required to evaluate all of the options and pick the best one for your organization.

It may be a good idea to consider outsourcing some of these services, especially ones that are very specialized and won't be utilized often. If you don't plan on doing computer forensics often, a trusted provider may be the best option for your organization.

Summary

This chapter explored some of the many products and tools that may be used by an incident response team. To use these tools effectively, there is no substitute for training, experience, and continuous challenge and verification of the results. This requires a strong, healthy relationship between the security team, the incident response team, and the constituency.

In the simplest form, everything with computers can be broken down into 1's and 0's. Similarly, computer security initiatives should always be able to be broken down into their simplest form, policies. Policies identify what is authorized and what is not, assign organizational responsibilities, communicate acceptable levels of risks, and much more. The policies may be expanded in the form of procedures, which provide the step-by-step guidelines for putting the policies into action. From there, it's a matter of implementing and configuring systems appropriately, purchasing and adding security tools to monitor and safeguard the systems, and training and authorizing end users to use the resources appropriately.

When the policies and procedures are violated, then a computer incident (e.g., unauthorized access, denial of service) may have occurred. To detect and respond to these violations of the organization's security policies, incident response policies and procedures should be in place. These policies may be in the form of stand-alone documentation, or they may be incorporated into other documentation such as company security policies or disaster recovery plans.

NOTE Unfortunately, not all organizations have existing computer security policies. Many people view the writing of a security policy as a huge undertaking that is nearly impossible to accomplish. Depending on the level of support from upper management, the task may be more daunting to complete in some organizations as compared to others. In the ideal situation, the organization has a security policy and is serious about covering all facets of the security equation. If the organization does not have existing policies, however, this omission should not stop the development of a CIRT. Ideally the organization will develop security policies in the near future or simultaneously as the CIRT is developed, but policies should not be viewed as a mandatory requirement for the formation of a CIRT.

This chapter focuses on the operational aspects of computer incident response. Considerations that should be given to specific incident-handling procedures will be described in detail, as will the life cycle of an incident. The information provided in this chapter can, in turn, be used to write computer incident policies and procedures. Together, these policies and procedures complete the incident response puzzle by filling in the center piece. Because computer security begins with policies, what better place to envision this piece of the puzzle than in the center where it belongs.

The Life Cycle of an Incident

The best way to determine the policies required for incident response is to examine the typical life cycle of computer incident response. Figure 8–1 provides a flowchart outlining the major phases of the incident response life cycle; each phase is described in detail in the sections that follow. Not all incidents are identical, of course: Many have unique attributes. Therefore, the steps outlined in this section will address the typical case. The incident handler, however, must always be prepared for the unexpected.

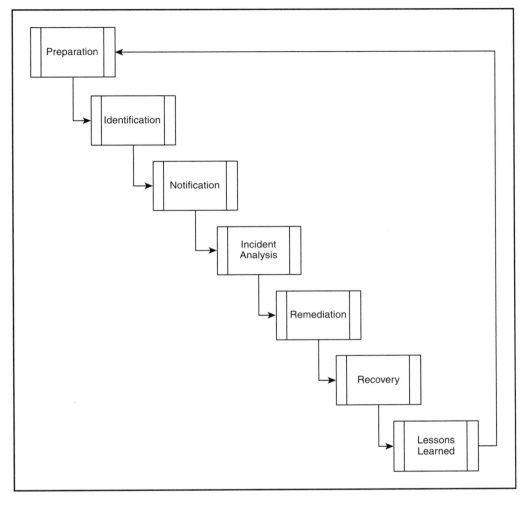

Figure 8-1   The Incident Response Life Cycle

The terms used to describe the various stages of incident response may vary somewhat from publication to publication. Despite the differing terminology used to describe the various phases, most agree that the process is cyclical and addresses many of the issues outlined in the different phases described in this chapter. The terms used to describe each phase and the number of phases may vary, but the basic elements will generally remain very similar.

The level and detail of response required in each phase depend on the type and severity of the incident. In the sections that follow, the worst-case scenario of a compromise has been used as the main focus for discussion points. Actual steps taken, however, may vary according to the type of incident, and some steps may be skipped or significantly condensed. In addition, if the reported activity turns out to not be an incident, the process may be aborted at any time, at which point the team resumes the preparation phase.

Step One: Preparation (Preparing for Compromise)

Incident response always begins with the steps taken to protect the organization's information resources before an incident takes place. These steps may be realized through the documentation of specific policies and procedures, end user awareness training, hardening of operating systems, installation of security tools, and the like. Just as security affects everyone in the organization at all levels, so should security safeguards be implemented at all levels.

Policies and Procedures.   Specific policies and procedures that should be documented for the organization in preparation for an incident include the following:

- Computer security policy or policies
- Incident response procedures
- Recall procedures
- Backup and recovery procedures

As previously noted, successful computer security begins with policies. The policies provide the foundation from which a security program is built, and provide "reference points for a wide variety of information security activities including: designing controls into applications, establishing user access controls, performing risk analyses, conducting computer crime investigations, and disciplining workers for security violations."[1] To be completely successful, the policies

---

1. Wood, Charles Cresson. *Information Security Policies Made Easy,* Version 7. Sausalito, CA: Baseline Software, 1999, p. 1.

must be clearly and concisely written, and enforced by management. To document policies but then not enforce them through human resource and legal action diminishes the writing of the policies to simply a paperwork drill.

Developing computer security policies involves identifying key business resources and supporting policies, defining specific roles in the organization, and determining the capabilities and functionality of those roles. One inclusive policy may be written for an organization or a shorter, overarching policy may be documented with smaller supporting policies written separately to address specific concerns. Examples of policies that could be addressed include the following: user account policy, remote access policy, acceptable use policy, firewall management policy, consent to monitoring policy, and special access policy.

The organization's security policy not only is important to communicate to the employees or members of the group what is authorized activity, but also may prove valuable should an authorized user intentionally abuse his or her privileges. Supporting documentation such as end-user agreements can prove quite useful for prosecuting or addressing an insider threat. Providing a copy of the security policy to end users and having them sign end-user agreements after they have read the policy is the approach taken by many proactive organizations that use such agreements. The security policy may also be summarized in an information packet or bulletin that provides a ready reference for end users in shorter fashion, thereby reinforcing the larger document, which may not be closely read. Some organizations choose to promote awareness of existing policies even further, by requiring employees to attend a "Security 101" course when they begin employment. The more ways in which the policy can be consistently communicated and reinforced, the better the chances for a successful implementation of the document.

Security policies should indicate management support for the computer incident response program, by identifying the incident response team as a key business resource. Security practices such as routinely changing passwords and using unique passwords should be specified in the appropriate policy documentation. The policies should also indicate the responsibility of the incident response team to perform the services assigned to it, such as vulnerability assessments, reporting requirements, and monitoring of systems.

Many security policies are supported through additional documentation in the form of written procedures. The procedures are intended to provide step-by-step guidelines for enforcing the policy. Every incident response team should have documented procedures available for immediate access by the team members. The procedures should identify the roles and responsibilities of the team, as well as offer step-by-step instructions for performing the assigned tasks. Flowcharts can be extremely useful tools for incident-handling procedures and can aid with the clarification of steps to be taken during a crisis situation. The procedures should address every service or responsibility of the team in detail, from start to finish. Examples of flowcharts and processes that may be addressed in the incident response procedures include the following:

- Responding to a "virus warning" inquiry or other request for information
- Monitoring intrusion detection systems
- Processing each type of event or incident that is reported (e.g., successful intrusion, attempted intrusion, denial-of-service attack, probes or scans)
- Eradicating a computer virus
- Entering information into the trouble ticket system or database
- Reporting incidents to law enforcement
- Reporting incidents to other teams
- Conducting penetration tests
- Responding to reported activity

Outlining processes in the form of a flowchart can be a quite valuable exercise in documenting the procedures, as it will force each step to be examined in detail. The simplified flowchart in Figure 8–2 shows how the flowchart can assist with outlining the procedures to be followed. Most flowcharts will not be so simple, however, and may actually require multiple pages to document. The simple version here is included to reinforce the point of using flowcharts. Note that flowcharts should also be accompanied by supporting verbiage and not used as the sole method of procedural documentation.

Incident-handling procedures should prioritize how incidents are to be managed when more than one response is needed. Depending on

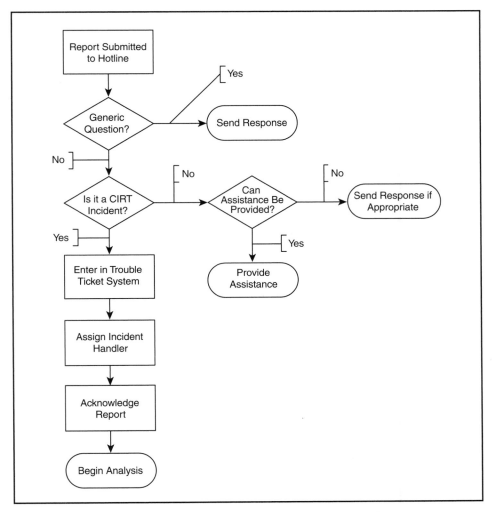

Figure 8-2 Sample Flowchart

the size of the team's constituency, it may not be uncommon for multiple incidents to be handled simultaneously. Prioritizing the order in which incidents are tackled can assist with resource assignment issues during peak periods. For example, the team may decide to prioritize the assignment of resources to incidents as follows:

1. Ongoing attack (intruder is currently in the system or resources are being denied on an increasing or large scale)

2. Successful attack on systems identified as critical to the business or operations
3. Root compromise
4. Level of severity of the attack (i.e., number of systems affected, type of attack)
5. External tip is received that requires investigation

The actual order of priorities chosen will vary between organizations, and each group must determine up front the best priorities for response for its particular constituency. Typically, the priorities assigned will reflect the location of the system, the type of data maintained on the system, and the potential impact of the loss of that system on overall operations.

Establish Response Guidelines.   In addition to determining the priorities of response, the team should discuss various response guidelines with upper management to determine actions that are deemed acceptable and those that may need consultation prior to the action being taken. For example, if a Web site is compromised, can the CIRT authorize the system being taken off-line without higher approvals?

One of the best methods to work out the acceptable response guidelines is to discuss various scenarios with upper management and walk through the possible response procedures that may be followed. Conducting tabletop exercises of various theoretical situations can be an excellent tool for developing response guidelines, as well as for training at various levels. Former New York City Mayor Rudolph Giuliani discusses how the use of tabletop exercises with his staff enabled him to remain calm during the attacks on the World Trade Center and thereafter in September 2001. Stated Giuliani, "We conducted tabletop exercises designed to rehearse our response to a wide variety of contingencies. We'd blueprint what each person in each agency would do if the city faced, say, a chemical attack or a biochemical attack. . . . The goal was to build a rational construct for myself, and for the people around me. I wanted them ready to make decisions when they couldn't check with me."[2] The middle of an incident is not the time to discuss

---

2. Giuliani, Rudolph. *Leadership.* New York: Miramax Books, 2002, pp. 62–63.

with management what options for response are available, unless it is a unique incident deemed critical to the business.

Establishing Contacts.   Points of contact outside of the immediate team and recall information for all team members should be readily available and kept current for when the need arises to make an immediate notification. The recall list should identify all team members and give a priority ranking for contacting them in an emergency situation should they need to be recalled to work. Co-locating this list with the written incident-handling procedures can assist with locating the information quickly in a stressful situation. Contact information for law enforcement agencies and emergency personnel (e.g., fire, police) should also be included in the outside contacts list.

NOTE   Some groups place the contact information within the procedures document. This approach is not recommended as it is more difficult to update the information when a change in the team occurs. By keeping the names and contact information separate, it is much easier to keep the list current. Additionally, the contacts are easier to locate in one central list as opposed to searching through the entire procedures document.

Backup Procedures.   Backup procedures should be documented and strictly followed. The importance of a good backup plan is never quite as evident as when a major incident has occurred and reliable data are needed quickly to restore operations. Multiple copies of backups should be maintained and stored off-site for added protection. The backup procedures and media should be periodically tested to help ensure their integrity.

Evaluate System Security.   Computer systems should be routinely evaluated for their overall level of security. Operating systems should be hardened to help protect against well-known vulnerabilities being exploited. ("Hardening an operating system" refers to locking down a system to ensure that it is not providing too much access or running unnecessary services.) Vulnerability assessments and penetration tests are the most common methods used to evaluate the security of a system. These tests can be performed by internal personnel or outsourced to a consulting firm.

Warning Banners.   Warning banners should be posted on systems at the "points of access." The purpose of the warning banner can vary, but it is normally used to indicate that the system is private and that use of the system is subject to monitoring. Figure 8–3 provides a sample warning banner. It is strongly recommended that the organization's legal counsel review the wording used in the banner to ensure that the goals for its use are met.

The placement of warning banners has been a topic of much debate between the security and legal communities for some time. The U.S. Department of Justice contends that the warning banner must be seen by the intruder upon entering the system for it to be recognized as "off limits" or subject to monitoring. With this idea in mind, the banner should be displayed on every point of access to the system (e.g., all open ports). The counter-argument cites the "no trespassing" sign analogy. If a "no trespassing" sign is posted on a fence, does it have to be posted at the very spot where an intruder jumps the fence

---

Users (authorized or unauthorized) have no explicit or implicit expectation of privacy.

Any use of this system and the files maintained or processed on this system may be intercepted, monitored, recorded, copied, audited, inspected, and disclosed to authorized management and law enforcement personnel, as well as authorized officials of other agencies. *By using this system, the user consents to such interception, monitoring, recording, copying, auditing, inspection, and disclosure at the discretion of management.*

Unauthorized or improper use of this system may result in administrative disciplinary action and civil and criminal penalties. By continuing to use this system you indicate your awareness of and consent to these terms and conditions of use. LOG OFF IMMEDIATELY if you do not agree to the conditions stated in this warning.

Figure 8–3   Sample Warning Banner

for him or her to be cited with trespassing? This sticking point, as with many security issues, will remain for the courts to iron out as more case law is established. In the meantime, it is recommended that warning banners be used and posted at as many points of entry to the network as possible.

Security Tools.   In addition to setting up the safeguards already mentioned, the preparation phase may include the implementation of specific security tools. Firewalls, intrusion detection systems, secure identification devices, biometrics, encryption programs, and other such tools may increase the overall security of the infrastructure. Completing a risk analysis as described earlier in this book can help with identifying the right tools for the organization. Ideally, several layers of security should be incorporated in the infrastructure to provide "defense in depth." The more layers a perpetrator has to transcend to reach the most sensitive information, the less likely he or she is to succeed.

Training.   Training requirements need to be considered and implemented for all levels of the organization. Computer security statistics from numerous surveys have helped to substantiate the threat posed by a lack of end-user awareness. End users need to be made aware of not only the basics of computer security, but also the presence of the incident response team and the need to notify the team of suspicious activity. Training is a security countermeasure that is estimated to require up to a 10 percent investment in resources and effort of the security/incident response team but will typically have a 90 percent return on investment if done correctly. Awareness training is a powerful tool that should not be overlooked.

Step Two: Incident Identification

Incident identification normally begins with someone or something noticing activity that appears suspicious. The following are examples of how this might occur:

- An end user notices that the system indicates an incorrect time for when he or she last logged into the system.

- A system administrator notices that an authorized user has higher privileges than were assigned.
- An end user notices that a file has been modified, yet no one else should have access to it.
- An outside organization notices probing activity against its site stemming from your site.
- System performance begins to unexpectedly slow down and the cause is not readily apparent.
- An intrusion detection system sends an alarm to the management console, drawing attention to a violation of the signature file.
- Firewall logs have a gap or period of time with no activity accounted for during normal operating hours.
- The organization's Web page is listed on a well-known "hacker Web site" as having been compromised.
- An end user reports additional files in a personal directory that he or she did not create or store there.

These are just a few examples of how suspicious activity may be noted. Once it is detected, the activity should be reported to the computer incident response team and investigated to determine whether an incident has occurred.

Every response team should have a report form that identifies the information needed to investigate and track an incident. The report form should be available to all members of the constituency and may be posted on an intranet, documented in security policies or procedures, or provided as a separate file or form. When suspicious activity is noted, the form should be completed and submitted to the team. Some of the information requested on the form may not be immediately available, but that omission should not hinder the reporting of the activity. Constituents should be encouraged to report the activity as quickly as possible so that the proper level of response can be initiated. Routinely, follow-up communications between the team and the person submitting the report will take place to gather further details.

Most incident response teams also provide a phone number for reporting suspicious activity verbally. Teams with a dispersed constituency should try to provide a toll-free number for such reporting. The e-mail address and phone numbers (local and toll-free) should try to follow the same naming convention, if possible. Using an easy-to-remember address and phone number will help the team to be more accessible during a crisis situation.

The information requested on the incident report form will vary from team to team. The CERT CC report form is available on its Web site at http://www.cert.org and may be used as a model for developing other forms. Appendix A also provides a sample incident report form that may be used or edited according to the requirements of the organization. The information requested in the form should mirror specific data fields in the incident tracking database or trouble ticket system. Whenever possible, excerpts of audit logs, copies of suspicious e-mails (including header information), and other supporting documentation should be submitted with the report form to help with the investigation.

> **NOTE** Extreme care should be given to not use the system that is being attacked to report the incident. Doing so may tip off the attacker that he or she has been discovered. Whenever possible, some form of out-of-band communications should be used. In other words, a different system, the phone, a fax machine, or a mode of communication other than the attacked system should be used to make the report.

The incident report form may be completed by someone external to the team and sent in, or it may be completed by a team member who receives a report via the phone or notices the suspicious activity directly. As soon as the report is received, it should be entered into the trouble ticket system and assigned a unique tracking number, and the team should acknowledge to the person sending the report that it has been received. The reporting party should be given the tracking number to use in case any further information or activity is detected. (The importance of acknowledging the receipt of reports will be addressed in more detail later in this chapter.)

At this point, the report should be reviewed to try and determine the circumstances surrounding the suspicious activity. If more information is needed to gain a clearer understanding of the events, then the appropriate party should be contacted and a request for information made. Depending on the nature of the report, the appropriate party may be an end user who submitted the report, someone from system administration who may have access to audit logs or other supporting evidence, or even an outside party such as the incident response team for an Internet service provider (ISP). Again, care should be taken to not divulge more information than is absolutely necessary. Sometimes the actual attacker may become involved in the incident communications without the incident handler realizing that he or she is talking to the attacker. It is always better to err on the side of caution throughout the incident-handling process.

Suspicious activity does not always equate to a computer incident (e.g., a misconfigured router reported as probing or scanning a network). As the information reported and obtained is reviewed, the incident handler should be able to determine whether an incident has occurred. If it appears that no incident has taken place, then the trouble ticket should be closed and the outcome should be communicated to the reporting party. If an incident has occurred, however, the trouble ticket should remain open until no further action is required on the part of the incident response team. Furthermore, if a successful attack (e.g., unauthorized access, denial of service) has occurred, the following steps should be taken:

1. A complete system backup should be made and stored in a safe location for further investigation and use.
2. All observations noted and steps taken in the course of investigating the incident should be logged as the analysis proceeds.
3. The appropriate notifications should be made.

Step Three: Notification

If an incident has occurred, the proper authorities need to be notified. Proper authorities may include upper management, law enforcement, another incident response team, or others as identified in the incident response procedures. It is extremely important that escalation procedures be documented up front, before an incident occurs. This will help to eliminate or reduce the room for error during a crisis situation. The procedures should address who is to be notified for each type of incident and at what point. The incident response team leader must always apply a certain amount of subjectivity, but the documentation of guidelines will cover the majority of situations. For the cases not covered, the best rule of thumb is to report the activity to upper management when in doubt.

As previously discussed, the integrity of the team can never be ignored. The level of trust that a team enjoys with its constituency and others will directly affect the team's level of success. Wrongful disclosure of incident information can quickly reduce the level of trust between the team and the people whom the team supports, as well as between the team and other teams and organizations. The incident response procedures should provide clear guidance on how and when information concerning an incident may be disclosed. This guidance should take into account any restrictions imposed on the team by upper management or outside organizations, and consider requests the team may receive for such information. For example, a government team should address Freedom of Information Act requests, a team in the health care industry should address requirements imposed by the Healthcare Information Portability and Accountability Act (HIPAA), and teams in financial organizations should address any requirements resulting from the Gramm-Leach-Bliley Act.

Teams should always hold the information reported to them in the strictest confidence. Many teams will not share the information beyond the immediate team members. Sometimes, however, information must be provided outside of the team (e.g., warning a site that it has been the victim of an attack or contacting law enforcement when it appears a computer crime has been committed or human life may be in danger, such as when an emergency response system has been disabled). When information does need to be shared, the purpose for disclosing the information, the requesting party, and the category of the information should be considered to determine if and how the information should be provided. More specifically:

- Disclosure of information concerning the incident should always be guarded and limited only to those with a valid "need to know." Even if people are aware of the incident and ask questions out of curiosity, the information should not be shared with them unless they have a valid reason for knowing the facts. This limitation even applies to incident response team members who may not have a role in the incident validating their awareness.

- The entity that is to receive the information will govern the amount or type of information to be provided. For example, a response to an inquiry received from the news media about a specific incident will drastically differ from the level of detail provided to upper management. Likewise, if the incident involves law enforcement, much more detail will be provided to the officer or agent working the case than possibly even the owner of the system, especially when an insider threat is suspected.

- The category of the information that is to be provided will also determine the extent and type of data to be disclosed. For example, information deemed necessary for public release will be more generic with less detail than that released internally to the organization.

In addition, it should always be remembered that once the information is shared or disclosed, control over that data is effectively lost. Therefore the information can easily be disclosed to other parties, and that spread can come back to haunt the incident response team.

The timing of when the information is provided should also be taken into consideration. Validating reports and facts to gain the full picture of what has taken place normally takes time. It would be nice to be able to delay reporting until the full picture is clear, but this option is not always prudent. Sometimes immediate notification must be made, such as when a potential threat to other systems or even human life is at stake. In these cases, an initial report should provide a "heads up" to the activity and annotate the fact that the investigation is still proceeding to gain further information.

How the information is reported or disclosed will vary as well. In some cases, the notification may occur through the completion of a report. If a specific report format must be used, that format should be identified in the incident response procedures with directions on what information is to be given in each section. The basic questions of *who, what, why, when,* and *how* can provide a simple format for reporting that covers the major elements. As with the initial report made to the team, care should be taken to not use the attacked system as the medium for submitting the report. If the report must be transmitted over a nonsecure medium such as the Internet, extra security precautions such as the use of encryption or a virtual private network (VPN) should be used to further protect against disclosure of the information. The report may also be made via a phone call. Again, if specific pieces of information will be provided in the phone notification, these elements should be documented and explained in the incident-handling procedures.

Although notification is listed as step 3 in this incident life cycle, with serious or large incidents this process will normally continue through the remaining steps. Successful attacks will typically require an initial notification as well as follow-up reports as the situation is investigated further. If multiple reports are provided, a method should be invoked for linking sequential reports together so that the flow of information can be followed and the potential for confusion is eliminated. Other papers or resources may include this phase with other phases in incident handling. It is broken out here to give it the attention it soundly deserves, as the notification and communication process can directly affect the success or failure of a response effort.

Step Four: Incident Analysis

The process for deciding how to handle an incident includes several aspects: characterizing the incident; considering the prevailing circumstances of the information asset or environment affected by it; and weighing the costs, merits, and drawbacks of various restoration or response options. The result of this process is a course of action that represents the incident response team's best judgment about how the incident should be addressed given the circumstances and options at the time.

Without a good understanding of the cause of an incident, it is extremely difficult to select a course of action that will effectively correct and securely restore the affected information resources. To diagnose an incident or attack, incident handlers attempt to determine whether the characteristics of the incident and circumstances surrounding it have a known or previously observed cause. Diagnosis can involve matching characteristics and circumstances with known conditions, or it could be a process of eliminating unlikely causes. Several factors influence the selection of the course of action to follow:

- The impact on and circumstances in the information environment at the time the suspicious activity occurred
- The criticality of affected information assets for business operations
- The real or potential damage caused by the incident
- The location of the system targeted

Evidence for the analysis may be provided through a variety of media, including alarms, logs, and remnant files. *Alarms* refer to the auditing data from security programs or tools that are programmed to trigger an alert when a specific event takes place. For example, the files provided by an intrusion detection system may be extremely valuable in determining the avenue used to gain access to a system. *Logs* refer to auditing files that track specific events as they occur. Both normal activity and malicious activity may be depicted in the audit logs. For example, many audit logs are set to record when users log onto the network or system. The activity of authorized users will not be of great importance to the incident analysis, unless an authorized user's account has been compromised and is used to gain access to the system. All too often, incident handling is analogous to "looking for the needle in the haystack." An audit log that notes an authorized user's account being accessed during a time period when the user is not at work or on vacation may be a clue to finding that "needle." Finally, *remnant files* refer to files or programs that an intruder may have left on the system once access was gained. Examples of remnant files include sniffer logs, password files, source code for programs, and exploit scripts that the intruder may have used to store his or her "goods" or to target other systems.

It is very common for intruders to install programs, create accounts, or open ports to allow for alternative points of access to the network while they are in the system. These changes enable later access should the intruder's initial avenue be shut off. Part of the incident analysis should include a vulnerability assessment of the targeted system to help identify avenues through which the attack may have been launched and any new vulnerabilities that may have been introduced as the result of the attack. Even if the incident appears to be clear on the surface, a vulnerability assessment should always be performed as part of the incident response.

In some cases, particularly those resulting from the actions of an insider or those through which physical access to the system was obtained, the evidence or clues to the case may be found in the surrounding area and may not be limited to computer media. For example, a torn printout in the trash can or a Post-it note with a user's account name and password may reveal how account information was used to gain access to the system. The main consideration when visiting the targeted system is to not limit your view to the system itself, but rather to take into consideration the surrounding environment and any clues it may provide.

If the incident involved an insider to the organization or any kind of illegal activity, a forensic analysis should be performed, preferably by personnel trained in computer forensics. This analysis will normally begin with photographing the "crime scene" from all directions (i.e., the computer system and surrounding area) and include imaging the computer media available in the environment. The use of forensic tools that have already been scrutinized in the legal system will increase the strength of the evidence that is preserved in this way if the case goes to trial. Additionally, the chain of custody of all evidence obtained must be strictly enforced and documented. (More information concerning computer forensics is provided in Chapter 11.)

Once the cause of the attack has been determined, the recommended course of action to remedy the situation may be determined and followed. Depending on the severity level and nature of the response, the course of action may first need approval from upper management.

Step Five: Remediation

The course of action and remediation phase normally begins by containing the incident (if applicable) and then removing the cause of the activity. To contain an incident means to limit the exposure or spread of the event. For example:

- If a system has been compromised or accessed by an unauthorized person, containment will mean either kicking the person out of the system or limiting the intruder's reach within the system to monitor his or her activity.
- In the case of a denial-of-service attack, containment may mean limiting the systems affected by blocking ports used in the attack or isolating access between affected and unaffected segments.
- If a virus or worm is affecting operations and the antivirus software is not limiting its spread, the containment may include disconnecting infected segments or systems from the network or disconnecting points of access to the network to minimize the possible spread.
- If an authorized user is suspected of using the system for unauthorized purposes, containment may require the employee to be placed on paid administrative leave until the situation can be fully investigated.

The method(s) of containment will typically be the focus of the course of action selected by the incident response team. Because isolating or removing a computer from a network or organization can directly affect the business operations, the recommended course of action should be explained to the owner or manager of the business unit prior to steps being taken if guidelines for that particular response have not previously been agreed to by upper management. The owner or manager should be able to judge how the action will further alter operations or hurt the business and if the recommendations are acceptable.

The steps that are taken on the network or system will normally be performed by the system administrator or IT staff responsible for the system, with the incident handler providing support. Therefore, once the course of action is determined and approved, the appropriate technical resource should be identified and requested to be on-site, if not already available. Working with the actual owners of the system(s) to perform the containment (and recovery) steps will normally be better received than having the incident response team show up and "take over" the system. Additionally, working with the technical staff or system administrators may yield additional clues about the incident. For example, they may help to identify configuration settings that may have resulted in a vulnerability that has been exploited or describe suspicious activity that may have been previously noted.

The most common method of containment is realized by completely removing a compromised system (or systems) from the network for further investigation. If resources allow, the system should be taken to a safe location to perform a root-cause analysis of the incident so as to validate the suspected source of the incident. A replacement system may be installed on the network, enabling operations to be restored while the team analyzes the compromised system. If a complete backup system is not available, then the same result may be accomplished by swapping the hard drive of the affected computer with a new hard drive.

Care must be taken with the new system to ensure that the intruder does not immediately gain access or deny services to the replacement. This consideration is particularly important if the exact cause of the incident was not fully determined in the analysis phase. The following steps may help to protect the replacement system:

- Move the host to a different IP address
- Require all users to change their passwords
- Install missing patches to guard against known vulnerabilities
- Examine trust relationships with other hosts for possible avenues to the targeted system

Containment may also mean isolating the affected computer system(s) in an effort to prevent further compromise, stop the spread of a virus or other form of malicious logic, or limit a denial-of-service attack. The isolation tactic may be taken when further evidence is desired to identify (and possibly prosecute) the intruder. There are multiple ways in which isolation of network segments may be realized. For example, adding a router or firewall to block access to other segments of a network may limit the reach of an intruder. Shutting down e-mail servers may help to stop the spread of a virus infection.

Disabling specific services or blocking ports on computer systems may help to slow down a denial-of-service attack.

Many people assume that the first step to take in the case of a successful compromise is to immediately "kick the intruder off the system or network." In reality, this is not always the case. If a computer crime appears to have been committed, the organization may decide to involve law enforcement and try to obtain further evidence that may later be used in a court of law to prosecute the intruder. Possibly a Title III (wiretap) order will be required and an intrusion detection system will be added to the compromised system to monitor for further activity. Access beyond the compromised system should be removed or restricted to limit potential exposure to other systems on the network while the monitoring takes place.

Passwords on compromised systems and systems that regularly interact with the compromised system should also be changed as part of the remediation phase. If, however, the decision has been made to "fishbowl" or monitor the intruder to gain further evidence, this step may be partially left for the recovery stage so as to not alert the intruder to the fact that he or she has been discovered. It is important to keep as low a profile as possible throughout this part of the incident life cycle. Additionally, any code that may have been compromised during the incident should be avoided while the system is still on-line, even if it has been isolated. The compromised code may include Trojan horses, which may either spread the incident further or alert the intruder to their discovery.

Once the situation has been contained and the cause of the incident is verified, then steps to remove the vulnerability should be taken. This removal may be done by changing system configurations, updating antivirus software signature files, blocking specific ports or services that are no longer needed, or undertaking more substantial work such as changes to application programs. If the incident resulted from a vulnerability for which a patch is available from the software manufacturer, then systems should be patched whenever possible before being placed back in production. Care should be taken during the patch process to ensure that the patch has not been altered (i.e., check MD5 checksums provided by the vendor prior to installation), and that it does not negatively affect the operation of applications that may be running on the system. Typically, it is best to test the installation of the patch on one or a few systems first, prior to large-scale patching. Once the vulnerability has been removed from the equation, the incident life cycle then leads into the recovery phase.

Step Six: System Restoration

In the worst-case scenario, restoring operations involves taking the system or systems off-line and rebuilding them. Rebuilding them may mean loading operating systems and programs from scratch or simply reloading files from backup sources. Depending on the amount of time that an intruder stayed in the system, the latest backup may not be the best one to use. The backup tape or other medium should be reviewed to determine its integrity and to decide whether it is the best source from which to restore operations. All too often, additional restoration work will be needed for the accounts or files that were affected during the incident. Nevertheless, the backup tape/medium should provide a foundation to begin that process.

In the simplest form, the typical recovery procedures can be broken down as follows:

1. Install an operating system from media that is known to be authentic, preferably from the vendor's original media.
2. Disable unnecessary services and apply secure configuration changes to applications.
3. Install appropriate vendor security patches to the operating system and all of the applications on the system.
4. Consult advisories, vendor bulletins, and security documentation.
5. Change passwords.
6. Reconnect the system.

Depending on the type of incident that has occurred, system restoration may be much easier to achieve. For example, a virus incident may just require antivirus signature files to be updated to achieve the system restoration. A scanning incident may not require any changes, if the potential vulnerability for which the person appears to have been searching is not present.

Once the system has been restored, configuration settings should be checked to ensure that they are equivalent to the initial state of the system prior to the incident. If the incident exploited a certain configuration setting, that setting should be changed accordingly to prevent a repeat occurrence. If not done before, all passwords on the compromised system should be changed, as well as any passwords on systems that regularly interact with that system. If a patch or fix exists for the vulnerability that was exploited to launch the attack, then the patch or fix should be made to the system. Finally, the system should be checked to ensure that it is operating normally.

In some cases, it may be appropriate to not restore the system immediately. For example, if the system is no longer needed, an upgrade to the system will be made in the near future, or the identified vulnerability cannot be readily fixed, management may decide to delay the recovery procedures. Restoring a system with the same vulnerability is an invitation to repeat the incident. Recovery should take place only when the reoccurrence of the incident can be prevented and/or the security of the system is strengthened. Once the system is restored, it should be closely monitored for repeat attempts or attacks, and for vulnerabilities that may not have been discovered during the incident analysis.

Step Seven: Lessons Learned

The final phase of the incident life cycle is always the "lessons learned" phase. Every incident that requires a response effort should be analyzed for lessons learned. The incident response team members should discuss the steps taken and address any concerns or problems encountered along the way. The review should focus on the facts and not place blame for steps that did not go well. Both the positive and the negative aspects of the incident response should be discussed. The following questions may be considered during this review:

- Were the response efforts provided appropriate? Did the selected course of action work?
- Was there enough information available to analyze the incident? If not, what else would have helped and how could that have been obtained?
- Were all appropriate parties kept informed of the status of the incident response? Was the information flow sufficient?

- Which steps went well? Which steps could be improved?
- Did the incident-handling procedures cover all needed steps or requirements? What documentation was the most helpful? Least helpful?
- Have steps been taken to prevent a reoccurrence of the incident?
- Should anyone else be alerted to the vulnerability exploited, such as a vendor?
- Might other systems within the constituency be vulnerable to the same attack? If so, what steps can be taken to mitigate the risks to those systems?
- Can the vulnerability exploited be addressed in organizational security policies? Do any policies need to be rewritten?
- Are there any other lessons learned that should be documented or acted upon?

Documentation changes identified during the review should be addressed as quickly as possible. The review may identify weaknesses in the organization's security policy or specific procedures that need to be addressed. It may not be the responsibility of the incident response team to correct these problems, but it is the responsibility of the team to notify the appropriate party of the deficiency. Providing recommended changes may help to speed the change being completed.

Another outcome of the review may be the identification of deficiencies in the incident-handling procedures. Those steps that worked well during the incident response and those that did not may be used to write improved procedures for future responses.

It may be determined that distributing an advisory is warranted to prevent a reoccurrence of the attack. This advisory may take the form of notifying a vendor of a newly discovered vulnerability, notifying the constituency of a specific vulnerability or threat, or notifying another organization of the incident or problem (e.g., CERT CC). The pertinent information should be obtained, documented clearly, and distributed as quickly as possible so that the problem may be addressed with all due speed.

Finally, a post-incident report should thoroughly document what took place and how the organization was affected by the event. The cost of the incident to the organization should be quantified (if possible), and any intangible damage or costs should be noted. These costs should be included in the incident database for tracking statistics and generic report generation. Copies of the report should be filed in a safe location for future reference, and submitted to management as required.

Upon completion of the report, the incident should be closed in any trouble ticket system, as no further action should be required of the incident response team. Of course, just because an incident is closed, it does not mean it cannot be reopened. On numerous occasions, incidents have been reopened due to new evidence, new activity, or a reoccurrence of activity that appears to originate from the same source. At this point, the incident life cycle begins again.

Sample Incidents

Building on the discussion of the incident life cycle just presented, let's examine the phases of this life cycle through a couple of hypothetical incidents. Because the preparation step will remain the same for all incidents, we will begin this discussion with step 2, identification. As previously noted, the discussion of each step focused on the system compromise, so our hypothetical cases will use other types of incidents for further review.

Unauthorized Use Example

1. *Identification:* An employee reports to her manager that a coworker is spending a great deal of time surfing the Internet instead of doing his job. The employee further states that some of the sites the coworker visits are offensive to her. The manager contacts human resources, which in turn asks the CIRT to investigate the situation further.
2. *Notification:* In this case, the manager is already aware of the report and does not need to be notified. If the employee is suspected of having or accessing child pornography, however, then upper management should be made aware of the potential violation.
3. *Analysis:* This type of incident will require a forensic examination of the employee's computer system and any other computer media he uses. The manager may provide the system to the CIRT for the

imaging and review, or the incident handlers may need to image the drives at the person's desk—possibly after hours, so as to not tip him off. If no unauthorized programs or files are found from the analysis, then the case may be closed and the team returns to the preparation phase.

4. *Remediation:* If unauthorized files or images are found on the employee's system, the focus would be on the human factor— that is, discussing the violation with the employee and human resources or management taking the proper steps to address the situation from their angle. For example, the employee may be given a written warning to not use the business computer for this sort of activity in the future.

5. *System Restoration:* System restoration in this case would require the hard drive or any other corrupt media to be cleaned and authorized software to be reinstalled.

6. *Lessons Learned:* The remediation steps taken depend on the proper policies (human resources or computer security) being in place. If a policy is lacking, then a lesson learned may be to strengthen the documented policy. If lack of awareness is an issue, then the lesson learned may be to enhance the awareness of existing policies.

Attempted Unauthorized Access

1. *Identification:* An employee reports to the CIRT that every morning when she comes into the office, her system is turned on and another user's ID appears in the login screen. She does not recognize the user's ID and she "swears" that she turned the computer off the previous night.

2. *Notification:* As this activity is not definitively an incident, the decision may be made to notify management when more information is obtained. Therefore, we will skip this phase and move right into the analysis.

3. *Analysis:* The employee's system may be examined for signs of attempted or unauthorized access. Any audit logs that are available should be checked for signs of suspicious activity. If nothing stands out and the suspicious activity continues, a video camera may be used to watch for someone accessing or attempting to

access the system after hours. If the activity stops or no substantial evidence of wrongdoing is found, the case may be closed and the team returns to preparing for the next incident.

4. *Remediation:* If an unauthorized individual is discovered as attempting to access the employee's system, physical security or other measures may be employed to keep the person out of the area in the future. For example, if the janitor is discovered to be the perpetrator, he or she may be relieved of these duties or moved to another location without computer systems. If the perpetrator is another employee, management may need to interview the individual to ascertain why the other person's system is used and counsel the worker if necessary to stop the activity.

5. *System Restoration:* As the system does not appear to have been successfully accessed, no restoration activity is needed.

6. *Lessons Learned:* If physical access to the system was not protected, some physical security measures may be implemented to bolster this protection. If awareness of authorized users is an issue, then training or counseling may be required.

Attempted Denial-of-Service

1. *Identification:* The intrusion detection system (IDS) alarm on suspicious activity sounds, indicating that a denial-of-service attack has been attempted. The attack appears to have come from an account at a large ISP. No degradation of system performance is noted. The IDS team reports the alarm to the CIRT.

2. *Notification:* Because the activity does not appear to have been successful, further notification of upper management may not be immediately required. Rather, the incident may be included in a weekly or monthly incident summary.

3. *Analysis:* The incident handlers should work with the operations personnel to check system logs in an attempt to verify the alarm as valid. If it appears to be a "false positive" or "false alarm," then the case should be closed and no further activity is required.

4. *Remediation:* If further information indicates that a denial-of-service attack was really attempted, then the team may consider contacting the ISP and reporting the activity to it. Many proactive and security-conscious ISPs will address abuses by their end

users. The amount of feedback received by the CIRT will vary, but the contact is worth a try. Most problems can be reported to the address of "abuse@" followed by the ISP's domain name.

5. *System Restoration:* As the attack does not appear to have been successful, no restoration activity is needed.

6. *Lessons Learned:* There may or may not be lessons learned in this hypothetical case. If contact with the ISP was successful, that fact may be noted for future incidents involving the ISP's users. Likewise, if the contact was not successful or included problems, that fact could be noted for future reference.

Incident Reporting

As previously noted in this chapter, every response team should have a report form that identifies the information it requires to investigate and track an incident. The information requested on the incident report form will vary from team to team, and should mirror specific data fields in the incident tracking database and/or trouble ticket system. Appendix A provides a sample form that may be used as a guide for an organization's own incident report form. The CERT CC report form is also available at http://www.cert.org and provides additional fields that may be considered.

The desired information should be clearly requested in the report form and allow little, if any, room for ambiguity. Pick lists or selection options can provide a tremendous advantage by eliminating confusion for both the reporting party and the incident handler. Pick lists are also extremely valuable in the incident database and trouble ticket systems. Without such lists, it's amazing how many different ways information may be defined and reported. Caution should be taken, however, to ensure that an "other" category is included for those cases that do not match any of the selections. The "other" selection should be accompanied by an area where specific comments may be made to expand upon the entry. Instructions for completing the report form should explain how to handle unclear areas or questions as they arise.

The report form should also ask for contact information for the reporting individual. In addition, the form should contain a place to indicate whether the e-mail address provided should not be used for communication regarding the incident. The ability to remain anonymous should also be considered, as some people may be reluctant to make a report if they have to provide their identity.

Feedback

Once the report form is completed and submitted to the incident response team, it should be acknowledged in some fashion. Lack of acknowledgment often leads to a feeling of helplessness and frustration on the part of the constituency. If the reporting party took the time to complete the report and submit it, then he or she should receive the satisfaction of a response indicating that someone was interested in the activity. The acknowledgment should include a unique incident or event tracking number and any pertinent information that needs to be passed on at that time. If additional information is needed, a request for it may accompany the response. At the same time, care should be taken to not disclose any information about the incident in the process of responding. The following provides a sample acknowledgment that may be used to respond to a report:

> Thank you for your incident report dated June 15, 2002. We are analyzing the information reported to ascertain what may have caused the suspicious activity noted, and we are tracking this activity as event #0601-25.
>
> We appreciate the inclusion of audit log excerpts with the report, but need to clarify the time zone for which these logs were recording activity. Please respond with the time zone used and reference the tracking number so we can update our records appropriately.
>
> If you discover any additional information concerning this activity or have any questions, please feel free to contact us at 800-123-4567.
>
> Regards,
> (Person responding or team signature)

In some cases little, if anything, can be done regarding the activity reported (e.g., a scan of network addresses). An acknowledgment or response to the report is still warranted, however. Without it, the person completing the report may be reluctant to continue reporting in the future. In addition, despite the limited response capability that may be provided to that report, the information may still be vital to the monitoring of the organization's information security. The following is a sample acknowledgment to this type of report:

> Thank you for your incident report dated December 1, 2002. We are tracking this event as incident #1201-01. Please reference this number should you discover any additional information concerning this incident.
>
> While we may not be able to take action against this source based on the information you provided, your reports, along with those of other system administrators, will help us to understand the scope and frequency of these problems. Your information will be added to our database so we can correlate it with past activity.
>
> If you discover additional information concerning this activity or have any questions, please feel free to contact us at 800-123-4567.
>
> Regards,
>
> (Person responding or team signature)

If activity is reported that turns out to not be an incident, then a response should be provided indicating that fact to the person who submitted the report. Depending on how the incident tracking numbers are assigned, the acknowledgment may include a tracking number. If applicable, the acknowledgment should be an awareness education opportunity in which feedback is provided describing why the activity was not considered to be an incident. If people are reporting nonincident activity, the education provided in the feedback can help to cut down on the number of unneeded reports.

Regardless of the type of acknowledgment sent, the response should be signed either by the incident handler who is responding to the report or with a team signature. Including an individual name can add to a sense of uniqueness to the process and detract from the feeling of a "canned" response, but it can also hinder follow-on communications regarding the incident. Specifically, if the person reporting discovers further information on the event and wishes to report it, that individual may believe that he or she can speak only with the person who signed the initial response. If that person is out for a few days or working a different shift, the unavailability can add to frustration for the reporting party and slow the communication. The person reporting should be encouraged to communicate with other members of the team as well, should they need to follow up on an incident.

Tracking Incidents

The number of incidents processed and responded to by every team will vary according to the size of the constituency. If an organization is large enough to establish its own incident response team, then the chances are very good that the team will need a database or mechanism to store and track incident data. Many larger teams have both a database and a trouble ticket system. The trouble ticket system helps with tracking the reports as they are received as well as already open items. Typically, an incident will be in one of three states from the incident response team's perspective:

- *Open:* The incident has not been resolved and an action is required of the response team.
- *Waiting or pending:* The incident has not been resolved, but the team is waiting for further information, an investigation to be conducted, or a response from another person or group.
- *Closed:* No further action is required of the incident response team.

The trouble ticket system should annotate the current state of each incident and indicate what action is pending. It should also identify the flow of steps taken, so an incident handler responding for the first time to an incident can quickly see the history of action taken to date.

The trouble ticket system is the tool used to triage the requests and reports as they are received. Normally, the system would assist with identifying those incidents that are in the open or waiting state. Depending on the programs used for the system and the database, the data from the trouble ticket may be directly ported into the database. Likewise, if a closed incident is reopened, information previously entered into the database should be able to be recalled through the trouble ticket system if needed.

Working in combination, these systems can be extremely important tools for incident handling. Not only can they be used to track open incidents (ensuring that a report does not fall through the cracks) and store incident data, but they can also aid in the correlation of activity. The "correlation of activity" refers to the process of looking for patterns in activity that may be attributed to either the same source or the same type of attack. Running queries on the database can automate the steps taken to identify attacks stemming from the same source, targeting the same destination, using the same port or service, occurring during the same time period, involving the same "handle," or following any other pattern. Without the database, this task can be tremendously time-consuming and the human eye may overlook important incident elements that are not readily apparent.

The database should be configured with enough storage to expand based on the number of records stored. As the incident response team becomes widely known and succeeds, the number of reports will increase exponentially, and the database must be able to support this growth. The statistics in Table 8–1 were taken from the CERT CC Web site and give the number of incidents processed over the years by that team. Although CERT CC can be considered as having the largest constituency and routinely handles more incidents than many other teams, the statistics should indicate how quickly the number of incidents can grow with time.

Another important use of the database is statistics generation. Statistics regarding the number of inquiries and incidents responded to can be used to help justify the hiring of additional people for the team or the purchase of additional resources. Statistics on parts of the organization experiencing the most successful attacks may indicate an area with training deficiencies or other problems that need to be resolved. Statistics indicating a decrease in successful incidents may be used to gauge the success of security programs or particular tools (e.g., antivirus software). Depending on the specific reporting needs of the organization, the data maintained in the database can be very useful for justifying the team's existence as well as pinpointing strengths and weaknesses in particular security programs.

Although an incident response team may use many tools, the database should be considered one of the (if not the) most important tool. Therefore, due consideration should be given to the type of data-

Table 8-1 Annual Number of Incidents Handled by the CERT CC

Year	Number of Incidents Reported
1988	6
1989	132
1990	252
1991	406
1992	773
1993	1,334
1994	2,340
1995	2,412
1996	2,573
1997	2,134
1998	3,734
1999	9,859
2000	21,756
2001	52,658
2002	82,094
Total	**182,463**

Source: http://www.cert.org/stats/cert_stats.html.

base purchased, the fields identified for tracking, and the hiring of a skilled database administrator for programming and maintaining the system. The database is not the area to cut costs or save dollars should funding problems emerge.

Keeping Current

One of the biggest complaints or problems facing system administrators today is keeping current with the latest vulnerabilities. With so many identified and noted in various forums, how do system administrators know which ones to address? The same dilemma faces incident response teams. For incident handlers, the situation is often even more complex because they have more operating systems about which to be knowledgeable. How does the team keep current?

Several resources may be used to accomplish this goal. Advisories and alerts provided by other teams and vendors can be excellent tools with which to keep abreast of the latest holes and fixes. CERT CC advisories, in particular, should be monitored closely for alerts of serious problems. Advisories or postings from other teams and security groups can also provide valuable information regarding a new vulnerability.

Vendor advisories for specific systems covered by the team should be monitored as well. Patches or fixes available from the vendor should be identified in the announcement. Many vendors forward their alerts to the CERT CC, which also posts their announcements on the center's Web site. Some vendors include special notes concerning the fix that should be carefully considered before any action is taken. For example, a vendor may indicate a temporary fix is available that has not been thoroughly tested. In this case, the potential threat posed by the vulnerability must be balanced against the potential problems that may be encountered by installing a temporary fix to determine whether action should be taken immediately.

Some vendors now offer alert services that are tailored to the organization. For a fee, this service provides daily, weekly, or monthly updates through a subscription-based service geared to the operating systems and programs present in the organization. Typically the updates will rank the severity of the threats identified. Some organizations offer the service with a focus on intelligence gathering, drawing information from additional resources that may provide indications and warnings of potential threats. The type of information and spin given to each advisory or report varies between service providers and should be selected based on the specific needs of the team.

The following avenues may also be used to keep current:

- Mailing lists and newsgroups available on the Internet provide additional sources of information for keeping current. Some lists and newsgroups are better than others, and sometimes the team must sift through a lot of information to find the most applicable or valuable pieces.
- Technical groups such as the Forum of Incident Response and Security Teams (FIRST) and InfraGard (both of which were described earlier in this book) can be valuable sources for establishing contacts to provide guidance on specific issues as well as updates to the latest vulnerabilities.
- Conferences can be a valuable source of information on the latest tools, attacks, and responses. Some conferences, such as those sponsored by the SysAdmin, Audit, Network, Security (SANS) Institute, offer training that can lead to certifications.
- Training from both internal and external sources can provide updates on vulnerabilities, threats, and the latest developments for addressing those threats.
- Trade publications, books, and magazines may be useful for researching various subjects.

A team cannot afford to rely strictly on one source of information to keep current with vulnerabilities and countermeasures. The best approach is to utilize a combination of resources with time slotted for team members to conduct research. Despite the best efforts to stay up-to-date, remember to always be prepared for the unexpected.

Writing Computer Security Advisories

Some teams decide to write their own advisories on vulnerabilities about which they want to alert their constituency. Other teams simply rely on forwarding advisories from other sources, such as those published by CERT CC or specific vendors. A few simple rules should be followed by teams chartered with writing their own advisories:

1. Keep it simple. The advisory should stick to the facts and avoid technical jargon.

2. Always include a fix or some steps to lessen the vulnerability. If a vulnerability does not have a readily available fix or countermeasure, the decision may be to not advertise the problem for further exploitation.

3. If a patch will be downloaded, include the MD5 checksum whenever it is available. The MD5 checksum is a digital signature or fingerprint of the patch and should be used to validate that the correct patch has been downloaded before it is installed on the system. Although the MD5 checksum is not foolproof, this step does significantly increase the overall security of the patch process. (Note: On some occasions, a patch has been compromised and modified to include a Trojan horse program when people are downloading it.)

4. Whenever possible, test the vulnerability and proposed fix in a lab environment to verify that the patch fixes the problem and doesn't inject other problems. This step may not always be possible, but it is a good security measure for protecting the team's integrity if it is an option.

NOTE For most teams that are internal to a specific company or organization, the testing of the patch is handled by the system administrators. The role of the CIRT is to identify and qualify the vulnerabilities, and then advise the appropriate entities of vulnerabilities, warnings, and informational bulletins. It is then the responsibility of the system administrators to test patches appropriately in their environment, troubleshoot any problems that arise, and be prepared with backups to restore the system if the patch goes bad.

The best format to follow with writing advisories has four parts:

1. *Problem:* Briefly describe the vulnerability—what it is and what can happen if it is exploited.

2. *Symptoms:* Identify any symptoms that may indicate the vulnerability has been exploited on a system.

3. *Fix:* Describe the steps that can be taken to prevent the

vulnerability from being exploited or to recover from an attack. Remember to include the MD5 checksum, if applicable.

4. *Point of contact information:* How can further information be obtained? Who can be contacted for questions or problems?

Advisories can be distributed to the constituency through several means. One of the most popular methods is through a list server, sending the advisory electronically through e-mail. Many teams also post copies of the advisory on their Web sites: on intranet sites, Web pages, or both. The final method is through paper versions, physically sending the report out to people or posting it on bulletin boards around corporate buildings. In this day of automation, the hard copy distribution is the method used the least, but it can be very valuable when a major event is taking place and people need to be made aware of it prior to turning computer systems on. For example, the Melissa virus made its debut on a Friday afternoon in March 1999. Offices that posted warnings on their doors before employees returned to work on the following Monday were able to give notice of the activity prior to computer systems being turned on. Very similar circumstances were experienced more recently when the Slammer worm spread in January 2003. The advisory steps taken by organizations in these cases may have helped to stop the further spread of the virus or worm by increasing the awareness of end users.

Summary

This chapter focused on the center of the incident response puzzle, the policies and procedures. The operational aspects of computer incident response were discussed in detail, with particular attention being given to the response life cycle. The phases addressed in detail regarding the life cycle of incident response may be summarized as follows: preparation, incident identification, notification, incident analysis, remediation, and lessons learned.

Often the lessons learned will feed directly into improvements that can be made to strengthen the security of the infrastructure, thus beginning the life cycle again. This outline may be used as a starting point for documenting the procedures that an incident response team should follow. It is reiterated here to reinforce the importance of these steps to the incident response puzzle.

This chapter also presented an overview of reporting criteria, addressing topics such as the report form, the importance of feedback, and the use of a trouble ticket system. The importance of a database for storing the incident data was discussed, pointing out the importance of this tool for incident correlation and statistic generation and tracking. Methods for keeping current with the latest vulnerabilities and trends once the team is formed were presented, as well as rules of thumb for writing and distributing advisories. Not every incident response team should write advisories. Several good sources of advisories are available that can just as easily be leveraged. Too many advisories can lead to the same problem experienced by many with respect to too many vulnerabilities: In time, people will tend to ignore the warnings if they are too frequent in distribution.

Combined, these topics outline many of the daily considerations that must be taken into account by the team in operation. They complete the overall picture of the incident response team puzzle. The remainder of the book provides more details on issues presented in this and earlier chapters. Although the elements described in Chapter 8 will assist with the task of writing policies and procedures for the response team, it is strongly recommended that you visit the remaining chapters before those procedures are documented or finalized. Additional details in the following chapters may provide further, more granular hints on developing your procedures.

CHAPTER

9

What Did That Incident Cost?

Your organization has been the victim of a computer incident, whether it be from malicious or nonmalicious intent. You have successfully identified the problem(s) and helped with the recovery process. Now you're asked what may be the most challenging question: "How much did the incident cost?" How do you respond? If the incident was a denial-of-service attack or major virus infection, do you take the payroll of all affected employees and tally the wages for the period of lost productivity? If it was industrial espionage, do you guess at the value of the information and provide that answer? If it was a compromise, do you total the person-hours and salaries for those involved with the response and provide that figure?

Unfortunately, there is no simple equation that can be used to estimate the costs of all computer incidents. That explains why this question is probably the most difficult to answer and is frequently left blank in survey responses. This chapter explores ways in which an answer to this question may be formulated. We'll attempt to demonstrate, through examples, some methods and tactics for estimating incident costs and losses. Although we would love to present one simple formula that could serve as a "one size fits all" solution to the question, that would be impossible.

Statistics and Cases

We start this chapter by exploring some estimates previously computed in response to surveys and real-world examples that reflect the financial impact of computer incidents to various organizations. Although these results and example cases do not reflect directly the methodology used in creating the damage estimates, they do help to identify the magnitude of the problem in computing incident costs. They also help to shed some light on how expensive computer crime and incidents can be to an organization. Ideally, this perspective will inspire more in-depth study of this aspect of computer incident response in the near future.

CSI/FBI Survey Results

The annual survey conducted by the Computer Security Institute, in conjunction with the FBI, is probably one of the best sources for incident-related statistics. Tables 9–1 and 9–2 were taken from the 2002 survey results and provide a breakdown of financial losses reported each year since the survey was initiated in 1997. The results of these surveys are noteworthy because they reflect not only an increase in those organizations recognizing financial losses due to computer crime, but also a wide variation in the losses reported. Note that the values were estimated and reported by personnel within each organization. As a consequence, the methods used to value the total loss vary as widely as the results themselves.

The combined financial losses reported in the surveys from 1997 through 2002 totaled $1,459,755,245 (nearly $1.5 billion)! Although this number seems quite high, it is actually low when you consider that fewer than 50 percent of those organizations acknowledging financial losses each year were actually able to put a price tag on that loss.

Some Example Cases

The following examples provide estimated damages for some computer incident cases that have occurred over the past few years. Although the manner in which the damage estimates were con-

Table 9-1   Number of Respondents with Quantified Losses

	1997	1998	1999	2000	2001	2002
Theft of proprietary information	21	20	23	22	34	26
Sabotage of data networks	14	25	27	28	26	28
Telecom eavesdropping	8	10	10	15	16	5
System penetration by outsider	22	19	28	29	42	59
Insider abuse of Internet access	55	67	81	91	98	89
Financial fraud	26	29	27	34	21	25
Denial-of-service	NA	36	28	46	35	62
Virus	165	143	116	162	186	178
Unauthorized insider access	22	18	25	20	22	15
Telecom fraud	35	32	29	19	18	16
Active wiretapping	NA	5	1	1	0	0
Laptop theft	165	162	150	174	143	134

Source: 2002 CSI/FBI Survey.

structed is not available for all of these cases, they should provide some indications as to the range of damage estimates that may be calculated.

- A former chief computer network program designer for Omega Engineering Corporation was convicted May 9, 2000, for intentionally causing an estimated $10 million in damage. The company's manufacturing software programs were permanently deleted

Table 9-2 Total Annual Losses Reported

	1997	1998	1999	2000	2001	2002
Theft of proprietary information	$20,048,000	$33,545,000	$42,496,000	$66,708,000	$151,230,100	$170,827,000
Sabotage of data networks	$4,285,850	$2,142,000	$4,421,000	$27,148,000	$5,183,100	$15,134,000
Telecom eavesdropping	$1,181,000	$562,000	$765,000	$991,200	$886,000	$6,015,000
System penetration by outsider	$2,911,700	$1,637,000	$2,885,000	$7,104,000	$19,066,600	$13,055,000
Insider abuse of Internet access	$1,006,750	$3,720,000	$7,576,000	$27,984,740	$35,001,650	$50,099,000
Financial fraud	$24,892,000	$11,239,000	$39,706,000	$55,996,000	$92,935,500	$115,753,000
Denial-of-service	NA	$2,787,000	$3,255,000	$8,247,500	$4,283,600	$18,370,500
Virus	$12,498,150	$7,874,000	$5,274,000	$29,171,700	$45,288,150	$49,979,000
Unauthorized insider access	$3,991,605	$50,565,000	$3,567,000	$22,554,500	$6,064,000	$4,503,000
Telecom fraud	$22,660,300	$17,256,000	$773,000	$4,028,000	$9,041,000	$346,000
Active wiretapping	NA	$245,000	$20,000	$5,000,000	$0	$0
Laptop theft	$6,132,200	$5,250,000	$13,038,000	$10,404,300	$8,849,000	$11,766,500

Source: 2002 CSI/FBI Survey.

when the former employee's "time bomb" program was activated. Damage estimates included figures for losses in sales and future contracts. The man was sentenced to 41 months in prison.[1]

- A Sacramento, California, man pleaded guilty to "three felony counts, including wire fraud; conspiracy to obtain unauthorized computer access to customer account information from a financial institution; and credit card fraud" on March 1, 2002. He had obtained account and credit card information from a credit union employee, then used that information to make fraudulent charges for hotel and airline reservations. The charges totaled $116,869.30. The man was sentenced to 27 months in prison with three years supervised release following that term, and ordered to pay $116,869.30 in restitution.[2]

- The creator of the Melissa virus, which wreaked havoc on thousands of e-mail systems on March 26, 1999, pleaded guilty in federal court on December 9, 1999. He was sentenced to 20 months in federal prison, with three years supervised release following that term. He was also fined $5000 and ordered to have "no involvement with computer networks, the Internet, or Internet bulletin boards unless authorized by the Court." Although the actual number of computer systems affected by the Melissa virus was not known, the individual admitted to more than $80 million in damage in cooperation with his federal plea agreement. He also faced sentencing at the state level.[3]

- An 18-year-old man pleaded guilty on December 6, 2000, to "six felony charges of breach of computer security and one felony charge of third-degree aggravated theft." Between November 1999 and January 2000, the individual had illegally obtained "access to computers belonging to the United States Postal Service, the State of Texas, the Canadian Department of Defence, and Glinn

---

1. U.S. Department of Justice press release, "Former Computer Network Administrator at New Jersey High-Tech Firm Sentenced to 41 Months for Unleashing $10 Million Computer 'Time Bomb'," February 26, 2002.

2. U.S. Department of Justice press release, "Twenty-Seven Month Sentence in Internet Fraud Scheme to Defraud Priceline.com and Others," May 17, 2002.

3. U.S. Department of Justice press release, "Creator of Melissa Computer Virus Sentenced to 20 Months in Federal Prison," May 1, 2001.

Publishing Company" and deprived the authorized users from being able to use these systems. He was "sentenced to two years in prison, on each of the six charges for breach of computer security, and 10 years on the theft charge. The prison sentences were suspended" and the individual was given five years supervised probation with his future use of computers restricted. He was also "ordered to pay $45,856.46 in restitution to the victims of his hacking."[4]

- Two former Cisco employees exceeded their authorized access levels "to illegally issue almost $8 million in Cisco stock to themselves." They had exceeded their authorized access levels so as "to access a computer system used by the company to manage stock option disbursals, used that access to identify control numbers to track authorized stock option disbursals, created forged forms purporting to authorize disbursals of stock, faxed the forged requests to the company responsible for controlling and issuing shares of Cisco Systems stock, and directed that stock be placed in their personal brokerage accounts." The total value of the Cisco stock taken over three separate occasions was approximately $7,868,637. That amount was based on the value of the stock at the time it was transferred. Each man was sentenced to 34 months in prison for the scheme. The two also agreed to the forfeiture of their assets that had been obtained during the investigation and will be responsible for paying restitution for the difference between the amount these items are sold for and the $7,868,637 in damages.[5]

The preceding examples were all taken from press releases available from the U.S. Department of Justice Web site. The total estimated damages were quite high for many of these cases due to the magnitude of the incidents. Many more cases with lower totals are cited as

---

4. U.S. Department of Justice press release, "Texas Hacker Pleads Guilty to 7 Charges of Unlawfully Obtaining Access to Computers Belonging to the U.S. Postal Service, the State of Texas, the Canadian Department of Defence and the Private Sector," December 6, 2000.

5. U.S. Department of Justice press release, "Former Cisco Systems, Inc. Accountants Sentenced for Unauthorized Access to Computer Systems to Illegally Issue Almost $8 Million in Cisco Stock to Themselves," November 26, 2001.

well. Because these cases were all prosecuted at the federal level, the minimum damage total $5000. For information on other cases and more examples, visit the Justice Department Web site at http://www.usdoj.gov/criminal/cybercrime and click on *cases*.

Forms of Economic Impact

The previous section indicated how widely damage estimates can vary for computer incidents. Unfortunately, as stated earlier, no single equation may be used to calculate the damages when an incident has occurred. The best approach is to identify all costs that result from the incident, then add those costs to determine a total. Even though this task sounds easy, it may not be when you take all the possible areas of expense into account. This section provides some guidance on ways that damages may be categorized and should help with identifying costs that may have not been previously considered.

Costs Associated with Time Frames

A successful computer attack can have three types or periods of economic impact on an organization: immediate, short-term, and long-term.[6] Immediate costs are normally associated with one-time incidents or large-scale incidents that occur within a short time frame. Major malicious logic infections such as the Love Bug and Melissa viruses are examples of attacks in which the costs provided would be considered the immediate impact of the incident. Normally, immediate costs are attributed to the problems that arise as a result of the incident from the time it occurs through the days following the event. For example, immediate costs can result from the sudden loss of computer resources for continuing business and may be attributed to deadlines missed, orders lost, lost productivity, and much more.

---

6. Erbschloe, Michael. *Information Warfare: How to Survive Cyber Attacks.* New York: McGraw-Hill, 2001, pp. 51–63.

Table 9–3   The Potential Impact on Revenue and Profits from Supply Chain Participation Being Disabled

Duration	$100,000,000 Annual Revenue	$10,000,000 Annual Profit	Percent Decline
One week	$1,900,000	$190,000	1.9%
Two weeks	$3,800,000	$380,000	3.8%
One month	$8,300,000	$830,000	8.3%
Two months	$16,600,000	$1,600,000	16.6%
Three months	$24,900,000	$2,490,000	24.9%

Source: Michael Erbschloe. *Information Warfare: How to Survive Cyber Attacks.* New York: McGraw-Hill, 2001.

"The short-term economic impact is what occurs over the first few weeks of sustained or random attacks. The long-term economic impact is the result of sustained attacks over weeks or months, or the aftermath of massive attacks that have ceased."[7] Logistical interruptions, lost contracts, or lost productivity in the workplace are all examples of short-term costs that may be attributed to a computer attack. Over a longer period of time, lost business and decreases in the valuation of stock or shareholder trust are examples of long-term economic impact.

To determine the full economic impact of an incident, organizations beyond the one directly targeted or affected by the computer incident may need to be considered. For instance, a ripple effect may occur as the result of an organization being "down" for a period of time; the costs to those organizations should be included as part of the overall impact as well. As an example, Table 9–3 provides the potential impact on revenue and profits for an organization influenced as part of a supply chain impaired by a computer attack.

---

7. Ibid., p. 51.

Tangible Versus Intangible Costs

In addition to costs broken up according to the period of time in which they occur, an organization normally incurs costs that fall into two distinct categories: tangible and intangible.

Tangible costs can be quantified in some way. These costs are normally easier to identify and associate a dollar figure with them. Examples of tangible costs follow:

- *Lost person-hours/productivity.* A specific dollar amount can normally be associated with the number of hours of production lost due to computer resources not being available. The cost may be determined in one of two ways. First, the hourly wages of the personnel directly affected by the down time may be used to compute the impact. (This assumes they were not able to do any other work during the down time.) Second, if the affected computer system had a direct income associated with it, the estimated or average income lost may be computed using the length of time during which the system was down.
- *Investigation and recovery efforts.* Some teams use the number of hours and salaries associated with those personnel directly involved in the investigation and recovery effort as part of the incident cost equation.
- *Loss of business.* If a direct loss of business can be associated with the computer incident, that figure should be used to determine the impact of the event. For example, if a contract was lost due to the computer incident, the amount of potential business lost should be accounted for.
- *Loss (or theft) of assets.* If hardware, software, or other tangible assets become lost or are stolen as part of the incident, the value of each item should be included in the cost figure. For example, the valuation of the stolen stock was used to determine the damages in the former Cisco employee case cited earlier in the chapter.

Intangible costs are normally more difficult to identify and quantify in terms of dollars. Examples of intangible costs follow:

- *Damage to corporate/organizational reputation.* Damage to an organization's reputation as the result of a computer incident can be very devastating and difficult to overcome. For example, if a financial institution becomes the victim of a computer crime, potential customers might lose faith in the ability of the company to protect their money and take their business to a competitor. If a retailer using the Internet as a source for sales becomes the victim of a computer incident in which credit card numbers are revealed, potential customers might not be confident enough to place orders on-line with that retailer. As a result, the retailer might lose potential business that cannot be easily measured. Similarly, if a hospital's computer systems are compromised and personal information on patients leaks to the press, some patients may avoid using that hospital in the future. The costs due to this loss of trust are normally recognized and felt by the organization, but it is very difficult to know how many would-be customers are diverted to a competitor as the result of the incident.

- *Loss of goodwill.* Goodwill is an item that is very difficult to define. It normally refers to the organization's standing within the business or other sector and the way the organization is supported and works based on the feelings of others. Other organizations may be reluctant to share information or connections with an organization that has experienced a computer incident. In this case, a loss of goodwill has occurred.
- *Psychological damages.* Those directly affected by the computer incident may feel victimized. This outcome may influence the overall morale of the organization and initiate fear in others.
- *Legal liability.* An organization that has experienced a computer incident may be open to legal liability claims. This liability may be tested in a civil or criminal case, depending on the nature of the incident, particularly if the prosecuting party can prove the organization did not secure its systems appropriately from the start.
- *Effect on shareholder value.* If a drop in the price of stock takes place immediately after an incident has been reported to the press, then that drop may be attributed to the incident and may be easier to measure. However, the effect may not be so quickly noticeable and will be more difficult to measure over the long term.

All too often, the intangible costs associated with an incident are ignored because it is too difficult to put a price tag on the damage or to prove a cause-and-effect relationship between the incident and the outcome. However, those challenged with determining the damage of an incident are encouraged to not omit these costs. Even if a price cannot be calculated, the costs should be noted in some way.

The categories and time frames presented in this section cover the major types of economic impact that should be considered when evaluating the cost of an incident. Labeling the costs appropriately as long-term, short-term, and immediate, or tangible and intangible, is not important. What *is* important is identifying all costs that result from a successful incident. The topics presented in this section should assist with this identification process. Typically, costs will be identified in multiple categories and not confined to only one area.

An Incident Cost Model

In an effort to develop an incident cost model for universities, the Committee on Institutional Cooperation (CIC) conducted the Incident Cost Analysis and Modeling Project (ICAMP) in the 1997–1998 time frame. Under the direction of Dr. Virginia Rezmierski from the University of Michigan, the study reviewed 30 computer incidents that had occurred at the participating university campuses. Each incident was studied in detail to help "develop a methodology for understanding the factors that influence the occurrence and costs of incidents in academic computing environments, and to provide a sense of the magnitude of overall loss to universities from particular information technology incidents."[8]

ICAMP is one of the most comprehensive studies done to date on calculating costs that result from computer incidents. The full study, which was released in 1998, may be obtained through the CIC at http://www.cic.uiuc.edu. A fee is charged for purchasing the report, but it is well worth the money for anyone wishing to delve deeper into this challenging task. This section presents some of the highlights of the survey, but the full report provides much greater detail, including a complete write-up on each incident used in the study.

---

8. CIC Security Working Group. *Incident Cost Analysis and Modeling Project, Final Report.* University of Michigan, 1998, p. 4.

Readers are strongly encouraged to obtain the complete report for further information.

The ICAMP researchers reviewed a total of 30 nonrandom computer-related incidents, including incidents attributed to hacker activity; theft of hardware, software, and/or information; infrastructure failures (i.e., due to loss of power or other physical processes); denial-of-service attacks; and nonmalicious data loss. Collectively, the 30 incidents involved a total of 210 employees at the various campuses who sought to investigate and resolve the events, accounting for a total of 9078 employee-hours. An estimated 270,805 computer and network users were affected as a result of these incidents, with a calculated overall cost of $1,015,810.

As a result of the survey, several factors were identified that seemed to affect the frequency of occurrence of the incidents in the university settings:

- Hacker communities: This study was focused on universities, which are particularly inviting to the hacker community.
- Openness of system(s): This factor has two aspects: (1) openness as it relates to the sharing of information and (2) the physical openness that allows systems to be easily accessed, which may include poor configurations.
- Training issues: This factor includes the training of personnel on handling and securing of resources, errors in operations management, and inadequate supervision.
- Policy issues: This factor refers to the lack of policies and standards that could have prevented some incidents from occurring. In these cases, the guidance for proper use of computer resources was missing.
- Physical security: Protection against theft of computer resources was inadequate.
- Hardware/software incompatibility: In some cases, incompatibility problems contributed directly to a loss.
- Hardware/software maintenance: This factor focuses on keeping the hardware and software at appropriate security levels.
- Lack of resources: This includes all types of resources—human, physical, and fiscal.

- Failure to comply with directions: In some cases, policies and guidelines were available, but were ignored and resulted in the incident.
- Appropriateness of level of security: The level of security present does not match the appropriate level of sensitivity for a resource, resulting in a loss.
- Appropriateness of use: When hardware or software is not used for its intended purpose, it may result in a vulnerability that permits an incident to occur.
- Faulty hardware and software: Sometimes the hardware or software does not work correctly or as intended (e.g., because of software bugs or system malfunctions).

Figure 9–1 and Table 9–4 provide a breakdown of how these factors were reflected in the 30 incidents studied. Note that some of these factors will vary for different industry segments. For example, the hacker community factor may not be as strong for the medical community. Likewise, some factors not listed here may be a consideration for other communities, such as organized crime and the financial community.

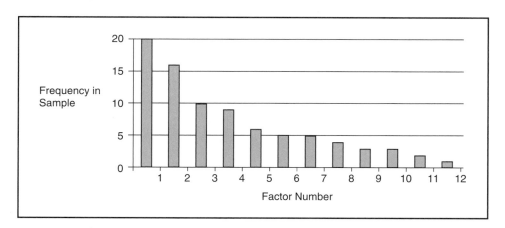

Figure 9-1   Frequency of Occurrence Factors in Incident Sample

Source: CIC Security Working Group. *Incident Cost Analysis and Modeling Project, Final Report.* University of Michigan, 1998.

Table 9-4   Factors with the Potential to Increase Incident Occurrence (as Noted in Figure 9-1)

1. Openness of system	7. Appropriate use
2. Community of hackers	8. Training
3. Lack of system maintenance	9. Faulty equipment
4. Level of security	10. Lack of resources
5. Directions followed	11. Policy
6. Physical security	12. Incompatibility

Source: CIC Security Working Group. *Incident Cost Analysis and Modeling Project, Final Report.* University of Michigan, 1998.

In addition to the frequency-of-occurrence factors, ICAMP noted several factors that have a potential for increasing the overall cost of an incident when it occurs:

- *Lack of knowledge.* This factor refers to knowledge required to handle, investigate, and manage an incident.
- *Capture versus closing holes.* This factor refers to the decision-making process to either close a hole once an incident has occurred or to leave the hole open and launch an investigation in an attempt to find the perpetrator.
- *No backup for reinstallation.* Usable backups to reinstall systems or documents may not be available because they are either nonexistent or too old and no longer valid.
- *Age of systems.* This consideration becomes a factor when the age of the system affects the overall cost of the incident recovery process.
- *Lack of resources.* These resources include human, physical, and fiscal resources.
- *Timing.* The time at which an incident happens can directly affect the cost due to variations in the number of potential users affected.

- *Loss of resources.* This factor includes the number of resources lost and the cost of replacing them, including data loss and the cost associated with reentry of those data.
- *Undocumented complex configurations.* Lack of documentation directly affects efforts to reestablish service.
- *Lack of continuity in staffing and responsibilities.* Costs of an incident are directly affected by rapid or uncoordinated personnel changes.
- *Age of incident relative to investigation.* The effort required to resolve an incident significantly increases when the investigation occurs well after the incident itself.
- *Level of personnel involved in investigation.* Personnel at higher levels (e.g., lawyers, media relations personnel, vice president) significantly increase the cost of the incident when they are involved with the investigation or recovery process.
- *Coordination of response from external organizations.* Involvement by external organizations increases the overall costs due to coordination efforts, time to resolve the incident, or needs for specific technical consultants.
- *Lack of monitoring and logging of information.* When machines are not logged, monitored, or analyzed for information, the time required to track needed data increases the overall costs.
- *Lack of coordination and duplication of effort.* This problem occurs when personnel duplicate or repeat specific tasks.
- *Software/hardware incompatibility.* Incompatibility in the hardware or software needed to resolve the incident typically lengthens the time required for incident response and increases the costs.

Figure 9–2 and Table 9–5 indicate how these factors tended to increase the overall costs of the incidents studied in the project. As noted with the occurrence factors, these variables may be different for other types of organizations.

ICAMP identified four main cost variables that contributed to the losses noted for universities: dollars, employee time, number of affected users, and unquantifiable costs. The unquantifiable or intangible costs were noted to possibly be more "expensive" in the long

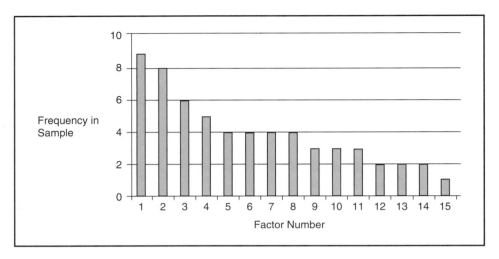

Figure 9-2   Factors Influencing the Costs of Incidents
Source: CIC Security Working Group. *Incident Cost Analysis and Modeling Project, Final Report.* University of Michigan, 1998.

Table 9-5   Factors with the Potential to Increase Incident Costs (as Noted in Figure 9-2)

1. Capture versus close	9. External response
2. Lack of knowledge	10. Age of incident
3. Coordination	11. Backup
4. Level of personnel	12. Age of systems
5. Loss of resources	13. Lack of resources
6. Complex configurations	14. Timing
7. Monitoring information	15. Continuity
8. Incompatibility	

Source: CIC Security Working Group. *Incident Cost Analysis and Modeling Project, Final Report.* University of Michigan, 1998.

term, through such areas as loss of prestige, user dissatisfaction, and lowered staff morale.

We will stop the discussion at this point to encourage the reader to obtain and review the full report. The personnel involved with the study did an excellent job of reviewing and breaking down the various cost factors. Although the report does not yield one equation that will work for every industry segment in computing the cost of incidents, it does reveal great insight into some of the many variables that should be considered when calculating the costs that may be attributed to an incident.

Summary

Answering the question of "How much did that incident cost?" is an extremely challenging task. Damage estimates will vary greatly from incident to incident. This chapter explored several aspects of costs associated with computer incidents and discussed one study performed for universities in detail. Although we cannot provide a single equation that will help to calculate the costs for all incidents, we have provided enough insight into areas of costs to make the task a little less challenging.

The most important thing is to identify all costs that result from the incident. This total will normally include the costs associated with identifying and recovering from an incident as well as any direct damages. Intangible costs, if known, should also be identified, even if the total loss associated with them cannot be quantified. As noted in the ICAMP report, some of these costs may prove more damaging in the long term, so they should not be overlooked.

We end this chapter with an interesting statistic from another study. The Omni Consulting Group conducted a survey of more than 3000 businesses worldwide, focusing on the economic impact of network intrusions and the ways in which security breaches happened. The conclusion of the survey was astounding: The network security breaches cost the businesses 5.57 percent of their annual gross revenue![9]

---

9. Savage, Marcia. "Network Breaches Hit the Bottom Line." *Plant IT,* February 12, 2001.

The Legal Eagles

The invention of the computer has had a major impact on our daily lives. It has brought many benefits to our way of living, but it has also led to negative consequences, such as computer crime. Just as it took time for people to develop safety features and establish laws for the negative consequences that accompanied the invention of the automobile, so it will require time for security safeguards and laws addressing the negative side effects of the computer to evolve. With this caveat in mind, enabling an incident response team to work with law enforcement can have very positive effects on the establishment of specific safeguards and case law.

The best approach to take when investigating any computer incident, particularly if it may involve a computer crime, is the three-expert approach. The three experts include a lawyer who is familiar with high-tech crimes and computer laws, a law enforcement agent, and a technical expert. Each has valuable knowledge and insight that can prove vital when taking a case to trial. This chapter explores the legal side of incident response and outlines considerations that should be addressed by the incident response team.

The comments and suggestions made in this chapter reflect the authors' experience in working with the legal community in various capacities over the years. We are neither lawyers nor law enforcement officials. Specific concerns or questions regarding computer crime laws should be addressed with the proper authority. The discussion presented here simply provides a high-level overview of considerations that apply when working with the legal community.

Working with the Legal Community

The Need for Legal Assistance

Law enforcement assistance may be required by the team if the organization decides to prosecute someone for committing a computer crime. When this occurs, issues such as evidence collection and preservation, the definition of a computer crime and interpretation of damage levels established in some laws, the ability to obtain a warrant to monitor activity, and much more will require the assistance of law enforcement.

More often than not, organizations choose to not report the suspected crime or incident, but rather deal with the issues that result directly from it. Even if the intent is to not prosecute, legal issues must be taken into consideration well ahead of time with respect to what can and cannot be done during an investigation. These considerations will normally be based on computer crime laws, privacy laws, industry regulations, and corporate policies. If the approach is not geared toward protecting the company's or organization's interest, problems will most likely be encountered at some later point if someone sues the company for wrongful dismissal, invasion of privacy, or some other issue. Therefore, it is in the best interest of the team and the organization to establish contacts with law enforcement and the legal community up front.

Protecting the organization's interest may also come into play with respect to civil litigation. The debate over holding organizations liable for not protecting their computer systems has been argued in many forums over the past few years. It is just a matter of time until a large company is held liable in a court of law for allowing its computer systems to be used as a jumping-off point for an attack on another organization. If the steps taken during an investigation have been carefully thought out and followed, then they may help to protect the organization from losing a large sum of money as the result of civil litigation.

Establishing Contacts

Some teams, such as those associated with government entities, are very fortunate in that they may have a dedicated law enforcement organization that can work side by side with the team. This approach offers many advantages in sharing techniques and information on new attacks and trends, as well as extending the reach of the team by opening up a new set of resources that may be used to respond to an incident. Of course, legal considerations must also be addressed as related to which privacy laws apply and what information can be shared. If considering the incorporation of law enforcement officials directly into the team, the first step would be to discuss these possibilities, concerns, and limitations with the appropriate legal organization.

If law enforcement officials cannot be directly included as part of the team, then contacts with local, state, and even federal officials should be established for when the need arises. Each level of law enforcement should be contacted during the early phases of establishing the team to determine the capabilities of each department and the specific requirements that it might have for handling computer crimes. The involvement of law enforcement in the team's planning phases can prove quite useful not only for establishing valuable points of contact, but also for identifying specific requirements and concerns that should be addressed when documenting incident-handling procedures.

Just as it is beneficial to include a law enforcement agent or official on the team, so a dedicated legal counsel trained in computer law should be considered if possible. "Every country, state, and company has its own regulations on employee privacy, and it seems that individual privacy concerns are getting more attention than ever before. Technical processes that may seem to be perfectly reasonable while responding to an incident may, in fact, be in violation of one or more local policies."[1] Having a dedicated legal counsel assigned to the team can help mitigate some of these concerns before further problems arise. In addition to addressing privacy concerns, sometimes guidance on the laws regarding computer crime may be quickly needed to help determine the best course of action to take in response to an incident. The team's lawyer can provide the "translation" needed for determining the best course of action. If a dedicated lawyer cannot be part of the team, then an avenue to some form of legal counsel should be identified, in which the lawyer is part of the overall organization or is contracted when needed.

The U.S. Department of Justice created the Computer and Telecommunications Coordinator (CTC) program in 1995 to address the overall increase in computer crime within the United States. The program has grown to include 137 attorneys, with each U.S. Attorney's Office (USAO) having at least one dedicated CTC. (More than 35 districts have two or more CTCs assigned.) The CTCs have four general areas of responsibility:[2]

- Prosecuting computer crime
- Serving as technical advisors for other prosecutors in the USAO.
- Serving as liaisons in the investigation and prosecution of computer crimes
- Provide training to other attorneys within the region

If the organization is having difficulty locating a legal counsel who is trained in prosecuting computer crime, the local CTC may be contacted as a point of reference.

Laws Pertaining to Computer Crime

Computer crimes have occurred for many years now, but they have not always been clearly identified as such in the courtroom. Many of the crimes have actually been prosecuted under other laws that did

---

1. Van Wyck, Kenneth, and Richard Forno. *Incident Response.* Sebastopol, CA: O'Reilly and Associates, 2001, p. 67.

2. Ibid.

not directly address computer crime. In fact, it wasn't until January 23, 1990, that the first person was convicted under the 1986 Computer Fraud and Abuse Act. That person was Robert T. Morris, Jr., the Cornell University graduate student responsible for releasing a worm on the Internet in late 1988. Initially, "he faced up to five years in jail, a $250,000 fine, and restitution for damages."[3] Morris was eventually sentenced to three years probation with a $91 charge assessed per month of the probation, fined $10,000, and ordered to serve 400 hours of community service.

Over the past decade, the laws used to prosecute computer criminals have been refined to bring the government regulations into the Information Age. The primary U.S. federal laws used to prosecute computer criminals are as follows (U.S.C. is an abbreviation for United States Code):

- 18 U.S.C. § 1029. Fraud and Related Activity in Connection with Access Devices
- 18 U.S.C. § 1030. Fraud and Related Activity in Connection with Computers
- 18 U.S.C. § 1362. Communication Lines, Stations, or Systems
- 18 U.S.C. § 2510 et seq.: Wire and Electronic Communications Interception or Oral Communications
- 18 U.S.C. § 2701 et seq.: Stored Wire and Electronic Communications and Transactional Records Access

Copies of the first three codes or laws (as they exist at the time of this writing) are provided in Appendix B. The Department of Justice Web site may be accessed to view the last two codes. (They were not included in Appendix B due to their length.)

In addition to these laws, several other codes are used to prosecute violations of intellectual property rights. The specific offenses and the corresponding laws used to prosecute people abusing these rights are listed in Table 10–1. The specific wording of each of these sections of code may be obtained from the Department of Justice Web site at http://www.cybercrime.gov.

---

3. Levine, Stacey. "U.S. Attorneys' Bulletin Computer and Telecommunications Coordinator (CTC) Program," www.cybercrime.gov.

Table 10-1   Laws Pertaining to Violations of Intellectual Property Rights

Category of Offense	Code	Specific Type of Offense Covered
Copyright offenses	17 U.S.C. 506	Criminal offenses
	18 U.S.C. 2319	Criminal infringement of a copyright
	18 U.S.C. 2318	Trafficking in counterfeit labels for phone records, copies of computer programs or computer program documentation or packaging, and copies of motion pictures or other audio visual works, and trafficking in computer program documentation or packaging
Copyright management offenses—Digital Millennium Copyright Act (DMCA)	17 U.S.C. 1201	Circumvention of copyright protection system
	17 U.S.C. 1202	Integrity of copyright management information
	17 U.S.C. 1203	Civil remedies
	17 U.S.C. 1204	Criminal offenses and penalties
	17 U.S.C. 1205	Savings clause
Bootlegging offenses	18 U.S.C. 2319A	Unauthorized fixation of and trafficking in sound recordings and music videos of live musical performances
Trademark offenses	18 U.S.C. 2320	Trafficking in counterfeit goods or services
Trade secret offenses	18 U.S.C. 1831	Economic espionage
	18 U.S.C. 1832	Theft of trade secrets
	18 U.S.C. 1833	Exceptions to prohibitions

Table 10-1 *(continued)*

Category of Offense	Code	Specific Type of Offense Covered
	18 U.S.C. 1834	Criminal forfeiture
	18 U.S.C. 1835	Orders to preserve confidentiality
	18 U.S.C. 1836	Civil proceedings to enjoin violations
	18 U.S.C. 1837	Applicability to conduct outside the United States
	18 U.S.C. 1838	Construction with other laws
	18 U.S.C. 1839	Definitions
Offenses relating to the integrity of IP systems	17 U.S.C. 506(c-d)	Criminal offenses
	17 U.S.C. 506(e)	Criminal offenses
	18 U.S.C. 497	Letters patent
	35 U.S.C. 292	False marking
Offenses relating to the misuse of dissemination systems	18 U.S.C. 1341	Frauds and swindles
	18 U.S.C. 1343	Fraud by wire, radio, or television
	18 U.S.C. 2512	Manufacture, distribution, possession, and advertising of wire, oral, or electronic communication intercepting devices prohibited
	47 U.S.C. 553	Unauthorized reception of cable service
	47 U.S.C. 605	Unauthorized publication or use of communications

In addition to the federal statutes, every state has formulated laws relating to computer offenses that may be used to prosecute computer crimes. State resources should be contacted to determine which laws pertain to events that occur within state boundaries. In some cases, local regulations may also need to be considered. For example, college students who violate campus regulations may be subject to administrative actions. Research on the set of laws and regulations that apply most often to the team's constituency should be done to identify specific legal concerns as they relate to the incident response process. If a legal counsel is available to the team, this research and preparation should be completed by him or her. Once identified, team members should be trained on any issues of concern of which they should be aware when determining the course of action to follow in responding to an incident.

In addition to the criminal law, a team must be prepared to address numerous regulations. The exact regulations depend on the organization's or company's industry and the type of information processed on the systems. For example, privacy regulations must be addressed by a multitude of organizations that maintain personal information. Those dealing with the health care industry must be prepared to follow the rules established by the Healthcare Information Portability and Accountability Act (HIPAA), whereas the financial community must address regulations levied by the Gramm-Leach-Bliley Act (GLB).

Needed—Case Law

For years, the hacker community has been known to share information on new exploits, work together to find new vulnerabilities, and share attack scripts. In contrast, the security community (the "white hats") has been very guarded about sharing information. As a result, the attackers have, in many cases, had the upper hand. Only recently has the security community as a whole banded together to address security concerns and increase the sharing of information. This teamwork and sharing of information cannot stop with just the "techie" community, but must include the legal community if we are to succeed in winning the war on computer crime. By joining forces, the computer security community can make a difference and help stem the tide of computer crime through the establishment of case law and stronger legislation.

Too many computer crimes have either gone unnoticed or not made their way into the courtroom. For case law to be established, the perpetrator and the case against that person must make it all the way into the courtroom. Plea bargaining prior to trial does not help to establish case law. Only when a significant number of sentences are administered will the needed deterrence to hacking activity truly be provided. That deterrence is the creation of case law.

Progress in this endeavor is beginning to be made. The Department of Justice Web site provides a sample listing of computer cases prosecuted over recent years. Although these cases do not represent a completely exhaustive list, they do provide some insight into the progresses being made with respect to computer crime as well as information on multiple cases prosecuted.

Reporting Computer Crime

Suspected computer crime should be reported to the appropriate law enforcement entity. Depending on the scope of the crime, the report may be made to authorities at the local, state, federal, or even international level. Typically it is best to start at the lowest level, unless the need for higher involvement is readily apparent. Pre-coordination efforts with law enforcement will help to identify at which level reporting should be initiated.

"Some federal law enforcement agencies that investigate domestic crime on the Internet include: the Federal Bureau of Investigation (FBI), the United States Secret Service, the United States Customs Service, the United States Postal Inspection Service, and the Bureau of Alcohol, Tobacco and Firearms (ATF). Each of these agencies has offices conveniently located in every state to which crimes may be reported. Contact information regarding these local offices may be found in local telephone directories."[4]

---

4. "Computer Crime Guidance," http://www.cybercrime.gov.

Normally, the FBI will have primary jurisdiction for investigating violations of federal laws, while the other agencies focus on particular types of crime. For example, if a case of suspected child pornography is being investigated and the offending material appears to have been imported, the U.S. Customs Service may become involved in the investigation or receive the initial report. In cases of fraud that involve media being sent via the U.S. postal system, the U.S. Postal Service may be contacted to report the activity. For cases of Internet fraud in general, the FBI, U.S. Secret Service, Federal Trade Commission, or Securities and Exchange Commission may be involved. Table 10–2 summarizes the types of crimes investigated by the various federal agencies. Most reporting of these crimes should be done through local offices, whenever possible. The U.S. Department of Justice Web site provides links to most of these agencies' Web sites for more information.

In addition to agencies at the federal level, many state and local entities are involved with investigating and prosecuting computer crimes. "The National Association of Attorneys General (NAAG) has compiled a list of prosecutors and investigators from state and local law enforcement agencies who are responsible for the investigation and prosecution of computer and computer-related crime within their respective jurisdictions."[5] For more information on these resources, contact the NAAG Web site at http://www.naag.org/.

The incident response team may be directly involved in the investigation of the computer crime prior to even realizing this fact. Once the event is reported, the law enforcement official cannot ask for further details or request specific searches be made without due authorization. Therefore, as much information as possible should be provided with the initial report to the law enforcement entity. It may include audit logs, notes of steps taken or observations made during the course of an incident response, queries ran on databases, pictures taken of the computer system and its surroundings, and more. Extreme care must be taken, however, to not taint any evidence in the process of trying to help the investigation. If any doubts arise as to the action being contemplated, erring on the side of caution is the

---

5. "How to Report Internet-Related Crime," http://www.cybercrime.gov.

Table 10-2 Types of Crimes Investigated by U.S. Federal Agencies

Federal Investigative Law Enforcement Agency	Types of Crime Investigated
Federal Bureau of Investigation (FBI)	• Computer intrusion
	• Password trafficking
	• Copyright (software, movies, sound, recording) piracy
	• Theft of trade secrets
	• Trademark counterfeiting
	• Counterfeiting of currency
	• Child pornography or exploitation
	• Internet fraud
	• Internet harassment
	• Internet bomb threat
	• Trafficking in explosive or incendiary devices or firearms over the Internet
U.S. Secret Service	• Computer intrusion
	• Password trafficking
	• Counterfeiting of currency
	• Internet fraud
U.S. Customs Service	• Copyright (software, movies, sound, recording) piracy—if imported
	• Trademark counterfeiting—if imported
U.S. Postal Inspection Service	• Child exploitation and Internet fraud matters that have a mail nexus

(continued)

Table 10-2 *(continued)*

Federal Investigative Law Enforcement Agency	Types of Crime Investigated
Federal Trade Commission	• Internet fraud
Securities and Exchange Commission	• Internet fraud—if it is a securities fraud
Bureau of Alcohol, Tobacco, and Firearms (ATF)	• Internet bomb threat
	• Trafficking in explosive or incendiary devices or firearms over the Internet

Source: http://www.cybercrime.gov/reporting.html.

best route. Additionally, team members should not try to take on the role of the law enforcement official. Those steps should be left to the appropriate authorities. Instead, response team members should perform only those tasks that would normally be undertaken during an incident response or during the normal course of protecting one's network.

One major complaint routinely expressed about reporting incidents to law enforcement is the period of time that any equipment provided may be kept. Tremendous improvements to shorten the time required to hold such equipment have been made in the recent past, but there is no guaranteed turnaround time. With this point in mind, installation of replacement equipment or hard drives should be implemented as quickly as possible to permit operations to continue. The business should not be placed on hold pending further investigation.

Another major concern expressed regarding reporting to law enforcement is the fear of information disclosure, particularly to the press. As stated in Chapter 5, once information about an incident is disclosed, the team's control over it is effectively lost. Of course, law enforcement officials will not stay employed for long if they lose the trust of those they are trying to serve. Leaks to the press do not routinely come from law enforcement personnel, but rather are typically attributed to other sources, such as company employees discussing matters in an open restaurant while others listen to the conversation. Most officials share the concern for the sensitivity of the information reported and can help to address any fears of reporting directly with the company.

Most organizations will not report all incidents that may have involved a computer crime. Upper management should be consulted up front to determine when law enforcement officials will be contacted and who should initiate the contact. For example, some organizations will report only crimes they are legally required to report, such as child pornography. Others may choose to report specific types of activity, such as child pornography, possible credit card theft, gambling, and copyright infringement. The type of activity to be reported and the possible side effects that may result (e.g., loss of equipment, information leaks to the press) from that report, should be thoroughly discussed up front when procedures are written. It is far better to plan for the crisis than react to it.

Summary

Law enforcement assistance may be required by the team if the organization decides to prosecute someone for committing a computer crime. When this occurs, issues such as evidence collection and preservation, the definition of a computer crime and interpretation of damage levels established in some laws, the ability to obtain a warrant to monitor activity, and much more will require the assistance of law enforcement. More often than not, organizations choose to not report the suspected crime or incident, but deal with the issues that result directly from it. Even if the intent is to not prosecute, legal issues must be taken into consideration well ahead of time with respect to what can and cannot be done during an investigation. The legal community can provide a great deal of insight into the best approach to computer incidents so that the organization's interest remain protected. Contacts with law enforcement officials at various levels and lawyers skilled in dealing with computer crimes can provide a great deal of guidance in determining the approach that should be followed for various types of incidents. These contacts will also prove extremely valuable when the need to report a crime arises.

The best route to take when responding to a successful computer incident utilizes a three-expert approach. The three experts include a technical resource, a law enforcement official, and a lawyer trained in dealing with high-tech crimes. Each of these individuals has a valuable role to play, and their combined knowledge can lead to the implementation of a better response plan.

A variety of laws and regulations are used to prosecute computer crimes and other offenses. These laws may be found at the local, state, and federal levels. The incident response team should have legal counsel available to help interpret these laws as needed in the course of responding to attacks. Without such guidance, problems can be further complicated by the response invoked.

Efforts such as those described in this chapter are beginning to make a difference. Teamwork between the three points of the response triangle (i.e., technical experts, lawyers, and law enforcement) should yield further improvements and help to stem the tide of computer crime. The establishment of case law is extremely important for providing a deterrent to much of the activity that the incident response team will address. By working together, the technical and legal communities can and will make a difference.

Computer Forensics: An Evolving Discipline

The computer security discipline has many subspecialties or areas of focus. One such subdiscipline that has emerged in recent years is that of computer forensics. Computer forensics combines the art of forensics with the discipline of computer security to address crimes committed using the medium of a computer. The due diligence given to investigating any crime using forensics techniques applies equally well to the world of computer forensics. This chapter begins by taking a look at forensics in general, then addresses specific considerations that must be taken into account when dealing with the computer crime scene. The methodologies and considerations addressed may, in turn, be used to identify specific forensics policies and procedures, or the need to outsource the function entirely.

The World of Forensics

What Is Forensics?

Forensics refers to the application of scientific methods to legal proceedings. Although these methods are normally applied to criminal cases, they may be used for civil cases as well. Forensics includes a combination of reasoning, investigative skills, and common sense, which are used to identify and explain any clues that may be present as the result of a crime. The forensics expert must be able to "think rationally and make distinctions among many variables in order to interpret the meaning of clues at a crime scene."[1] Various forms of reasoning may be used throughout the investigation, including induction, deduction, and reduction. The final result is a theory that defines the *who, what, when, why,* and *how* elements of the crime. The theory must be substantiated and thoroughly supported to withstand cross examination or testing by others, normally through the course of a trial in a court of law.

Science can be described simply as the "knowledge gained from careful observation and measurement, based on deduction from physical laws and proven with experimentation. The aim is to approach the facts with a method that can be replicated by peers, which often means to take something into a laboratory to control conditions."[2] "Science is not necessarily about certainty. The goal is to devise a hypothesis that best fits the full array of facts, without crunching the facts to fit a theory."[3]

'Scientific' has come to mean being grounded in the methods and procedures of science, and 'knowledge' must be stronger than subjective belief or speculation. . . . The judge has only to focus on the methodology, not on the conclusion, and must determine:

- Whether the theory can be tested
- Whether the potential error rate is known
- Whether it was reviewed by peers and has attracted widespread acceptance within relevant scientific community
- Whether the issue is relevant to the issue in dispute
- Whether there are standards that control the technique's operation"[4]

---

1. Ramsland, Katherine. *The Forensics Science of C.S.I.* New York: Berkley Publishing Group, 2001, pp. 128–129.

2. Ibid., p. 124.

3. Ibid., pp. 124–125.

4. Ibid., pp. xiii–xiv.

Given the observation, measurement, testing, and theory concepts of forensics, it can indeed be described as a form of science.

Katherine Ramsland presents an interesting overview of the forensics discipline by using examples from the television show *Crime Scene Investigator* in her book *The Forensics Science of C.S.I.* Several points from her book are used throughout this section to present an overview of forensics. Regardless of whether the forensics investigator is viewed as a scientist or a technician, according to Ramsland the forensics investigator "works according to Einstein's three rules:

- Out of clutter, find simplicity.
- From discord, make harmony.
- In the middle of difficulty, find opportunity."[5]

She further points out that "intuition without science is blind; science without intuition is stagnant."[6]

The Forensics Investigation

Before any investigation can take place, "the investigator must decide whether a search warrant is needed. If a search or seizure of evidence is made without protecting the rights of the people involved, then the evidence can be thrown out of court—along with anything deduced from the evidence."[7]

"If the person who controls the property offers permission to search, then the search is legal. If not, a warrant must be obtained from a judge. To get a warrant from a judge, investigators must prepare an affidavit that details exactly what they are looking for, where they need to search, and why they think the item(s) are in that location. In other words, they must supply probable cause. A 'no-knock' warrant is issued only if there is compelling reason to suppose that the evidence may be destroyed if any warning is given or that the

5. Ibid., p. 81.

6. Ibid., p. 124.

7. Ibid., p. 7.

officer may be in danger. Any search must be confined to the location and items listed on the warrant. In the case of an obvious crime, searchers may look for all evidence associated with the crime. If they want to return to a scene, they need to post an officer there to indicate that the search based on that warrant is still in progress, or else get a new warrant."[8]

Of course, in the case of some corporations and agencies, the organization owns the computer system and the data residing upon it, so some of the legal technicalities mentioned above may not apply.

The center of any forensics work is the crime scene or location where the illegal act took place. The crime scene is normally "analyzed through a combination of steps involving both criminology and criminalistics. Criminalistics refers to the application of science to any physical evidence. Criminology includes the psychological angle, which involves studying the crime scene for motives, traits, and behavior that will help to interpret the evidence."[9] Profiling represents one aspect of criminology and is a subspecialty of the broader discipline of forensics psychology. It may be performed or practiced by psychiatrists, psychologists, neuropsychologists, or social workers.

The primary focus or concern for a crime scene is the preservation of evidence. How the evidence is preserved and handled depends on the type of evidence that exists and the type of crime that has been committed. "Investigators must assume that whoever was at the scene has left something there or taken something away, and probably both."[10] The most difficult aspect of any crime scene is defining its boundaries. In some cases, boundaries are marked by yellow tape, indicating the lines that should not be crossed by people other than those authorized or involved in the investigation (i.e., it keeps onlookers out). In addition to the crime scene itself, another area may be marked off "for taking breaks, storing equipment, and briefing the various personnel who come in. Sometimes a mobile crime lab is set up there for quick processing of certain types of evidence."[11]

---

8. Ibid., p. 8.

9. Ibid., pp. 1–2.

10. Ibid., p. 3.

11. Ibid., p. 7.

"The first twenty-four-hour period after a crime is considered the most crucial because the evidence is relatively undisturbed and witnesses have better memories."[12] Once the boundaries of the crime scene have been determined, the investigator will normally take notes about the scene reflecting what is found or any details that may help to piece together the events. The crime scene is also usually photographed before any evidence is moved or collected. The photographs are an important part of the documentation, depicting how the scene was left. After the photographs and notes have been taken, then the actual search for evidence can begin. A plan of operation is typically formed to determine the order in which the search should proceed so as to minimize potential contamination of evidence.

Evidence handling is a primary concern for the forensics expert, as every step taken in the course of an investigation can be questioned in a court of law. The jury must be confident that the evidence presented did, in fact, come from the crime scene and has not been tampered with by anyone (or anything) since it was secured or seized. "Courts are notoriously conservative, but it's also true that many 'experts' hawk their theories as 'scientific,' and judges don't have time to thoroughly examine each and every one. Claiming expertise does not make one an expert in the eyes of the law, and just because some technique of collections or analysis is 'scientific' does not make it automatically admissible."[13]

"There are two types of evidence: testimonial and physical. Testimonial comes from anyone who was near the scene and saw something. . . . Physical evidence is grouped into one of five categories:

- Temporary (may change or be lost)
- Conditional (associated with specific conditions at the crime scene)
- Associative (links a suspect or a victim to a scene)
- Pattern (blood, impressions, tire treads, residue or evidence of the modus operandi)
- Trace/transfer (produced by physical contact with some surface)"[14]

---

12. Ibid., p. 7.
13. Ibid., p. xii.
14. Ibid., pp. 8–9.

The "evidence collected at the scene may serve several purposes:

- Prove that a crime has been committed
- Indicate key aspects of the crime
- Establish the identity of the victim or suspect, or determine what kind of investigation must be done to identify them and see how they interacted
- Corroborate (or not) any testimony given by witnesses
- Help exonerate a suspect who is innocent
- Provide leads for further investigation
- Pressure suspects into giving confessions"[15]

"Initial collection and preservation of evidence, as well as the chain of custody, will be scrutinized by defense lawyers for weaknesses. Proper protocol must be followed to the letter. Chain of custody means that each person who handles the evidence signs off on it, records what is done with it on what dates, and replaces it in its secure storage location. The evidence that is submitted to court must be the same evidence that was collected and the district attorney must be able to prove this."[16]

To help identify and prove the guilt of the perpetrator, pieces of evidence need to be individualized. That is, the evidence needs to be directly linked to the individual. For example, fingerprints are a type of evidence that can be clearly linked to an individual. In contrast, evidence that may be linked to more than one person (e.g., shoeprints, fibers from clothing) is referred to as "class evidence," which means the item can be grouped with a class of items like it. Class evidence is not as strong in a court of law as individual evidence.

Once the evidence has been collected, it must be examined and tested to develop the theory of what took place. The investigator must take care to keep an open mind when piecing the forensics puzzle together, as experience may cloud judgment or cause the investigator to pursue the wrong path. For example, previous cases that may seem similar in nature cannot be assumed to be a repeat of the same crime

---

15. Ibid., p. 11.
16. Ibid., p. 26.

or perpetrated by the same person. Every crime scene is unique in some way and must be approached as such.

This section has presented a high-level overview of forensics in general. Although many of the issues discussed will apply equally well to computer forensics, some aspects are more difficult to define or identify when dealing with the "computer crime scene." With this caveat in mind, we will move into the subdiscipline of computer forensics.

Overview and Importance of Computer Forensics

Computer forensics can be defined as the process of extracting information from a computer crime scene and guaranteeing its accuracy and reliability. Typically, the information is extracted from computer media, such as hard drives, Zip drives, and other storage devices. It may also include other sources of evidence, such as photographs of the physical system components or the connections among devices, and surveillance videotapes of someone accessing the system.

The computer forensics expert must be able to prove, beyond "any shadow of a doubt," that the information extracted is exactly as it was on the computer once the investigation began. Elements such as time stamps, file names, file contents, audit log entries, and more must not have been modified or changed in any way. Furthermore, the chain of custody of that evidence, once obtained, must also be protected so that no one other than the forensics expert(s) or other designated personnel have had access to the evidence to modify it. If any of these aspects cannot be guaranteed, then the strength of the evidence is significantly reduced and the likelihood of success in a court of law is diminished.

Computer Forensics Challenges

Several challenges exist with respect to computer forensics. One of the biggest is the overall need for a paradigm shift in responding to computer incidents. It is human nature to want to identify what caused a problem and fix it so that operations may be quickly restored. All too often, system administrators rush to identify how an attack occurred and to rebuild the system, destroying evidence in the process. This helpful, quick response must be balanced with the realization that a computer can, in fact, be a crime scene. As such, it cannot be touched until the proper steps have been taken to preserve any evidence that may be present.

Potential damage to evidence can also be attributed to end users. If a computer system is not blocked off, just as yellow tape is normally placed around other crime scenes, then the computer system may be accessed by personnel who are either curious to see what has happened or who may not know about the potential existence of evidence. Even the simple act of turning the system on can corrupt evidence. Therefore, when a computer crime is suspected, steps must be taken quickly to block physical access to the system so that the evidence may be preserved. (Note that, although the term "computer crime" is used frequently in this chapter, the same steps and safeguards can apply to instances when evidence is needed to support human resources requirements or for civil litigation.)

Another major obstacle for computer forensics is overcoming the hesitation to report computer crimes. Reporting computer crimes to law enforcement can help with the establishment of case law, as discussed in detail in Chapter 10. As a follow-up to that discussion, note that there are many reasons why organizations might choose not to report suspected crimes:

- *Misunderstanding of the scope of the problem.* Organizations do not realize that a crime has been committed and therefore do not report the activity.
- *Belief that these sorts of things don't happen to other organizations.* Some in management may believe that they are dealing with an isolated case and that similar activity does not happen to other organizations. This feeling of isolation can lead to frustration and a feeling of embarrassment that deters reporting the activity.
- *Fear of damage to company integrity due to media reports.* Fear of bad publicity is a major reason why organizations do not report computer crime. Many considerations play into this factor, such as fears that the stock value will decline, that customers (both existing and potential) will be lost, and that the organization's brand

image may suffer. In fact, many organizations in recent years have been able to receive positive responses by reporting the crimes. An organization can highlight its proactive reporting and handling of the incident to put a positive spin on any media reports. Of course, reports to media are inappropriate until after the case has been resolved.

- *Desire to handle things internally.* Some organizations simply prefer to handle matters internally and do not permit any potential delay to the restoration of operations by getting law enforcement agencies or other forensics resources involved. There may also be a fear that if external resources are contacted for forensics support, the hardware and software involved may be taken for a long period of time, affecting operations even further. (This delay was a major problem with some well-known, early computer crime cases investigated.) Organizations need to remember that system administrators are not forensics experts or specialists, unless they have had specialized training or experience!

- *Lack of awareness of the attack.* Unfortunately, some computer crimes go unreported simply because the organization is unaware that they have taken place. Without proactive measures to detect and respond to unauthorized activity, it is often difficult to properly identify crimes even when they are committed.

The final challenge for computer forensics comes in the actual courtroom. Members of a jury or even judges may not have a computer background or enough expertise to interpret audit log files or other forms of evidence that may be presented. Therefore, the evidence must be simplified to the greatest extent possible and clearly explained to convey its importance. All too often, defense attorneys are able to create "doubt" in the preservation of the evidence and the interpretation of it. For these reasons, the chain of custody and processing of the evidence are even more crucial.

Computer Evidence

Several key factors should be remembered with respect to the discipline of computer forensics. For instance, computer evidence is fragile and can easily be modified. A sound methodology for taking a "snapshot of the crime scene" must be adhered to at all times during an investigation. Some very good forensics programs can make the evidence collection process easier. The evidence may be hidden, deleted, or camouflaged in some way, so the technical investigator must have a firm understanding of the various storage mediums to uncover it. Warren G. Kruse and Jay G. Heiser present an excellent overview and in-depth guidance on how to preserve evidence in *Computer Forensics Incident Response Essentials*. Those wishing to delve deeper into the world of computer forensics are encouraged to read this book.

Any person investigating a computer crime must have a firm grasp of the storage media to be examined. Bill Betts wrote an outstanding article on computer forensics, published in *Information Security* magazine in March 2000. The text of the Storage Overview sidebar was included with that article and offers an overview of computer storage media.

The importance of documentation when investigating a computer crime cannot be emphasized strongly enough. Whether you are a system administrator, incident response team member, law enforcement agent, or some other entity involved in an investigation, the steps taken and notes made throughout the investigation can serve as the "missing link" needed to solve the crime. Every incident should be approached from the start as if it will go to trial. This view will help to preserve evidence that might otherwise be lost early in a case. No matter how minuscule an action may seem, it should be noted for recollection later. Typically, the case will not go to trial for a long period of time (months or even years); without the assistance of notes, it will be difficult to recall some steps that were taken or evidence that was noted. Care should be taken with the physical notes as they themselves can become evidence for a court. Specifically, the notes should be protected as any other piece of evidence to prevent tampering with them.

Documentation through photographs can be equally important for a computer crime. As noted earlier in this chapter, crime scenes are normally photographed before any evidence is collected or moved. Likewise, a computer system should be photographed from all angles to note the connections and any physical evidence that may be present. These photographs can play a valuable role in testing derived theories in court, as well as reassembling the system in a secure location when it is moved.

Storage Overview

Storage Media Primer

Before conducting a computer forensics investigation, you must have a good grasp of the media you'll be examining.

Magnetic/Hard/Physical Disk: This is the primary computer storage device. Like tape, it is magnetically recorded and can be re-recorded over and over. Disks are rotating platters with a mechanical arm that moves a read/write head between the outer and inner edges of the platter's surface. Finding a location can take between 1 millisecond (on an ultra-fast hard disk) and 1 second (on a floppy disk).

Tracks: The disk surface is divided into concentric tracks (circles within circles). The thinner the tracks, the more storage. The smaller the spot, the more bits per inch, and the greater the storage. Most disks hold the same number of bits on each track, even though the outer tracks are physically longer than the inner ones. Some disks pack the bits as tightly as possible within each track.

Sectors: Tracks are further divided into sectors, which hold the least amount of data that can be read or written at one time (e.g., READ TRACK 7 SECTOR 24). To update the disk, one or more sectors are read into the computer, changed, and written back to the disk. The operating system figures out how to fit data into these fixed spaces.

Cluster: Also called an allocation unit, a cluster is some number of disk sectors that are treated as a unit. This is the smallest unit of storage the operating system can manage. For example, on a PC with a 200MB hard disk, the smallest cluster is 8 sectors (8×512 bytes) or 4KB. On a 2GB disk, the cluster is 32KB. That means a 1KB file takes up 32KB on the disk, wasting an inordinate amount of space. In mid-1996, Windows 95 installed on new PCs introduced a 32-bit file allocation table (FAT32), which decreased the cluster size to 4KB.

File Slack: This refers to the space available from the end of the file to the end of the cluster. If the cluster size is 512 bytes, and the file size is 101 bytes, then the unallocated space in that cluster is 411 bytes.

Free or Unallocated Space: This is the available space on computer storage media, such as a hard drive or floppy drive. This space may be available after files were erased or deleted. These areas can reveal lots of forensics evidence.

Hash: An MD5 hash is a 128-bit number that uniquely describes the contents of a file. MD5 hashes are used to verify that the contents of the original file and the bitstream backup are the same. If the hash values of two files match, the file contents match as well.

BIOS: BIOS is the Basic Input/Output System of a PC. It refers to the number of machine code routines that are stored in the ROM and available for execution at boot time.

Boot Sector: This is the very first sector of a physical disk. It contains machine code to enable the computer to find the partition table and the operating system.

Cyclical Redundancy Check (CRC): CRC is used to verify the integrity of a block of data. Most hard drives store one CRC for every sector (512 bytes). A CRC is order-sensitive, so "1234" and "4321" will not produce the same CRC. When a "read error" message is generated from a disk, it means that the CRC value in the suspect hard drive does not match the value that is recomputed by the drive after the sector is read.

File Allocation Table (FAT): The FAT is an array of numbers that sits near the beginning of a DOS volume. Depending on the size of the volume, these numbers can be 1.5 bytes (12 bits), 2 bytes (16 bits), or 4 bytes (32 bits) long. This is why volumes are referred to as FAT12, FAT16, or FAT32. FAT identifies whether a cluster is free, bad, or the last cluster in a file.

File Signature: Many, but not all, file types contain a few bytes at the beginning that constitute a unique signature of the file. Most graphical and document file types contain this signature. For example, the first 6 bytes at the beginning of a .gif file are either GIF89A or GIF87A. This allows forensics software to sense the true type of a file, regardless of the file extension.

Logical Volume: A logical volume is a concept, not a physical device. As hard disks have grown in size, it's become convenient to partition the physical drive into a series of logical volumes. Up to 24 logical volumes can exist on a hard drive and show up as drive "C," "D," "E," etc. . . . up to "Z."

RAM (Random Access Memory): Each computer has a certain amount of volatile read/write memory. This memory is lost when the power is turned off. The operating system, programs, and drivers are all loaded into RAM at the same time.

ROM (Read-Only Memory): These memory chips contain a permanent program that is burned in the factory and maintained when the power is turned off. The information on these chips can only be read, not written to. These chips usually exist on the motherboard, and contain small programs that the computer needs to boot.

Source: Adapted from Bill Betts. "Crime Seen." *Information Security*, March 2000.

Methodologies

If you are an IT person, the steps you take in responding to a computer incident may make the difference for prosecution. The technologies used and procedures followed early in an investigation may determine how successful an organization is in identifying and prosecuting the attacker, whether an insider or an external source. Organizations that proactively implement and maintain security processes have a better chance of catching an attacker and limiting the potential damage. This section outlines some specific methodologies that may be applied to investigate a suspected incident or computer crime.

The basic tactic that should be followed can be summarized as "the three A's:

1. Acquire the evidence without altering or damaging the original.
2. Authenticate that your recovered evidence is the same as the originally seized data.
3. Analyze the data without modifying it."[17]

The first and most important consideration before initiating any investigation is to ensure that you have the proper approval needed to proceed. Without the proper authority, the person wishing to investigate the incident or possible crime may end up in as much trouble as the attacker. The appropriate personnel (e.g., human resources, legal) and law enforcement (if necessary) should be notified as soon as possible. In some cases, the fact that a computer crime has been committed may not be readily apparent. Some investigation may be warranted by authorized internal personnel before notifying law enforcement. When notification to law enforcement is mandated, the lowest appropriate level should be contacted first. For example, if the alleged crime has been conducted on a university's computer systems, campus police may be contacted first. If the crime appears to include child pornography within state boundaries, then the state police might be notified. If the alleged crime involves a financial institution, then federal authorities should be contacted. Regardless of the level of law enforcement contacted, if the investigation needs to go to a higher authority or a different agency, the law enforcement agency involved will normally contact the appropriate source and hand over the case.

When an investigation is initiated or circumstances are being closely evaluated, this activity should not be advertised. Only those personnel with a valid "need to know" should be made aware of the activity. Advertising or discussing the investigation too much could tip off the attacker, particularly if the person is inside the organization.

Once the appropriate approvals have been received (preferably in writing), then the investigative steps may be started. Typically a com-

---

17. Kruse, Warren G. II, and Jay G. Heiser. *Computer Forensics: Incident Response Essentials.* Boston: Addison-Wesley, 2002, p. 3.

puter system (if running) will be shut down first,[18] then moved to a safe location for further examination. Pictures should be taken of the computer system before it is dismantled or moved. All connections to the computer should be photographed so that the system can be put back together in exactly the same manner. All steps taken should be documented as well as any changes made to configuration settings. The notes should reflect the time and date of the actions taken, and they should be kept in a safe place where they can be readily found but not tampered with by anyone else.

Care should be taken when shutting down the computer. Attackers have been known to rig a system so that files are altered or destroyed if a safe shutdown is attempted. Simply pulling the plug is often the best method of shutdown for PCs, although this method can result in the loss of some random access memory (RAM). Pulling the plug on larger corporate systems can actually be more dangerous, as Redundant Array of Inexpensive Disks (RAID) drives that have been running for some time may not recover. (RAID drives are used in networking and mission-critical applications. RAID is a method of using several hard disk drives in an array to provide fault tolerance should one fail.[19])

Once the computer has been shut down and moved to a safe location (with limited physical access) for further investigation, the system should be reconnected as it was originally found and started from an appropriate known-good boot diskette or CD. The suspect hard drive should *not* be used for restarting the computer to avoid possible contamination of the evidence. In fact, the hard drive may need to be removed from the system prior to restarting it.

At least two backups of the suspect hard drive should be made to help preserve the evidence. Some very good computer forensics software programs are available that may be used to make the bitstream backups. (Some of these programs were mentioned in Chapter 7.) One backup may be evaluated for evidence, while the other can be

---

18. There are significant differences of opinion on if, and how, a system is to be shut down; all have merit. If a system is shut down, forensic information contained in memory are erased. Also, shutting down a system "gracefully" changes the disk contents and may trigger more programs to run, possibly destroying information in which you may be interested. Some security experts recommend simply "pulling the plug" on the system to begin this phase of forensic analysis. We won't belabor this technical quandary further in this book.

19. Dyson, Peter. *Novell's Dictionary of Networking.* San Jose: Sybex, 1994, p. 235.

preserved for a trial. All evidence, including backup tapes, should be sealed and stored in a controlled location with limited access. The fewer people with access to the storage medium, the better. As was described in the forensics overview section, proper protocol must be followed to the letter when obtaining and preserving any evidence. The chain of custody must be documented, identifying each person who has handled the evidence, what was done with it on what dates, and when it was replaced in its secure storage location. This documentation is vital to proving in court that the evidence submitted is the same evidence that was collected and that it has not been tampered with in any way, even to preserve the original media when possible.

Once the backups are made, the search may begin for evidence. If found, it should be documented for presenting in court, if needed. In addition to making the backups, forensics software can be used to ease and expedite the investigation process. Specifically, the software can be used for the following purposes:[20]

- Analyze free space on the media for signatures that may indicate the presence of data
- Examine slack areas of files for hidden or deleted data
- Analyze swap files
- Locate deleted files
- Run a hash of the suspect hard drive and backup tape to prove the reliability of the evidence
- Document the system date and time
- Use keyword searches to look for suspect data
- Locate and search free and slack space for deleted files

Whether the team is using a forensics program or searching the backup directly, each element listed above should be investigated for possible evidence. Depending on the size of the files and the number of systems involved, this process may take some time. The search represents the heart of the computer forensics investigation and can be compared to "searching for a needle in the haystack."

---

20. Betts, Bill. "Crime Seen." *Information Security,* March 2000 pp. 33–46.

Education

Just as end users need to be made aware that they should report suspicious activity to the appropriate contact in an organization, so computer security awareness training should include the value of computer forensics and the potential for computer crime. Awareness training is actually the best route to start a paradigm shift of viewing the computer as a potential crime scene when warranted. End users should recognize how easily computer evidence can be altered through simple actions and should be directed to not use a computer system if an incident (including possible computer crime) has occurred. Computers should not be restarted by anyone other than those directly authorized to conduct an investigation, and files should not be deleted or altered in any way. Under no circumstances should end users attempt to perform an investigation on their own. Instead, the suspicious activity must be reported to the appropriate authority within the organization.

The world of computer forensics is a newer area of expertise, and the number of computer forensics experts at the time of this book's publication was far smaller than the number of computer security personnel. If forensics expertise does not exist internally within an organization, a forensics specialist should be contacted or brought in to assist with any investigation. In recent years, a few companies have been formed by former law enforcement agents who can provide valuable insight to members of the commercial sector during the course of an investigation. Many law enforcement agencies also have their own computer crime investigation units and will provide the forensics expertise as part of the investigation.

Summary

Now that you've read an overview of computer forensics and a short summary of some of the issues involved, you probably have a question hanging in your mind: Why do you need to consider computer forensics for your organization? Computer forensics are used in organizations for many reasons: to solve the mystery of exactly what a particular user did to the system, to recover "deleted" data, to ensure compliance with policies, to investigate possible misuse of the organization's systems, and to prepare evidence for an internal or even a court case.

Computer forensics is the process of extracting evidence from computer storage media and guaranteeing its accuracy and reliability. The rules and methodologies followed with any forensics investigation equally apply well to the world of computer forensics. The steps taken during an investigation may make the difference for prosecution, and information technology personnel must keep this idea in mind. If the IT staff does not have appropriate forensics experience, it is better to bring in a forensics expert to handle the investigation instead of trying to preserve the evidence internally.

For deterrence of computer crime to be successful, a paradigm shift is needed. If a computer crime has been committed, people must realize that the computer is the crime scene. As with any forensics investigation, defining the boundaries of the crime scene can pose the greatest challenge. The broad reach of the Internet can make this challenge even greater.

Computer evidence is fragile and can easily be modified. Extra care should be taken to preserve the evidence exactly as it was, typically through the use of multiple copies of system backups. One copy should be preserved for any trial that may take place, while other copies are used for the actual investigation. Forensics software can ease the investigation process and aid with the preservation and review of evidence.

The best approach to take in tackling any computer crime is the three-expert approach. The three experts include a technical expert, a law enforcement official, and a lawyer. Each plays a vital role in the investigation, and technical personnel should not try to cover all three bases themselves. Once a computer crime has been substantiated or evidence supporting the suspicion of a crime noted, the appropriate level of law enforcement officials should be notified. Given the heavy workloads experienced at the federal level, it is often best to start with the lowest level of law enforcement as applicable.

The world of computer forensics can be a fascinating area in which to work and will undoubtedly see an increased demand for its services in the years to come. Anyone intrigued with the world of incident response and interested in computer crime will find this subdiscipline very fascinating.

CHAPTER
12 Conclusions

In March 1882, George Parmalee set a cotton-spinning factory on fire in Bolton, England. He did so as part of a sales pitch to try and convince factory managers to buy sprinkler systems. "In 90 seconds, flames and billows of thick black smoke engulfed the mill. After two minutes, 32 automated sprinklers kicked in and extinguished the fire."[1] At the time, many managers were as uncertain about spending money on fire sprinklers as some information technology and corporate managers are uncertain or reluctant to spend money on computer security today.

The computer is like any other invention that has had a major impact on our daily lives in that it has both benefits and negative consequences. Just as it took society some time to respond to the negative effects (e.g., auto accidents, auto theft) that accompanied the invention of the automobile, so too will it take time for us to fully appreciate and implement the safeguards that are being developed for computer systems and the information stored on them. One safeguard that can

---

1. Berinato, Scott. "Finally, a Real Return on Security Spending." *CIO Magazine,* February 15, 2002.

be put in place to protect our information systems is the development of a computer incident response team.

At the time this book was written, very few resources were available to help a manager put together a computer incident response team. Technical books that describe the processes involved with incident response were beginning to appear, but no real guides on how to form such a team existed. For these reasons, we decided to build on our experiences in the security field and put this book together. Although the book was initially intended for managers, several points covered in it apply equally well to those fulfilling the role of system administrators, incident handlers, end users, and students of computer security.

The world of computer incident response can be very challenging, exciting, and even frustrating. In describing the many considerations that should be taken into account when forming an incident response team, we have used the analogy of putting a puzzle together. Many pieces to the puzzle must be considered, and this book has tried to address many of them in detail.

The book began with a short history of computer security incidents that have raised challenges to the Internet community. These spectacular cases prompted the formation of some of the first incident response teams. These examples of teams are included as a basis of comparison—so that you can compare and contrast your team organization with them, and learn by example. The book also introduced several organizations that provide help, guidance, and information about vulnerabilities, crime information, and notes for comparing with other teams. Ultimately, a group of teams working together is much more effective than a team that works in a vacuum. Several sections of the book also emphasized the importance of including the legal and law enforcement communities when considering how to build a computer incident response team.

The statistics included in this book are not intended to frighten you—they're provided as reference material to help you identify some of the problems that have been reported in the past. We've attempted to answer questions such as "How often?", "How much?", and "What do these incidents really cost my organization?" You can use this information to make informed decisions about the many different issues that your team may pursue.

Terminology was discussed in depth in Chapter 3. This chapter can be used in several ways: as a guide to help group your incidents, and as a common language that your team can use to describe incidents when reporting them to another team or legal entity. Although this terminology might not be something that will prove useful at a cocktail party, it provides a common, consistent, and widely accepted description of the issues with which your team will be concerned.

When describing computer attacks and analyzing them, many factors must be considered. The human factor is one of the most unpredictable factors to be considered in analyzing these events. Here is where the credibility of your team will be tested. Can your organization rely on your team to provide accurate and timely information regarding the latest virus hoax? Such information can most certainly keep your constituency from hanging around the water cooler and talking about something that isn't even an issue!

The formation of the incident response team is the main focus of this book. Topics included items such as roles, staffing, funding, training, outsourcing, and tools for such a team. The ultimate goal of the team is very much like insurance—to prevent incidents by using the skills that it has in its arsenal, and to efficiently investigate and address incidents that are impossible or impractical to prevent. As with any business decision, risk is always present. Having an idea of what the risks are, how to safeguard against those risks that can be efficiently prevented, and how to efficiently address the risks that your organization has chosen to accept are certainly goals that all business managers endeavor to achieve.

In addition to highlighting the many roles that your team should consider, we've made an effort to reinforce the fact that the team's mission, strategy, credibility, and support by the organization are all issues that are of critical importance when forming the team.

An incident response team is a group of professionals. They're trained, experienced personnel who are often on the leading edge of technology. That's why it's important to have a plan to retain them. An effective compensation structure, career path, and strategies to keep your team alert and well trained are truly the key to keeping your investment sound. In our careers, we've seen several organizations put enormous effort into keeping their staff trained, only to have their personnel leave for reasons such as "the job got boring" or "there was no recognition of our efforts." We certainly hope that this point is well taken when you're reading this book. Your personnel are the most valuable assets for a successful team.

The operational factors of a team—the incident life cycle, incident tracking, and continuous teamwork—are all outlines that you'll need to refine and incorporate into your particular organization. We've provided suggestions and, in many places, examples of some of the successful implementations that we've encountered.

In many places, we've chosen to blur the line between an "incident response team" and a "security team." Should they be separate and distinct teams? The answer to that question will depend on your organization, your constituency, and, in some cases, the clientele served by your organization. In any case, your organization should take into consideration all of the capabilities and roles described in the book.

The importance of working with law enforcement has been stressed throughout the book. Just as it took time for society to establish laws for illegal acts related to any recent invention, so it will take time to establish laws concerning crimes committed through the avenue of the computer and the network to which it may be connected. Only by teaming up with law enforcement experts will we be able to push for the development of more case law faster. Such case law is sorely needed—not only to set a precedent regarding what an intruder can expect when he or she is apprehended, but also to serve as a deterrent to continued or increased computer crime.

We've provided appendices with sample formats and information that may be used in the formation and operation of a team. Appendix A provides a sample report form that illustrates the information that should be collected when an incident is reported. Appendix B identifies some of the major laws pertaining to computer crime. Appendix C provides a sample set of frequently asked questions (FAQ). This FAQ may be modified and used on a site's intranet to help address questions concerning the team. Appendices D and E provide country codes and port numbers that may be used by the team for training purposes and in daily operations.

The world of computer incident response is complex, for both managers and incident handlers alike. It is not an easy undertaking to form such a team. With the right mix of people, patience, and support, however, a team can be successfully formed and make a real difference for the organization. Just as the sprinkler system is poised to extinguish the fire when it breaks out, so the incident response handlers stand ready to solve the incident mystery and restore computer operations when the time comes. Remember, with computer incidents, it is not a question of "if," but rather "when" an incident will occur.

The following fields represent some of the information that may be desired when receiving reports on suspicious activity. Collection of this information should be automated to track in a triage or trouble ticket system of some type and a database for storage, retrieval, and correlation of information. Whenever possible, it is strongly recommended that automated versions of the report include a pull-down or pick list from which answers may be selected. Pick lists greatly reduce the chance for data integrity to become an issue.

The following points should also be tracked by a trouble ticket system:

- Incident handler entering the report
- Date on which the report was entered or created
- Date on which the report was last modified
- Status of the report: open, pending more information, closed, or cancelled
- Was a response sent to the submitter of the report?
- Which incident handler has been assigned the report?
- Has the report been validated to be an incident?

Other sample report forms are available from various sources. This list may be edited as needed to meet the needs of the organization.

Ticket ID: This should be a unique tracking number for the report submitted

Organization/department/division:

Point of contact:

- Name:
- Phone number:
- Fax number:
- E-mail address:
- Mailing address:

Is this the same person who completed and submitted this report? If not, name and phone number of person submitting report:

Alternate point of contact:

- Name:
- Phone number:
- Fax number:
- E-mail address:
- Mailing address:

Type of activity suspected:

- Unauthorized access
  - Level of access suspected? (root, end user, supervisory, etc.)
- Denial-of-service attack
  - Successful?
- Probe or network scan
- Attempted access

- Malicious logic infection

- Other (specify):

How was this activity detected?

- Audit logs

- Intrusion detection system

- Degradation in system performance

- Notified by another site (specify site making the notification):

- Unauthorized change in system settings or user parameters

- New (unaccounted for) files

- End user

- Other (specify):

Apparent source of the activity:

- IP address:

- Host name:

Target:

- IP address:

- Subnet (if internal):

- Operating system (including version and patches applied):

- Applications running on the system (including versions and patches applied):

- Type of data stored on the system:

How many systems/sites were affected by this activity?

How were the systems or sites affected?

Are there any audit logs reflecting suspicious activity?
If so, they should be submitted with the report.

Any other suspicious activity noted?

Any previous activity noted?

- What?

- When was it reported?

- Was it resolved?

Who has been notified of the activity?

Is there a need to report to law enforcement?
Has this activity been reported?

What actions have been taken to respond to the activity to date?

Probability of media attention:

- High

- Medium

- Low

Estimated cost of the damage or down time:

- Estimated dollar amount if known:

- Number of person-hours spent resolving the problem:

- Number of lost work hours due to system being down:

- Cost of equipment purchased for replacements:

- Other:

  What steps have been taken to resolve the problem?

  Is technical assistance needed? Yes/No

B Federal Code Related to Cyber Crime

The following code was taken from the U.S. Department of Justice Web site and is reiterated here to provide an overview of the primary laws pertaining to computer crimes. Although other laws may be used to prosecute individuals who break the law by using computers, these sections represent the primary set of codes used to prosecute activity normally considered to be cyber crime. Changes to these codes that resulted from the U.S. Patriot Act of 2001 are described in detail on the U.S. Department of Justice Web site.

18 U.S.C. 1029. Fraud and Related Activity in Connection with Access Devices

§ 1029. Fraud and related activity in connection with access devices

(a) Whoever—

(1) knowingly and with intent to defraud produces, uses, or traffics in one or more counterfeit access devices;

Appendix B source: http://www.cybercrime.gov.

(2) knowingly and with intent to defraud traffics in or uses one or more unauthorized access devices during any one-year period, and by such conduct obtains anything of value aggregating $1000 or more during that period;

(3) knowingly and with intent to defraud possesses fifteen or more devices which are counterfeit or unauthorized access devices;

(4) knowingly, and with intent to defraud, produces, traffics in, has control or custody of, or possesses device-making equipment;

(5) knowingly and with intent to defraud effects transactions, with one or more access devices issued to another person or persons, to receive payment or any other thing of value during any one-year period the aggregate value of which is equal to or greater than $1000;

(6) without the authorization of the issuer of the access device, knowingly and with intent to defraud solicits a person for the purpose of—

    (A) offering an access device; or

    (B) selling information regarding or an application to obtain an access device;

(7) knowingly and with intent to defraud uses, produces, traffics in, has control or custody of, or possesses a telecommunications instrument that has been modified or altered to obtain unauthorized use of telecommunications services;

(8) knowingly and with intent to defraud uses, produces, traffics in, has control or custody of, or possesses a scanning receiver;

(9) knowingly uses, produces, traffics in, has control or custody of, or possesses hardware or software, knowing it has been configured to insert or modify telecommunication identifying information associated with or contained in a telecommunications instrument so that such instrument may be used to obtain telecommunications service without authorization; or

(10) without the authorization of the credit card system member or its agent, knowingly and with intent to defraud causes or arranges for another person to present to the member or its agent, for payment, one or more evidences or records of transactions made by an access device; shall, if the offense affects interstate or foreign commerce, be punished as provided in subsection (c) of this section.

(b)

(1) Whoever attempts to commit an offense under subsection (a) of this section shall be subject to the same penalties as those prescribed for the offense attempted.

(2) Whoever is a party to a conspiracy of two or more persons to commit an offense under subsection (a) of this section, if any of the parties engages in any conduct in furtherance of such offense, shall be fined an amount not greater than the amount provided as the maximum fine for such offense under subsection (c) of this section or imprisoned not longer than one-half the period provided as the maximum imprisonment for such offense under subsection (c) of this section, or both.

(c) Penalties.

(1) Generally. The punishment for an offense under subsection (a) of this section is—

    (A) in the case of an offense that does not occur after a conviction for another offense under this section—

        (i) if the offense is under paragraph (1), (2), (3), (6), (7), or (10) of subsection (a), a fine under this title or imprisonment for not more than ten years, or both; and

        (ii) if the offense is under paragraph (4), (5), (8), or (9) of subsection (a), a fine under this title or imprisonment for not more than fifteen years, or both;

    (B) in the case of an offense that occurs after a conviction for another offense under this section, a fine under this title or imprisonment for not more than twenty years, or both; and

    (C) in either case, forfeiture to the United States of any personal property used or intended to be used to commit the offense.

(2) Forfeiture procedure. The forfeiture of property under this section, including any seizure and disposition of the property and any related administrative and judicial proceeding, shall be governed by section 413 of the Controlled Substances Act, except for subsection (d) of that section.

(d) The United States Secret Service shall, in addition to any other agency having such authority, have the authority to investigate offenses under this section. Such authority of the United States Secret Service shall be exercised in accordance with an agreement which shall be entered into by the Secretary of the Treasury and the Attorney General.

(e) As used in this section—

(1) the term "access device" means any card, plate, code, account number, electronic serial number, mobile identification number, personal identification number, or other telecommunications service, equipment, or instrument identifier, or other means of account access that can be used, alone or in conjunction with another access device, to obtain money, goods, services, or any other thing of value, or that can be used to initiate a transfer of funds (other than a transfer originated solely by paper instrument);

(2) the term "counterfeit access device" means any access device that is counterfeit, fictitious, altered, or forged, or an identifiable component of an access device or a counterfeit access device;

(3) the term "unauthorized access device" means any access device that is lost, stolen, expired, revoked, canceled, or obtained with intent to defraud;

(4) the term "produce" includes design, alter, authenticate, duplicate, or assemble;

(5) the term "traffic" means transfer, or otherwise dispose of, to another, or obtain control of with intent to transfer or dispose of;

(6) the term "device-making equipment" means any equipment, mechanism, or impression designed or primarily used for making an access device or a counterfeit access device;

(7) the term "credit card system member" means a financial institution or other entity that is a member of a credit card system, including an entity, whether affiliated with or identical to the credit card issuer, that is the sole member of a credit card system;

(8) the term "scanning receiver" means a device or apparatus that can be used to intercept a wire or electronic communication in violation of chapter 119 or to intercept an electronic serial number, mobile identification number, or other identifier of any telecommunications service, equipment, or instrument;

(9) the term "telecommunications service" has the meaning given such term in section 3 of title I of the Communications Act of 1934 (47 U.S.C. 153);

(10) the term "facilities-based carrier" means an entity that owns communications transmission facilities, is responsible for the operation and maintenance of those facilities, and holds an operating license issued by the Federal Communications Commission under the authority of title III of the Communications Act of 1934; and

(11) the term "telecommunication identifying information" means electronic serial number or any other number or signal that identifies a specific telecommunications instrument or account, or a specific communication transmitted from a telecommunications instrument.

(f) This section does not prohibit any lawfully authorized investigative, protective, or intelligence activity of a law enforcement agency of the United States, a State, or a political subdivision of a State, or of an intelligence agency of the United States, or any activity authorized under chapter 224 of this title. For purposes of this subsection, the term "State" includes a State of the United States, the District of Columbia, and any commonwealth, territory, or possession of the United States.

(g)

(1) It is not a violation of subsection (a)(9) for an officer, employee, or agent of, or a person engaged in business with, a facilities-based carrier, to engage in conduct (other than trafficking) otherwise prohibited by that subsection for the purpose of protecting the property or legal rights of that carrier, unless such conduct is for the purpose of obtaining telecommunications service provided by another facilities-based carrier without the authorization of such carrier.

(2) In a prosecution for a violation of subsection (a)(9) (other than a violation consisting of producing or trafficking), it is an affirmative defense (which the defendant must establish by a preponderance of the evidence) that the conduct charged was engaged in for research or development in connection with a lawful purpose.

18 U.S.C. 1030. Fraud and Related Activity in Connection with Computers: As amended October 11, 1996

§ 1030. Fraud and Related Activity in Connection with Computers

(a) Whoever

(1) having knowingly accessed a computer without authorization or exceeding authorized access, and by means of such conduct having obtained information that has been determined by the United States Government pursuant to an Executive order or statute to require protection against unauthorized disclosure for reasons of national defense or foreign relations, or any restricted data, as defined in paragraph y. of section 11 of the Atomic Energy Act of 1954, with reason to believe that such information so obtained could be used to the injury of the United States, or to the advantage of any foreign nation, willfully communicates, delivers, transmits, or causes to be communicated, delivered, or transmitted, or attempts to communicate, deliver, transmit, or cause to be communicated, delivered, or transmitted the same to any person not entitled to receive it, or willfully retains the same and fails to deliver it to the officer or employee of the United States entitled to receive it;

(2) intentionally accesses a computer without authorization or exceeds authorized access, and thereby obtains—

(A) information contained in a financial record of a financial institution, or of a card issuer as defined in section 1602(n) of title 15, or contained in a file of a consumer reporting agency on a consumer, as such terms are defined in the Fair Credit Reporting Act (15 U.S.C. 1681 et seq.);

(B) information from any department or agency of the United States; or

(C) information from any protected computer if the conduct involved an interstate or foreign communication;

(3) intentionally, without authorization to access any nonpublic computer of a department or agency of the United States, accesses such a computer of that department or agency that is exclusively for the use of the Government of the United States or, in the case of a computer not exclusively for such use, is used by or for the Government of the

United States and such conduct affects that use by or for the Government of the United States;

(4) knowingly and with intent to defraud, accesses a protected computer without authorization, or exceeds authorized access, and by means of such conduct furthers the intended fraud and obtains anything of value, unless the object of the fraud and the thing obtained consists only of the use of the computer and the value of such use is not more than $5000 in any one-year period;

(5)

(A)

(i) knowingly causes the transmission of a program, information, code, or command, and as a result of such conduct, intentionally causes damage without authorization, to a protected computer;

(ii) intentionally accesses a protected computer without authorization, and as a result of such conduct, recklessly causes damage; or

(iii) intentionally accesses a protected computer without authorization, and as a result of such conduct, causes damage; and

(B) by conduct described in clause (i), (ii), or (iii) of subparagraph (A), caused (or, in the case of an attempted offense, would, if completed, have caused)—

(i) loss to one or more persons during any one-year period (and, for purposes of an investigation, prosecution, or other proceeding brought by the United States only, loss resulting from a related course of conduct affecting one or more other protected computers) aggregating at least $5000 in value;

(ii) the modification or impairment, or potential modification or impairment, of the medical examination, diagnosis, treatment, or care of one or more individuals;

(iii) physical injury to any person;

(iv) a threat to public health or safety; or

(v) damage affecting a computer system used by or for a government entity in furtherance of the administration of justice, national defense, or national security;

(6) knowingly and with intent to defraud traffics (as defined in section 1029) in any password or similar information through which a computer may be accessed without authorization, if—

    (A) such trafficking affects interstate or foreign commerce; or

    (B) such computer is used by or for the Government of the United States;

(7) with intent to extort from any person, any money or other thing of value, transmits in interstate or foreign commerce any communication containing any threat to cause damage to a protected computer;

shall be punished as provided in subsection (c) of this section.

(b) Whoever attempts to commit an offense under subsection (a) of this section shall be punished as provided in subsection (c) of this section.

(c) The punishment for an offense under subsection (a) or (b) of this section is—

(1)

    (A) a fine under this title or imprisonment for not more than ten years, or both, in the case of an offense under subsection (a)(1) of this section which does not occur after a conviction for another offense under this section, or an attempt to commit an offense punishable under this subparagraph; and

    (B) a fine under this title or imprisonment for not more than twenty years, or both, in the case of an offense under subsection (a)(1) of this section which occurs after a conviction for another offense under this section, or an attempt to commit an offense punishable under this subparagraph; and

(2)

    (A) except as provided in subparagraph (B), a fine under this title or imprisonment for not more than one year, or both, in the case of an offense under subsection (a)(2), (a)(3), (a)(5)(A)(iii), or (a)(6) of this section which does not occur after a conviction for another offense under this section, or an attempt to commit an offense punishable under this subparagraph;

(B) a fine under this title or imprisonment for not more than five years, or both, in the case of an offense under subsection (a)(2) or an attempt to commit an offense punishable under this subparagraph, if—

(i) the offense was committed for purposes of commercial advantage or private financial gain;

(ii) the offense was committed in furtherance of any criminal or tortious act in violation of the Constitution or laws of the United States or of any State; or

(iii) the value of the information obtained exceeds $5000;

(C) a fine under this title or imprisonment for not more than ten years, or both, in the case of an offense under subsection (a)(2), (a)(3), or (a)(6) of this section which occurs after a conviction for another offense under this section, or an attempt to commit an offense punishable under this subparagraph; and

(3)

(A) a fine under this title or imprisonment for not more than five years, or both, in the case of an offense under subsection (a)(4) or (a)(7) of this section which does not occur after a conviction for another offense under this section, or an attempt to commit an offense punishable under this subparagraph; and

(B) a fine under this title or imprisonment for not more than ten years, or both, in the case of an offense under subsection (a)(4), (a)(5)(A)(iii), or (a)(7) of this section which occurs after a conviction for another offense under this section, or an attempt to commit an offense punishable under this subparagraph; and

(4)

(A) a fine under this title, imprisonment for not more than ten years, or both, in the case of an offense under subsection (a)(5)(A)(i), or an attempt to commit an offense punishable under that subsection;

(B) a fine under this title, imprisonment for not more than five years, or both, in the case of an offense under subsection (a)(5)(A)(ii), or an attempt to commit an offense punishable under that subsection;

(C) a fine under this title, imprisonment for not more than twenty years, or both, in the case of an offense under subsection (a)(5)(A)(i) or (a)(5)(A)(ii), or an attempt to commit an offense punishable under either subsection, that occurs after a conviction for another offense under this section.

(d)

(1) The United States Secret Service shall, in addition to any other agency having such authority, have the authority to investigate offenses under this section.

(2) The Federal Bureau of Investigation shall have primary authority to investigate offenses under subsection (a)(1) for any cases involving espionage, foreign counterintelligence, information protected against unauthorized disclosure for reasons of national defense or foreign relations, or Restricted Data (as that term is defined in section 11y of the Atomic Energy Act of 1954 (42 U.S.C. 2014(y)), except for offenses affecting the duties of the United States Secret Service pursuant to section 3056(a) of this title.

(3) Such authority shall be exercised in accordance with an agreement which shall be entered into by the Secretary of the Treasury and the Attorney General.

(e) As used in this section—

(1) the term "computer" means an electronic, magnetic, optical, electrochemical, or other high-speed data processing device performing logical, arithmetic, or storage functions, and includes any data storage facility or communications facility directly related to or operating in conjunction with such device, but such term does not include an automated typewriter or typesetter, a portable handheld calculator, or other similar device;

(2) the term "protected computer" means a computer

(A) exclusively for the use of a financial institution or the United States Government, or, in the case of a computer not exclusively for such use, used by or for a financial institution or the United States Government and the conduct constituting the offense affects that use by or for the financial institution or the Government; or

(B) which is used in interstate or foreign commerce or communications, including a computer located outside the United States that is used in a manner that affects interstate or foreign commerce or communication of the United States;

(3) the term "State" includes the District of Columbia, the Commonwealth of Puerto Rico, and any other commonwealth, possession, or territory of the United States;

(4) the term "financial institution" means

(A) an institution with deposits insured by the Federal Deposit Insurance Corporation;

(B) the Federal Reserve or a member of the Federal Reserve including any Federal Reserve Bank;

(C) a credit union with accounts insured by the National Credit Union Administration;

(D) a member of the Federal home loan bank system and any home loan bank;

(E) any institution of the Farm Credit System under the Farm Credit Act of 1971;

(F) a broker-dealer registered with the Securities and Exchange Commission pursuant to section 15 of the Securities Exchange Act of 1934;

(G) the Securities Investor Protection Corporation;

(H) a branch or agency of a foreign bank (as such terms are defined in paragraphs (1) and (3) of section 1(b) of the International Banking Act of 1978); and

(I) an organization operating under section 25 or section 25(a) of the Federal Reserve Act;

(5) the term "financial record" means information derived from any record held by a financial institution pertaining to a customer's relationship with the financial institution;

(6) the term "exceeds authorized access" means to access a computer with authorization and to use such access to obtain or alter information in the computer that the accesser is not entitled so to obtain or alter;

(7) the term "department of the United States" means the legislative or judicial branch of the Government or one of the executive departments enumerated in section 101 of title 5;

(8) the term "damage" means any impairment to the integrity or availability of data, a program, a system, or information;

(9) the term "government entity" includes the Government of the United States, any State or political subdivision of the United States, any foreign country, and any state, province, municipality, or other political subdivision of a foreign country;

(10) the term "conviction" shall include a conviction under the law of any State for a crime punishable by imprisonment for more than one year, an element of which is unauthorized access, or exceeding authorized access, to a computer;

(11) the term "loss" includes any reasonable cost to any victim, including the cost of responding to an offense, conducting a damage assessment, and restoring the data, program, system, or information to its condition prior to the offense, and any revenue lost, cost incurred, or other consequential damages incurred because of interruption of service; and

(12) the term "person" means any individual, firm, corporation, educational institution, financial institution, governmental entity, or legal or other entity.

(f) This section does not prohibit any lawfully authorized investigative, protective, or intelligence activity of a law enforcement agency of the United States, a State, or a political subdivision of a State, or of an intelligence agency of the United States.

(g) Any person who suffers damage or loss by reason of a violation of the section may maintain a civil action against the violator to obtain compensatory damages and injunctive relief or other equitable relief. A civil action for a violation of this section may be brought only if the conduct involves one of the factors set forth in clause (i), (ii), (iii), (iv), or (v) of subsection (a)(5)(B). Damages for a violation involving only conduct described in subsection (a)(5)(B)(i) are limited to economic damages. No action may be brought under this subsection unless such action is begun within two years of the date of the act complained of or the date of the discovery of the damage. No action may be brought under this subsection for the negligent design or manufacture of computer hardware, computer software, or firmware.

(h) The Attorney General and the Secretary of the Treasury shall report to the Congress annually, during the first three years following the date of the enactment of this subsection, concerning investigations and prosecutions under section 1030(a)(5) of title 18, United States Code.

Section 814(e) Amendment of Sentencing Guidelines Relating to Certain Computer Fraud and Abuse

Pursuant to its authority under section 994(p) of title 28, United States Code, the United States Sentencing Commission shall amend the Federal sentencing guidelines to ensure that any individual convicted of a violation of section 1030 of title 18, United States Code, can be subjected to appropriate penalties, without regard to any mandatory minimum term of imprisonment.

18 U.S.C. 1362. Communication Lines, Stations, or Systems

Whoever willfully or maliciously injures or destroys or attempts willfully or maliciously to injure or destroy any of the works, property, or material of any radio, telegraph, telephone or cable, line, station, or system, or other means of communication, operated or controlled by the United States, or used or intended to be used for military or civil defense functions of the United States, whether constructed or in process of construction, or willfully or maliciously interferes in any way with the working or use of any such line, or system, or willfully or maliciously obstructs, hinders, or delays the transmission of any communication over any such line, or system, shall be fined under this title or imprisoned not more than ten years, or both. In the case of any works, property, or material not operated or controlled by the United States, this section shall not apply to any lawful strike activity, or other lawful concerted activities for the purposes of collective bargaining or other mutual aid and protection which do not injure or destroy any line or system used or intended to be used for the military or civil defense functions of the United States.

APPENDIX

C

Sample Frequently Asked Questions

This appendix provides a sample set of frequently asked questions (FAQ). We have used a fictitious company named SecureCo for the purpose of creating this sample. The answer to each question should be modified appropriately for the organization. For example, the types of incidents to be reported and incident definition will vary for each response team. Although this FAQ may not be fully inclusive of all questions that might possibly arise, it provides a good foundation from which to modify and build a FAQ specific to a company or group.

What is SCIRT?

SCIRT stands for the SecureCo Incident Response Team. It was formed to provide a computer incident response capability for problems experienced within our computer systems. The SCIRT works closely with our legal department, system administrators, and management to respond to computer abuses from both internal and external sources.

What is the mission of SCIRT?

The mission of SCIRT is to identify and protect SecureCo's computer infrastructure from vulnerabilities that would allow unauthorized access, use, or denial of service of our computer resources. When unauthorized activity on our computer systems is accomplished, SCIRT provides technical assistance to isolate, contain, and recover from the attack.

Where is SCIRT?

The SCIRT is physically located at our headquarters in Arlington, Virginia. The team manager works directly for the Chief Information Security Officer (CISO).

What is a computer incident?

A computer incident may be defined differently by different organizations. SecureCo management considers unauthorized access to the company's computer resources, denial-of-service attacks on those resources, and computer viruses to be computer incidents. The incidents may be caused by internal or external resources. If internal resources are found to maliciously and purposely cause a computer incident, then human resources will be involved with the resolution of the incident.

What company resources or guidelines provide more information on the SCIRT?

The purpose and mission of SCIRT is identified in SecureCo's Corporate Computer Security Policy. This policy is supplemented with specific incident response guidelines by the SCIRT Procedures and Guidelines. The Corporate Computer Security Policy may be obtained from the internal Web site, http://www.secureco.com, or from the office of the CISO.

How do I know if I've had a computer incident or if my system has been attacked?

Sometimes it is very difficult for an end user to know that his or her computer system has been attacked. If the system starts acting in a suspicious way or manner out of the ordinary, then SCIRT should be made aware of this problem. For example, if a message suddenly appears on the screen while you are working or if files are unexpectedly changed or deleted, the activity should be reported to the SCIRT. Likewise, more subtle activity should also be reported. For example, our systems display the time and date that you previously logged into the system when the system is accessed. If a time and/or date appears that does not accurately reflect your previous session, that fact should also be reported. Not all activity reported will, in fact, be a computer incident. However, it is better to report the activity and be safe.

How do I report suspicious activity or an incident to the SCIRT?

The SCIRT may be contacted via any of the following means:

E-mail: abuse@secureco.com

Phone: 1-800-XXX-XXXX

Fax: 1-XXX-XXX-XXXX

Report forms are available on the SecureCo internal Web site as well and may be downloaded for completion and faxing, or they may be completed directly and submitted.

Why should I report suspicious activity to the SCIRT?

SecureCo, like many other companies, relies heavily on our computer systems for our daily business operations. If these computers are accessed by an outsider, company secrets may be divulged, records and information may be corrupted, or our resources may be suddenly shut down. All of these events could have a devastating effect on our bottom line. Each employee at SecureCo is part of our first line of defense against such attacks. Even the smallest piece of information that does not look right may help to prevent damage to our information, our reputation, and our business as a whole when it is reported. By reporting suspicious activity, you help to protect our company.

Who gets my incident report?

SecureCo has hired a very technically trained group of professionals who work together to form the SCIRT. Reports are received and processed by this group. The SCIRT is separate from the system administration group and completely devoted to responding to such reports. Once the report is received, you should receive feedback from the SCIRT in the form of e-mail, a phone call, or a visit to investigate the activity further.

How do I contact the SCIRT?

The SCIRT may be contacted via any of the following means:

E-mail: abuse@secureco.com or SCIRT@secureco.com
Phone: 1-800-XXX-XXXX
Fax: 1-XXX-XXX-XXXX

How can I get information from the SCIRT?

If reporting suspicious activity, the means of contacting and reporting that activity described above should be used. For all other questions, the e-mail address SCIRT@secureco.com may be used. E-mails to this address will be directed and responded to as appropriate.

How can I keep up to date with the latest information regarding viruses and other attacks?

The SCIRT has a Web site on the company's intranet with information concerning the latest security vulnerabilities, ways to report incidents, and more. The site also includes several resources that may be accessed for more information on viruses, virus myths or hoaxes, and other pertinent information.

Does the SCIRT offer any security training?

The SCIRT works with our training department and the office of the CISO to develop and offer training pertinent to SecureCo employees regarding computer security threats. All training is coordinated by the training office.

If I receive a warning of a virus, should I forward it to others?

No. If you have not received any official word on the warning from your manager and if there are no news bulletins posted on the warning on the corporate intranet, then forward the warning to the SCIRT. The team will validate the warning and take the appropriate response for you. Under no circumstances should these warnings be forwarded to others without validation by the SCIRT.

How can I work in the SCIRT? Are there jobs available to join the team?

If you are interested in becoming a member of the SCIRT, contact your human resources representative and let him or her know of your interest. Openings will be posted as appropriate by human resources as they occur with all other positions that are open.

APPENDIX

D

Domain Name Extensions Used for Internet Addresses

One of the initial steps normally taken during the course of incident response is to determine the apparent source of the activity. This step will typically be accomplished by reviewing audit logs for an Internet Protocol (IP) address. The IP address will then be translated into its domain name by using one of the Internet registration resources to determine the source of the attack. Just because a signal comes from a specific IP address, however, it does not mean that the perpetrator is coming directly from that spot. Intruders often jump from IP address to IP address to hide their tracks. Nevertheless, the following codes can help to determine the country in which an address is registered.

There are three main types of top-level domains used to indicate the use and/or assignment of a domain name: country codes, generic names, and Internet structure. The top-level name normally appears at the end of the domain name such as .com, .edu, or .gov. The most frequently used types of top-level domains are country codes and generic names. The country codes were created for individual countries to use as they deemed appropriate. The generic codes were created for general Internet use and are the ones familiar to most people. The third type of top-level domain name is used for the Internet infrastructure (.arpa) and will rarely show up during incident response.

A quick reference to the country codes and the generic top-level domain names could prove useful to an incident response team in resolving the source and/or target of suspicious activity. It can also prove useful in determining which database to use to conduct a domain name lookup for contact and further information.

The following codes are used within the domain names to denote various countries around the world. They are included here for use in training incident response personnel and for use in written procedures. Most organizations within North America will use the more generic codes of .com, .net, .edu, .mil, and .gov. These extensions are used by entities worldwide as well.

Codes for European Countries

Country	Extension
Albania	AL
Austria	AT
Belarus	BY
Belgium	BE
Bosnia-Herzegovina	BA
Bulgaria	BG
Croatia	HR
Cyprus	CY
Czech Republic	CZ
Denmark	DK
Estonia	EE
Finland	FI
France	FR

Codes for European Countries *(continued)*

Country	Extension
Georgia	GE
Germany	DE
Great Britain	GB
Greece	GR
Hungary	HU
Iceland	IL
Ireland	IE
Italy	IT
Latvia	LV
Liechtenstein	LI
Lithuania	LT
Luxembourg	LU
Macedonia	MK
Malta	MT
Moldova	MD
Netherlands	NL
Norway	NO
Portugal	PT
Romania	RO
Russia	RU
Slovakia	SK

(continued)

Codes for European Countries *(continued)*

Country	Extension
Slovenia	SI
Switzerland	CH
Ukraine	UA
Yugoslavia	YU

Codes for African Countries

Country	Extension
Algeria	DZ
Angola	AO
Botswana	BW
Burkina Faso	BF
Burundi	BI
Cameroon	CM
Chad	TD
Comoros	KM
Congo	CG
Djibouti	DJ
Egypt	EG
Ethiopia	ET
Gabon	GA

Codes for African Countries *(continued)*

Country	Extension
Gambia	GM
Guinea	GN
Kenya	KE
Lesotho	LS
Liberia	LR
Libyan Arab Jamahiriya	LY
Malawi	MW
Mauritania	MR
Mauritius	MU
Morocco	MA
Mozambique	MZ
Namibia	NA
Niger	NE
Nigeria	NG
Sierra Leone	SL
Soa Tome and Principle	ST
Somalia	SO
South Africa	ZA
Sudan	SD
Swaziland	SZ
Togo	TG

(continued)

Codes for African Countries *(continued)*

Country	Extension
Tunisia	TN
Yemen	YE
Western Sahara	EH
Zaire	ZR
Zambia	ZM
Zimbabwe	ZW

Codes for Asian Countries

Country	Extension
Afghanistan	AF
Bangladesh	BD
Bhutan	BT
Brunei	BN
Cambodia	KH
China	CN
Christmas Island	CX
Cocoa Island	CC
East Timor	TP
Hong Kong	HK
India	IN

Codes for Asian Countries *(continued)*

Country	Extension
Indonesia	ID
Kazakhstan	KZ
Kyrgyz	KG
Laos	LA
Macau	MO
Malaysia	MY
Maldives	MV
Mongolia	MN
Nepal	NP
North Korea	KP
Pakistan	PK
Philippines	PH
Russia	RU
South Korea	KR
Sri Lanka	LK
Tajik	TJ
Thailand	TH
Turkmenistan	TM
Uzbek	UZ
Vietnam	VN

Codes for Middle Eastern Countries

Country	Extension
Armenia	AM
Bahrain	BH
Iran	IR
Iraq	IQ
Jordan	JO
Kuwait	KW
Lebanon	LB
Oman	OM
Qatar	QA
Saudi Arabia	SA
Syria	SY
Turkey	TR

Codes for Central American Countries

Country	Extension
Anguilla	AI
Antigua/Barbuda	AG
Aruba	AW
Bahamas	BS
Barbados	BB

Codes for Central American Countries *(continued)*

Country	Extension
Belize	BZ
Bermuda	BM
British Virgin Islands	VI
Cayman Islands	KY
Costa Rica	CR
Cuba	CU
Dominican Republic	DO
Grenada	GD
Guadeloupe	GP
Guatemala	GT
Haiti	HT
Honduras	HN
Jamaica	JM
Martinique	MQ
Montserrat	MS
Panama	PA
Puerto Rico	PR
St. Kitts-Nevis	KN
St. Lucia	LC
St. Vincent and Grenada	VC
Trinidad and Tobago	TT

(continued)

Codes for Central American Countries *(continued)*

Country	Extension
Turks and Caicos Island	TC
U.S. Virgin Islands	VG

Codes for South American Countries

Country	Extension
Argentina	AR
Bolivia	BO
Brazil	BR
Chile	CL
Colombia	CO
Ecuador	EC
Falkland Islands	FK
French Guiana	GF
Guyana	GY
Paraguay	PY
Peru	PE
Suriname	SR
Uruguay	UY
Venezuela	VE

The following is a reiteration of the same country codes, provided in alphabetical order of the codes themselves. This format is provided as a cross reference for ease of use. Either format may be used by a team. The format selected is strictly a matter of preference.

Country	Country Code	Geographical Location
Afghanistan	AF	Asia
Antigua/Barbuda	AG	Central America
Anguilla	AI	Central America
Albania	AL	Europe
Armenia	AM	Middle East
Angola	AO	Africa
Argentina	AR	South America
Austria	AT	Europe
Aruba	AW	Central America
Bosnia-Herzegovina	BA	Europe
Barbados	BB	Central America
Bangladesh	BD	Asia
Belgium	BE	Europe
Burkina Faso	BF	Africa
Bulgaria	BG	Europe
Bahrain	BH	Middle East
Burundi	BI	Africa
Bermuda	BM	Central America
Brunei	BN	Asia

(continued)

Country	Country Code	Geographical Location
Bolivia	BO	South America
Brazil	BR	South America
Bahamas	BS	Central America
Bhutan	BT	Asia
Botswana	BW	Africa
Belarus	BY	Europe
Belize	BZ	Central America
Cocoa Island	CC	Asia
Congo	CG	Africa
Switzerland	CH	Europe
Chile	CL	South America
Cameroon	CM	Africa
China	CN	Asia
Colombia	CO	South America
Costa Rica	CR	Central America
Cuba	CU	Central America
Christmas Island	CX	Asia
Cyprus	CY	Europe
Czech Republic	CZ	Europe
Germany	DE	Europe
Djibouti	DJ	Africa
Denmark	DK	Europe

Country	Country Code	Geographical Location
Dominican Republic	DO	Central America
Algeria	DZ	Africa
Ecuador	EC	South America
Estonia	EE	Europe
Egypt	EG	Africa
Western Sahara	EH	Africa
Ethiopia	ET	Africa
Finland	FI	Europe
Falkland Islands	FK	South America
France	FR	Europe
Gabon	GA	Africa
Great Britain	GB	Europe
Grenada	GD	Central America
Georgia	GE	Europe
French Guiana	GF	South America
Gambia	GM	Africa
Guinea	GN	Africa
Guadeloupe	GP	Central America
Greece	GR	Europe
Guatemala	GT	Central America
Guyana	GY	South America
Hong Kong	HK	Asia

(continued)

Country	Country Code	Geographical Location
Honduras	HN	Central America
Croatia	HR	Europe
Haiti	HT	Central America
Hungary	HU	Europe
Indonesia	ID	Asia
Ireland	IE	Europe
Iceland	IL	Europe
India	IN	Asia
Iraq	IQ	Middle East
Iran	IR	Middle East
Italy	IT	Europe
Jamaica	JM	Central America
Jordan	JO	Middle East
Kenya	KE	Africa
Kyrgyz	KG	Asia
Cambodia	KH	Asia
Comoros	KM	Africa
St. Kitts-Nevis	KN	Central America
North Korea	KP	Asia
South Korea	KR	Asia
Kuwait	KW	Middle East
Cayman Islands	KY	Central America

Country	Country Code	Geographical Location
Kazakhstan	KZ	Asia
Laos	LA	Asia
Lebanon	LB	Middle East
St. Lucia	LC	Central America
Liechtenstein	LIh	Europe
Sri Lank	LK	Asia
Liberia	LR	Africa
Lesotho	LS	Africa
Lithuania	LT	Europe
Luxembourg	LU	Europe
Latvia	LV	Europe
Libyan Arab Jamahiriya	LY	Africa
Morocco	MA	Africa
Moldova	MD	Europe
Macedonia	MK	Europe
Mongolia	MN	Asia
Macau	MO	Asia
Martinique	MQ	Central America
Mauritania	MR	Africa
Montserrat	MS	Central America
Malta	MT	Europe
Mauritius	MU	Africa

(continued)

Country	Country Code	Geographical Location
Maldives	MV	Asia
Malawi	MW	Africa
Malaysia	MY	Asia
Mozambique	MZ	Africa
Namibia	NA	Africa
Niger	NE	Africa
Nigeria	NG	Africa
Netherlands	NL	Europe
Norway	NO	Europe
Nepal	NP	Asia
Oman	OM	Middle East
Panama	PA	Central America
Peru	PE	South America
Philippines	PH	Asia
Pakistan	PK	Asia
Puerto Rico	PR	Central America
Portugal	PT	Europe
Paraguay	PY	South America
Qatar	QA	Middle East
Romania	RO	Europe
Russia	RU	Europe
Russia	RU	Asia

Country	Country Code	Geographical Location
Saudi Arabia	SA	Middle East
Sudan	SD	Africa
Slovenia	SI	Europe
Slovakia	SK	Europe
Sierra Leone	SL	Africa
Somalia	SO	Africa
Suriname	SR	South America
Soa Tome and Principle	ST	Africa
Syria	SY	Middle East
Swaziland	SZ	Africa
Turks and Caicos Island	TC	Central America
Chad	TD	Africa
Togo	TG	Africa
Thailand	TH	Asia
Tajik	TJ	Asia
Turkmenistan	TM	Asia
Tunisia	TN	Africa
East Timor	TP	Asia
Turkey	TR	Middle East
Trinidad and Tobago	TT	Central America
Ukraine	UA	Europe
Uruguay	UY	South America

(continued)

Country	Country Code	Geographical Location
Uzbek	UZ	Asia
St. Vincent and Grenada	VC	Central America
Venezuela	VE	South America
U.S. Virgin Islands	VG	Central America
British Virgin Islands	VI	Central America
Vietnam	VN	Asia
Yemen	YE	Africa
Yugoslavia	YU	Europe
South Africa	ZA	Africa
Zambia	ZM	Africa
Zaire	ZR	Africa
Zimbabwe	ZW	Africa

The following table provides a breakdown of the top-level domain names used for generic purposes. The general use for the name and the sponsor or group responsible for assignments within the domain is also provided.

Generic Domain Names

"The .arpa domain is the **A**ddress and **R**outing **P**arameter **A**rea domain and is designated to be used exclusively for Internet-infrastructure purposes. It is administered by the IANA in cooperation with the Internet technical community under the guidance of the Internet Architecture Board."[1]

Incident response teams frequently need to identify the registered owner of an IP address or determine who is the registered owner of a

---

1. http://www.iana.org/assignments/port-numbers.

Generic Domain	Reserved for or Used by	Sponsor
.aero	Members of the air-transport industry	Societe Internationale de Telecommunications Aeronautiques (SITA)
.biz	Business	NeuLevel, Inc.
.com	Commercial entities	VeriSign Global Registry Services
.coop	Cooperative associations	Dot Cooperation
.info		Afilias Limited
.museum	Museums	Museum Domain Management Association
.name	Individuals	Global Name Registry
.net		VeriSign Global Registry Services
.org	Intended for noncommercial community; however, some commercial organizations are registered with the .org domain	Public Interest Registry
.pro	Credentialed professionals and related entities	RegistryPro
.gov	United States government	U.S. General Services Administration
.edu	Degree-granting educational institutions of higher education accredited by one of the six U.S. regional accrediting agencies	Educase
.mil	United States military	U.S. Department of Defense Network Information Center
.int	Registering organizations established by international treaties between governments	Internet Assigned Numbers Authority (IANA)

specific domain name. A "who is" database is normally accessed to complete this task. Several "who is" databases may be used to do this research, including the following Regional Internet Registry resources:

- ICANN (Internet Corporation for Assigned Names and Numbers): Nonprofit corporation that is assuming responsibility from the U.S. government for coordinating certain Internet technical functions, including the management of the Internet domain name system
- APNIC (Asia Pacific Network Information Centre): Asia/Pacific Region
- ARIN (American Registry for Internet Numbers): Americas and sub-Saharan Africa
- LACNIC (Regional Latin American and Caribbean IP Address Registry): Latin America and some Caribbean islands
- RIPE NCC (Réseaux IP Européens): Europe, the Middle East, Central Asia, and African countries located north of the equator

Links to most of these sites are available on the IANA Web site at http://www.iana.org. IANA also operates a "who is" service for .int addresses that may be accessed at http://whois.iana.org. The ICANN site may be accessed via the InterNIC site at http://www.internic.net or directly at http://www.icann.org. The InterNIC site also provides a link to the Universal "Who Is" for Internet Domains site, which can provide more information on any of the domains listed. These names are broken down by geographic region for ease of use.

In addition to the Regional Internet Registry resources, several accredited registry directories may be used to conduct research. A listing of several directories is available from the InterNIC registry at http://www.internic.net/alpha.html.

Well-Known Port Numbers

A listing of port numbers can be a useful tool for an incident response team when responding to an incident or reviewing audit logs. The port numbers available on computer systems range from 0 through 65535, and can be divided into three main groups:

- Well-known ports: 0 through 1023
- Registered ports: 1024 through 49151
- Dynamic and/or private ports: 49152 through 65535[1]

"The Well Known Ports are assigned by the InterNet Assigned Numbers Authority (IANA) and on most systems can only be used by system (or root) processes or by programs executed by privileged users."[2] A complete listing of the port numbers and their assigned usage can be obtained from the IANA at http://www.iana.org/assignments/port-numbers. The table following on the next page is a small sampling of the information provided at the Web site.

The list of port numbers may be used for training incident handlers and can serve as a handy guide for incident response. These codes can be a quite valuable resource when reviewing audit log

---

1. http://www.iana.org/assignments/port-numbers.

2. http://www.iana.org/assignments/port-numbers.

entries in particular. (Note: Port numbers that are not needed for authorized applications and systems should not be active on properly configured computer systems.)

Keyword	Port/Protocol	Description
ftp-data	20/tcp	File Transfer [Default Data]
ftp	21/tcp	File Transfer [Control]
ftp	21/udp	File Transfer [Control]
ssh	22/tcp	SSH Remote Login Protocol
telnet	23/tcp	TELNET
smtp	25/tcp	Simple Mail Transfer
http	80/tcp	World Wide Web HTTP

Glossary

access   Establishing a logical or physical connection to a computer resource.

accountability   In computer security terms, the ability to link computer or network activity to an authorized user. This is normally done by logging events that occur on a system, such as access to a critical database.

alarm   The auditing data from security programs or tools that are programmed to trigger an alert when a specific event takes place.

application   A software program that runs on a computer system. Application security, along with network security and operating system security, provides the focus for a well-balanced security program.

architectural review   A process of evaluating the hardware, software, network, policies, and management of a system or group of systems to ensure that it does what is intended, and does not do what is not intended.

audit   A straightforward review of an information system used to determine how an organization meets specific standards. A checklist is normally used to complete the audit.

authentication   The act of ensuring an entity is who or what it claims to be.

authorization   In computer security terms, the privileges that a computer user is assigned on a computer system. It is used to maintain the appropriate level of access to a computer system.

availability   In computer security terms, the measurement that a computer system is able to be used for its intended purpose. An example of a risk to availability is a denial-of-service attack.

CERT Computer Emergency Response Team. This term is often used interchangeably with IRT, but CERT has been trademarked by Carnegie Mellon University to describe its team that provides computer security incident analysis, reports, and alerts to the public.

chain of custody The controlled handling of evidence, documented to reflect every person who handled the evidence, what they did with it, and where the evidence was stored.

CISA Certified Information Systems Auditor.

computer forensics The process of extracting information from a computer crime scene and guaranteeing its accuracy and reliability.

computer incident An unauthorized activity directed toward an organization's computer resource(s). There is no universally accepted definition for an incident, and many organizations will define an incident by the types of attacks that may occur.

confidentiality The act of sharing information with only the necessary and authorized entities.

denial-of-service (DoS) attack An attack in which the targeted system resources are overwhelmed or saturated to a point where their availability to legitimate users is either diminished or ceased.

distributed DoS (DDoS) attack A denial-of-service attack involving the services of many dispersed compromised systems to launch the attack.

fat-finger Slang for mistyping on a keyboard.

FBI United States Federal Bureau of Investigation. In this book, it has been used as an example of a national-level law enforcement agency that has capabilities to investigate computer-based crime. In other countries, there are also some excellent examples.

flood Accessing a computer resource repeatedly to overload the system's capacity.

GIAC Global Information Assurance Certification.

hardening The process of locking down a system to ensure that it does not provide too much access or run services that are not needed.

incident   See *computer incident.*

InfraGard   A cooperative effort between law enforcement and the technical community with the participants dedicated to increasing the security of critical infrastructures within the United States. InfraGard is often likened to a neighborhood watch program where businesses and agencies with similar interests share information and experiences to help reduce the risks of a networked community.

integrity   In computer security terms, safeguards to ensure that the information stored on a computer system is accurate and is the information that was intended to be stored.

IRT   Incident response team.

ISACA   Information Systems Audit and Control Association.

logic bomb   A program in which the payload is delivered when a particular logical condition occurs—for example, not having the author's name in the payroll file. Logic bombs are a kind of Trojan horse.

logs   Typically, computerized files that store activity. Logs are crucial to investigating an incident.

malware   Software used for malicious intent, including Trojan horses, viruses, worms, logic bombs, exploit scripts, and time bombs.

MSSP   Managed security services provider. An outside company hired to provide specific security resources. These resources vary significantly in the services that they offer.

out-of-band communications   A method of communicating other than by using the compromised system. In other words, a different system, the phone, a fax machine, or a mode of communication beside the attacked system should be used to communicate.

payload   The unauthorized or unwanted activity of malicious software. It can also be described as the malicious portion of network traffic. Example: The packet contained a virus payload.

penetration   Unauthorized access to a computer system or resource.

penetration test   A covert test in which a consultant or trained insider plays the role of a hostile attacker who tries to compromise system security. The test is normally carried out without warning.

policy   A set of rules created by an organization for the organization to follow. In computer security terms, *policy* can refer to a standard method of configuring a computer system, or a set of rules about what sorts of network traffic may flow through the networks. An example of a policy statement would be "Customer data may only be stored in encrypted format."

probe   Sending a signal to a computer resource in an attempt to determine its characteristics.

remnant files   The files or programs an intruder may have left on the system once access was gained. Examples of remnant files include sniffer logs, password files, source code for programs, and exploit scripts that he or she may have used to store the intruder's "goods" or to target other systems.

risk   A measurement (either qualitative or quantitative) of an event occurring.

risk assessment   A process of rating and evaluating the potential exposure of a system. This process takes the results of a vulnerability assessment and adds in an analysis of threats, the value of the information, and the safeguards used to protect the information. Its purpose is to help make informed decisions on the best balance between the risk that is posed to the organization's information and the benefit of protecting it.

safeguard   In computer security terms, an action taken to prevent misuse of a computer system. An example of a safeguard is the action of locating a critical computer system in a locked area. A safeguard helps reduce risk caused by threats or vulnerabilities.

scan   To access or probe a set of computer targets in a sequential order in an attempt to determine specific characteristics of the system or systems.

shoulder surfing   An activity in which one person watches someone else type a password, user name, or other critical information into a computer system.

spoof To masquerade or assume the appearance of a different person or entity in network communications.

social engineering A popular method used to bypass or exceed normal computer access by convincing others that you don't have the access that you legitimately need and that they should give it to you. It can sometimes involve lying about your identity, position, location, or many other factors to convince others that access should be granted.

SPAN network Space Physics Analysis Network.

threat A capability of exploiting a vulnerability. In some risk assessment models, threats are used as part of the calculation or estimate that a vulnerability may be exploited in a certain environment. For example, if you're storing milk, spoilage is the risk. To reduce the risk, you may consider heat and time as threats. Safeguards that you may choose to employ are refrigeration and a policy to use the milk within a certain amount of time to reduce the risk of spoilage.

Trojan horse A program or routine concealed in software that appears to be harmless. Trojan horses are not viruses and do not replicate like viruses. However, they may contain or include a worm or virus as part of the package.

urban legend Similar to a virus hoax, except that it forwards a warning about some other major event, problem, or impending catastrophe.

USC United States Code. A collection of laws for the United States. In particular, several laws are concerned with computer-based crime: 18USC§1029 and 18USC§1030 (Title 18 United States Code, section 1030).

virus A self-replicating program whose purpose is to propagate to as many different places as possible. Viruses do so by modifying other programs to include copies of themselves through an (unknowing) act of a user.

virus hoax A false warning of some "new" virus rumored to be in circulation on the Internet.

vulnerability   A point where a system is susceptible to an attack.

vulnerability assessment   Evaluating a system for possible susceptibility to be accessed in an unauthorized way or to have authorized access denied. Many commercial and free vulnerability assessment tools can help streamline this process, although it does still require a certain amount of experience to use these tools effectively.

worm   "An independent program that reproduces by copying itself from one system to another, usually over a network. Like a virus, a worm may damage data directly or it may degrade system performance by tying up resources and even shutting down a network."[1]

zombie   A program inserted into a vulnerable system to await further instructions; usually part of a distributed denial-of-service attack.

---

1. Russell, Deborah, and G. T. Gangemi, Sr. *Computer Security Basics*. Sebastopol, CA: O'Reilly & Associates, 1991, p. 426.

Bibliography

Books

Andress, Mandy. *Surviving Security: How to Integrate People, Process, and Technology.* Indianapolis: SAMS Publishing, 2002.

Baker, Richard H. *Network Security: How to Plan for It and Achieve It.* New York: McGraw-Hill, 1995.

Bosworth, Seymour, and M. E. Kabay, eds. *Computer Security Handbook,* 4th ed. New York: John Wiley & Sons, 2002.

Chirillo, John. *Hack Attacks Denied.* New York: John Wiley & Sons, 2001.

Dyson, Peter. *Novell's Dictionary of Networking.* San Jose: Sybex, Novell Press, 1994.

Erbschloe, Michael. *Information Warfare: How to Survive Cyber Attacks.* New York: McGraw-Hill, 2001.

Giuliani, Rudolph. *Leadership.* New York: Miramax Books, 2002.

Kruse, Warren G. II, and Jay G. Heiser. *Computer Forensics: Incident Response Essentials.* Boston: Addison-Wesley, 2002.

Mandia, Kevin, and Chris Prosise. *Incident Response Investigating Computer Crime.* Berkeley, CA: Osborne/McGraw-Hill Publishing, 2001.

Norton, Peter, and Mike Stockman. *Peter Norton's Network Security Fundamentals.* Indianapolis: SAMS Publishing, 2000.

Ramsland, Katherine. *The Forensics Science of C.S.I.* New York: Berkley Boulevard Books, 2001.

Russell, Deborah, and G. T. Gangemi Sr. *Computer Security Basics.* Sebastopol, CA: O'Reilly & Associates, 1991.

Shaffer, Steven L., and Alan R. Simon. *Network Security.* Cambridge, MA: Academic Press, 1994.

Skardhamar, Rune. *Virus Detection and Elimination.* Cambridge, MA: Academic Press, 1996.

Stallings, William. *Network and Internetwork Security: Principles and Practice.* Englewood Cliffs, NJ: Prentice Hall, 1995.

Stoll, Clifford. *The Cuckoo's Egg.* New York: Pocket Books Publishing, 1990.

Van Wyk, Kenneth R., and Richard Forno. *Incident Response.* Sebastopol, CA: O'Reilly & Associates, 2001.

Wood, Charles Cresson. *Information Security Policies Made Easy.* Version 7. Sausalito, CA: Baseline Software, 1999.

Reports and Articles

Bennett, Madeline. "Virus Costs Keep Rising." *IT Week,* March 31, 2003. http://www.itweek.co.uk/News/1139852.

Berinato, Scott. "Finally, a Real Return on Security Spending." *CIO Magazine,* February 15, 2002.

Betts, Bill. "Crime Seen." *Information Security,* March 2000.

Bouchard, Mark. *Global Networking Strategies.* Meta Group, October 31, 2001.

CIC Security Working Group. *Incident Cost Analysis and Modeling Project, Final Report.* University of Michigan, 1998.

Grossman, Lee. "Attack of the Love Bug." *Time,* May 15, 2000.

Kurtz, George, and Chris Prosise. "Part 3: Penetration Testing Exposed." *Information Security,* September 2000.

Levine, Stacey. "US Attorneys' Bulletin Computer and Telecommunications Coordinator (CTC) Program," www.cybercrime.gov.

Levy, Steven, and Brad Stone. "Hunting the Hackers." *Newsweek,* February 21, 2000.

Postel, J., ed. "Transmission Control Protocol—DARPA Internet Program Protocol Specification," STD 7, RFC 793. USC/Information Sciences Institute, September 1981.

Postel, J. "User Datagram Protocol," STD 6, RFC 768. USC/Information Sciences Institute, August 1980.

Power, Richard, ed. "2002 CSI/FBI Computer Crime and Security Survey." *Computer Security Institute,* spring 2002.

Savage, Marcia. "Network Breaches Hit the Bottom Line." *Plant IT,* February 12, 2001.

U.S. Department of Justice press release, "Creator of Melissa Computer Virus Sentenced to 20 Months in Federal Prison." May 1, 2001.

U.S. Department of Justice press release, "Former Cisco Systems, Inc. Accountants Sentenced for Unauthorized Access to Computer Systems to Illegally Issue Almost $8 Million in Cisco Stock to Themselves." November 26, 2001.

U.S. Department of Justice press release, "Former Computer Network Administrator at New Jersey High-Tech Firm Sentenced to 41 Months for Unleashing $10 Million Computer 'Time Bomb'." February 26, 2002.

U.S. Department of Justice press release, "Texas Hacker Pleads Guilty to 7 Charges of Unlawfully Obtaining Access to Computer Belonging to the U.S. Postal Service, the State of Texas, the Canadian Department of Defence and the Private Sector." December 6, 2000.

U.S. Department of Justice press release, "Twenty-Seven Month Sentence in Internet Fraud Scheme to Defraud Priceline.com and Others." May 17, 2002.

Winkler, Ira. "Part I: Audits, Assessments & Tests (Oh, My)." *Information Security,* July 2000, pp. 80–85.

Web Sites

CERT Coordination Center: http://www.cert.org

Common Vulnerability and Exposures (CVE): http://cve.mitre.org

Forum of Incident Response and Security Teams: http://www.first.org

Information Systems Audit and Control Association and Foundation (ISACA): http://www.isaca.org

InfraGard: http://www.infragard.net/history_main_pg.html

International Information Systems Security Certification Consortium (ISC)[2]: http://www.isc2.org

SysAdmin, Audit, Network, Security (SANS) Institute: http://www.sans.org

U.S. Department of Justice: http://www.usdoj.gov/criminal/cybercrime

Index